PEACEBUILDING AND CATHOLIC SOCIAL TEACHING

PEACEBUILDING AND CATHOLIC SOCIAL TEACHING

THEODORA HAWKSLEY

University of Notre Dame Press
Notre Dame, Indiana

University of Notre Dame Press
Notre Dame, Indiana 46556
undpress.nd.edu
All Rights Reserved

Copyright © 2020 by the University of Notre Dame

Published in the United States of America

Library of Congress Control Number: 2020945494

ISBN: 978-0-268-10845-8 (Hardback)
ISBN: 978-0-268-10846-5 (Paperback)
ISBN: 978-0-268-10848-9 (WebPDF)
ISBN: 978-0-268-10847-2 (Epub)

Let us then pursue what makes for peace and mutual upbuilding.

—Romans 14:19

CONTENTS

ACKNOWLEDGMENTS

This book began life at the University of Edinburgh as part of the project Peacebuilding through Media Arts. That project would not have happened without the vision of Jolyon Mitchell, director of the Centre for Theology and Public Issues, whose encouragement led me to begin work in this field and thus to a task and a calling I might not otherwise have discovered. The project was made possible by the generous support of the Binks Trust and Alison and Jo Elliot.

The peacebuilding scholars and practitioners who attended the interdisciplinary workshops of the Peacebuilding through Media Arts project were inspiring, and their writing and conversation have shaped and sharpened my thinking. I owe warm thanks to my former colleagues at the Centre for Theology and Public Issues and the School of Divinity for their support, companionship, and good humor during my time in Edinburgh. I learned much from the team at the Kroc Institute for International Peace Studies at the University of Notre Dame, and Scott Appleby deserves special thanks here for his encouragement.

Jolyon Mitchell, Scott Appleby, Ashley Beck, Anna Rowlands, and Susanna Hawksley were kind enough to read parts of the manuscript at various stages, and I am grateful for the generous engagement of the anonymous reviewers for the University of Notre Dame Press. Thanks also to Georgetown University Press for permission to reuse material in chapter 5. My thinking and writing owe much to the wisdom, friendship, and conversation of Cecelia Clegg, John Knowles, and Nick Austin S.J. In a different and life-changing way, the Amerindian peoples of the Rupununi and Pakaraimas taught me much about power, peace, and the struggle for justice.

During the period I was finishing the book, the Congregation of Jesus was home, and I would like to thank Provincial Superior Frances Orchard C.J. for encouraging me to finish the book and the sisters of the English Province for all their mercies, great and small. This book is dedicated to them.

Introduction

In April 2019, the leaders of South Sudan met at the Vatican for a spiritual retreat led by the archbishop of Canterbury, Justin Welby, and Pope Francis. Since 2013, South Sudan has been embroiled in a civil war that has killed hundreds of thousands of people and displaced millions more. The peace deal, which was brokered in 2018 between the president, Salva Kiir, and his erstwhile deputy turned rebel leader, Riek Machar, remains fragile. Pope Francis's remarks to the two leaders were uncompromising. Telling them that God's gaze was on them, he added, "There is another gaze directed to you: it is the gaze of your people, and it expresses their ardent desire for justice, reconciliation, and peace." The pope continued, "I urge you, then, to seek what unites you, beginning with the fact that you belong to one and the same people, and to overcome all that divides you. People are wearied, exhausted by past conflicts: Remember that with war, all is lost!" Then, kneeling with some difficulty, he kissed the feet of each of the leaders in turn, begging them, "I am asking you as a brother to stay in peace. I am asking you with my heart, let us go forward."[1]

After Islamic State forces had been driven out of the Nineveh Plains of Iraq in 2017, returning Christian communities were faced with scenes of destruction. Homes, churches, and schools had been badly damaged,

1

and a major task of reconstruction lay ahead. No less important was the task of human and spiritual rebuilding. Fr. Araam Hanna, a Chaldean priest in Alqosh, noticed how profoundly people had been traumatized by their experience: they were irritable, deeply fearful, and disposed to violence. After years of insecurity, they lacked trust in political processes and hope for the possibility of a different future. In response, Hanna founded the New Hope Trauma Centre of Iraq, which offers mental health services for those suffering from trauma; courses on topics such as anger management, grief, coping skills, and communication; and education and arts workshops.[2] The Centre's programs are open to all, and it serves the local Yazidi population as well as the Christian community. While acknowledging that the broader political situation is out of their control, and the future still very uncertain, Hanna reinforced the importance of building a more positive future on a local level: "We may not be able to give them hope in politicians, or hope in lasting security, but we can at least give hope in themselves and in each other, and that's a start."[3]

In conflict zones around the world, from South Sudan to Colombia to the Philippines and the Nineveh Plains of Iraq, the Catholic Church is deeply embedded in the task of peacebuilding.[4] In these locations and hundreds more, local Catholic communities, including laypeople, priests, religious, and bishops, as well as Catholic aid agencies and nongovernmental organizations (NGOs), are engaged in courageous, difficult, and imaginative work in the service of peace: everything from facilitating national peace dialogues to negotiating for the release of hostages, caring for refugees, and overseeing demobilization. From the Vatican to the grassroots, the Catholic Church is making a significant contribution to the work of peacebuilding in the twenty-first century, in the face of what Pope Francis has repeatedly referred to as a "piecemeal World War III."[5]

The Catholic Church's capacity to act as a force for peacebuilding is immense. The Church has a two-thousand-year history of teaching and theological and moral reflection, vibrant traditions of spirituality, and a global presence in a dizzying variety of cultural contexts. Among the biggest religious groups on the planet, it is unique in being organized under a single head, with a single centralized teaching authority that serves to unify, even if only sometimes loosely, its 1.4 billion members. Allied with this hierarchical structure is a huge and diverse range of institutions and networks through which the Church is present and active on a local level. All of these features make the Catholic Church a potentially world-changing force for justice and peace. So what would it take for the Catholic Church to realize fully its potential as a force for peacebuilding? What kind of transformation would it require? And what kind of growth and transformation might it require of the tradition of Catholic social teaching itself?

These questions are what drive this book, and they give me two major tasks to pursue in what follows. First, if the Church is to become a major force for peacebuilding, then its teaching on peace needs to become better known and embedded, as David O'Brien puts it, "Church wide and parish deep."[6] Most Catholics are fairly well informed about what the Church teaches about high-profile life issues like abortion and euthanasia, and many non-Catholics would also be able to give a basic account of the Church's teaching on these matters. Far fewer people, either within the Church itself or in society more widely, would be aware of what it teaches about workers' rights or economic justice. The same is true of the Church's teaching on peace. While just war reasoning is fairly common currency in society at large, few Catholics, and even fewer non-Catholics, would be able to articulate how the just war tradition fits into the Church's teaching on peace more widely or what the Church teaches on key issues such as nuclear weapons and postconflict reconciliation. The Church's teaching on peace is simply not well known and, partly because it is so little known, few Catholics would think of a commitment to peacebuilding as being central to the practice of their faith. So the first task is to reverse this tendency, by re-presenting the tradition of Catholic social teaching on peace and making the case that the "ministry of reconciliation" (2 Cor 5:18) entrusted to us is a key dimension of our Christian vocation and an indispensable part of the Church's mission and identity.[7]

Second, if the Church is to become a major force for peacebuilding, then Church teaching on peace needs to continue to grow and develop. To borrow a phrase from John Courtney Murray, the Church's teaching on peace represents a "growing edge" of the tradition, and this growth needs to be encouraged and nurtured.[8] The shape of violent conflict has changed significantly over the course of the past fifty years, and Church teaching needs to respond to these new signs of the times and the distinctive challenges that contemporary violent conflict poses for the task of peacebuilding. Church teaching also needs to grow and develop in light of the experience of Catholics who are already engaged in the task of peacebuilding in conflict situations around the world. This means exploring how Church teaching is illuminated and challenged by the insights of those engaged in the messy and difficult realities of violent conflict. Their experience can help us to see more clearly the points in the Church's teaching on peace where new resources, new emphases, or fresh theological development are needed.[9] Exploring the theologies and spiritualities that motivate and sustain the work of grassroots peacebuilders also offers insights that can enrich and theologically deepen the Church's formal teaching tradition.

IN "A UNIVERSITY WAY"

This book works in the spaces between the potential of the Church's teaching on peace and the many complex and difficult situations in which the practice of peacebuilding takes shape. Much of this kind of work is being undertaken by those engaged directly in the work of peacebuilding in situations of violent conflict. These are the people who are awakening the Church's potential as a force for peacebuilding, and these are the people who put into practice, day by day, the Church's teaching on topics like solidarity, hope, and reconciliation and thereby discover firsthand its strengths and its weak points. My work in this volume is undertaken in conversation with their experience, but it is undertaken in what Jon Sobrino S.J. calls "a university way."[10] My focus is on the tradition of Catholic teaching on peace, on the coherence, strength, and vitality of that tradition, and on critical and constructive theological interaction with it.

At this juncture, it is worth noting two points about how I approach the tradition of Church teaching on peace, because my approach and points of emphasis themselves constitute an argument about how the tradition should be read. First, I deliberately read the tradition of Catholic teaching on peace as a complex whole. One occasionally encounters the view that the Catholic Church only had teaching on war until the mid-twentieth century, after which it developed teaching on peace; one also occasionally encounters the view that the just war tradition is the really authoritative tradition and that what follows Vatican II is idealistic liberal filler material. Both notions should be resisted: the Church's teaching on peace needs to be read as a whole, albeit a complex whole with many seams and shifts and not a few points of tension. Second, while I interact with the classic sources of the Church's teaching on peace, particularly Augustine and Aquinas, I foreground the tradition of Catholic social teaching. In a certain sense, this stretches back to the earliest Church, but in a more specific sense, "Catholic social teaching" names the tradition of magisterial social teaching inaugurated by Pope Leo XIII's *Rerum novarum* in 1891. I choose to foreground this material partly because it is comparatively understudied.[11] Much Catholic reflection on war and peace centers on questions of ethics, interacts largely with just war doctrine in one guise or another, and arises in the context of specific debates about the rightness or wrongness of a particular military intervention or initiative. This means that sustained theological reflection on the tradition of Church teaching on peace often falls by the wayside, along with reflection on what that tradition has to say about peacebuilding over the long term: in the face of urgent decisions about whether or not to intervene in a conflict, it is easy to forget that the Church's teaching on peace is not *just* just war. This tradition of social teaching on peace needs to become better known, so that it becomes part of the toolbox for which we instinctively reach in the face of such urgent decisions. It needs to become understood as a set of resources for a way of life rather than primarily as a set of instructions for what to do in an emergency.

Second, although my work focuses on the tradition of Catholic teaching on peace, in particular, the magisterial tradition of social teaching, I also draw on the work of Catholic theologians of peace more widely, on resources from theologians of other Christian denominations, and on assorted interdisciplinary resources, from ethics to social science and beyond. Catholic theological reflection on peace has always benefited richly from such "over the fence" conversations, and there is every reason to continue both critiquing and developing the Church's teaching through exchanges of this kind. Moreover, as Scott Appleby points out, in the various conflict settings around the world in which Catholic peacebuilders are engaged, the Catholic Church is by no means the only voice—indeed it is quite often a minority voice—in conversations about peace, conflict, development, politics, and justice.[12] Explaining, exploring, critiquing, and developing the Church's formal teaching on peace demands that we engage with these other voices.

PEACEBUILDING

My determination to read the tradition of Church teaching on peace as a whole also partly explains my use of the term "peacebuilding," which is not yet commonly used within the tradition itself.[13] Theological and ethical reflection on the Church's teaching on peace often gets mired in debates between just warriors and pacifists, which all too readily take on the tone of the "culture wars" between Catholic liberals and conservatives, with each insisting that its viewpoint is the most—or only—faithful way to read the tradition. As Lisa Sowle Cahill points out, the term "peacebuilding" "represents a convergence of thinking from both directions and a new social movement." "Peacebuilding," she adds,

> unites convictions within traditional just war theory with commitments from nonviolent pacifism. With just war thinkers, peacebuilders agree that politically motivated violence must be limited and restrained, and that societies can move past injustice to justice. Peacebuilders share the convictions of pacifists that peaceful cooperation is a state to which all societies must aspire, and that ending violence requires a conversion of hearts and minds.[14]

Peacebuilding therefore provides a lens through which nonviolence and just war—both of which the Church's teaching commends—can be seen as different approaches to a shared quest to bring about a world of greater justice and peace.[15] The varied resources of the Church's teaching need not be seen as competing, although they may exist in tension with one another: they can be understood as corresponding to different approaches, phases, or roles within the broader shared task of peacebuilding.[16]

Peacebuilding is not just a convenient term by which Catholic hawks and doves can be described as at least members of the same family; it is a discipline in its own right. As contemporary peacebuilders are important conversation partners in what follows, it is worth providing an initial working definition of what peacebuilding is before pressing any further. Simply put, peacebuilding is an approach to transforming conflict and creating sustainable peace that encompasses a range of practices aimed at reducing direct violence, increasing justice, and healing the wounds of conflict over the long term.[17] This condensed definition needs some unpacking. Because peacebuilding aims at the reduction of direct violence, it includes practices we might think of as typically "peacemaking," including dialogue and mediation between parties in conflict and facilitating negotiations between military and political leaders at the national and local levels. Because it also aims at the long-term transformation of the causes of violent conflict, peacebuilding simultaneously moves beyond an exclusive focus on short-term state diplomacy and military intervention, to include a broader range of practices aimed at transforming inhumane social, political, or economic structures and destructive patterns of relating.[18] Its ultimate aim is a positive and just peace, characterized by the presence of constructive and flourishing human relationships at all levels of society.[19] This means that peacebuilding also encompasses activities and practices often thought of as "postconflict," including the facilitation of truth and reconciliation processes, trauma healing, and initiatives aimed at building up civil society.

In short, "peacebuilding" names a collection of strategies and practices aimed at fostering a sustainable, dynamic, and just peace. Its ultimate goal is so ambitious, and its approach so comprehensive, that it can be hard to distinguish the tasks of peacebuilding from those of pursuing social justice more widely, and the term can become something of a catchall.[20] However, the comprehensive nature of its goals and practices reflect not impractical utopianism but the recognition that peace is not sustainable without a comprehensive approach that seeks to address the injustice and insecurity that drive violent conflict and the grievances and trauma that result from it. If peacebuilding occasionally sounds soft to the point of being fluffy, it is not because of its practitioners' distance from the complex realities of conflict but precisely because of their proximity to them. The work of building peace is not ultimately a matter of social engineering conducted from without but of working with and transforming persons and relationships in ways that may be hard to quantify but that are no less real for being hard to measure.[21] Appleby and Lederach emphasize the importance of this kind of attention to the human and personal dimension of conflict and peacebuilding, arguing that "promoting reconciliation and healing as the sine qua non of peacebuilding is predicated on a hard-won awareness that violent conflict creates a deep disruption in relationships that then need radical healing—the kind of healing that restores the soul, the psyche and the moral imagination."[22] To put the same point in the language of Catholic social teaching, the task of peacebuilding must be shaped around the recognition that reconciliation cannot be less profound than the division itself.[23]

In what follows, I explore the aims, insights, and practices of peacebuilding in greater depth, but for now it will be helpful to comment briefly on the relationship between the discipline of peacebuilding and the Church's teaching. As with any discipline, the goals and processes of peacebuilding are a matter of debate among theorists and practitioners alike, and the definition of peacebuilding I have just given reflects one particular understanding of its aim and tasks. Every understanding of peacebuilding inevitably bears with it implicit beliefs about the nature of the human person, what a flourishing society looks like, what causes conflict, and what peace means, as well as how it is best achieved. One does not have to be a theologian to harbor beliefs about such matters.[24] It will be clear from the understanding of peacebuilding I have set out above that I have highlighted an approach whose understanding of the human person makes room for a spiritual dimension, whose understanding of society emphasizes mutual flourishing over bare social contract, and whose understanding of peace resonates with—indeed owes much to—biblical themes. Although I have emphasized the natural convergence between peacebuilding and Catholic social teaching in this way, my aim is not to forge an uncritical alliance between the two but rather to draw the thinking and experience of a range of peacebuilders into a broader conversation about how the Catholic Church's teaching on peace might need to grow, develop, and respond to new signs of the times in order to make the Church an ever more courageous and effective witness of peace.[25]

COHERENCE, STRENGTH, VITALITY

The convictions that drive this volume and its two principal tasks should now be clear. It remains only to name some of my overarching concerns in the book and give a brief overview of the ground covered in each chapter.

My overarching concerns are with the coherence, strength, and vitality of the tradition of Catholic social teaching on peace. I have already noted my commitment to treating the Church's teaching on peace as a whole, but this concern with coherence does not mean treating the tradition as monolithic. As I explore in the first two chapters, the tradition is a complex whole, bearing the marks of the historical contexts in which it emerged and the theological shifts that accompanied them. My commitment to coherence means exploring how the various aspects of the tradition, from Augustine to John XXIII and beyond, fit together and paying critical and constructive attention to the points of tension that arise as the tradition shifts and changes over time. It means, too, showing how the central concepts of Catholic social thought—solidarity, subsidiarity, human dignity, and the common good—take shape in the Church's teaching on peace and exploring how new and stronger connections can be forged between peacebuilding and the broader social teaching tradition.

My concern for the strength of Church teaching on peace follows on from this, and all of the chapters that follow are concerned with discerning where and how the resources of the Church's teaching on peace might need to develop in order to respond to the realities of contemporary conflict and the challenge of contemporary peacebuilding. Many of the chapters engage directly with the experience of peacebuilders and explore how the Church's teaching might better address the difficulties, both practical and theological, that arise in the course of their work.

My concern for the vitality of the Church's tradition of teaching on peace takes shape as a particular concern for the "liveability" of that tradition. The Church's teaching on peace holds up high ideals and, as a result, is sometimes criticized for being insufficiently realistic. It does hold that human beings naturally desire peace and that, possessed of sufficient goodwill, they can move toward more peaceful and just social and political lives. At least on one reading, it reflects a profoundly optimistic view of what human beings can achieve within the confines of history. My concern is not whether or not Church teaching is "realistic," in the sense of offering sensible hopes, achievable goals, or reasonable proposals for moral action: to the extent that Catholic teaching on peace is governed by the logic of the gospel, its demands will never be sensible, achievable, or reasonable by any ordinary standards. My concern is with whether or not Church teaching on peace offers an inhabitable, imaginable moral universe. There is a world of difference between a moral ideal that while unachievable in its fullness nevertheless concretely structures the way one lives and acts and a moral ideal that floats above the world in which one lives and acts and bears no practical relation to it. A vital tradition is one that is living and lived, and the Church's teaching on peace must be both.

THE PATH AHEAD

The aim of the first two chapters is to offer an analytical survey of the tradition of Catholic teaching on peace, exploring not just how it changes shape over time, but why it changes. Each chapter covers a considerable historical sweep, the first from the early Fathers to Aquinas, and the second from the discovery of the "New World" to the present day. The intent is not to offer an encyclopedic and comprehensive overview of the Church's teaching on peace in each historical period; rather, the purpose of these chapters is to identify the major theological shifts that have formed the teaching as we have it today and, in so doing, to identify some of the significant points of tension in the tradition and some of the key areas for development. In addition to introducing the overall shape of the tradition, this helps situate the particular interventions in the subsequent chapters.

The third chapter begins by discussing the changing shape of conflict across the past one hundred years, from the interstate conflicts characteristic of the early part of the twentieth century to the complex intrastate and internationalized conflicts of the late twentieth and early twenty-first century. The impact of such conflicts is often devastating on a local level, and grassroots peacebuilding is also key to transforming them. The chapter goes on to propose pastoral accompaniment as a key practice of Catholic peacebuilding in contexts like these. In the first part, drawing on the work of Héctor Fabio Henao, I describe pastoral accompaniment as an intentional practice of peacebuilding. I then suggest that a theology of consolation can support and resource this practice, giving it scriptural roots and a richer theological rationale and helping to develop a spirituality of accompaniment. In the second half of the chapter, I develop a theology of consolation for pastoral accompaniment, beginning with the meaning of consolation in the Hebrew scriptures before going on to explore Isaiah's theology of consolation and how it shapes the gospel writers' presentation of the person and work of Jesus. Such a theology of consolation, I argue, can help Church communities in situations of violence understand their vocation as one of comforting and relenting: comforting, in the sense of being alongside people in their suffering, in ways that help to transform it; and relenting, in the sense of fidelity to a vision of restoration and peace that encourages communities to remain and creatively resist the forces of violence and death.

The fourth chapter focuses on one of the key concepts of Catholic social teaching: solidarity. Contemporary strategic peacebuilding high-lights the importance of midlevel and grassroots peacebuilding initiatives and their capacity to initiate, cultivate, and sustain conflict transfor-mation on a local level. Catholic social teaching on peace, by contrast, tends to focus on macro level solutions to conflict, through the creation and strengthening of political institutions capable of resolving disputes rationally and peacefully. This macro-level focus is paired with the call for individual transformation and conversion, but midlevel peacebuilding initiatives and the experience of those who engage in them are scarcely in view. I argue that Catholic social teaching on solidarity offers some resources for engaging with this middle level of social transformation. After briefly exploring the development of the concept, I go on to show how John Paul II's work on solidarity offers the beginnings of a stronger account of the kinds of cultures, groups, attitudes, and abilities needed to sustain peace on the local level and in the long term. This survey also illustrates some of the ways in which Church teaching on solidarity itself might need to develop to support the practice of peacebuilding, and I draw attention to the need for a richer Christological dimension to the concept. In the last section, I explore how one example—the Jesuit martyrs of Universidad Centroamericana (UCA) El Salvador—offers a theologically rich understanding of solidarity that shows how Church teaching might better address and support those caught up in all the risk, ambiguity, and cost of peacebuilding in situations of violent conflict.

The fifth chapter engages an important topic on the "growing edge" of the tradition of Catholic social teaching: social sin. The emerging concept of social sin has provided the Church with important tools for engaging with situations of both direct and structural violence, but its development and application have been necessarily limited by the fundamental understanding of sin in Catholic moral theology: a knowing act of offense against God for which, in the final analysis, an individual agent is always responsible. Drawing on some insights from peacebuilders engaged with describing and transforming sectarianism in Northern Ireland, I argue that the concept of social sin needs some work if it is to engage effectively with the embedded and unconscious nature of what Church documents call "situations of sin" or "structures of sin." Through exploring contemporary ethnographic insights into the narrative nature of the social, I argue that approaching social sin as kind of "narrative verdict" on the sinfulness of a situation of structural or direct violence can offer important insights into the nature of social sin at the same time that it offers us a helpful tool for naming and transforming it. I also suggest that Karl Rahner's work on concupiscence, transposed into a social key, helps us to view the transformation of social sin in eschatological perspective.

The sixth chapter addresses one of Catholic social teaching's most exportable assets: the theology of reconciliation. The popularity of reconciliation language and processes in the political sphere over the past few decades gives the Church the opportunity to make a distinctive and rich contribution to the discussion. Yet, as the survey in the first part of the chapter shows, the Church's theology of reconciliation as it stands remains tightly tied to its sacramental form, and its connections to the Church's teaching on peace are not as well developed as they could be. In the second part of the chapter, I explore Paul's theology of reconciliation in depth and draw out some of his key themes—that reconciliation is God's initiative, cosmic, and eschatological in its scope and that it involves the overcoming of human boundaries. From there, I develop a broader understanding of the ministry of reconciliation as belonging to the whole Church and connect it with the practice of active nonviolence. In 2017, Pope Francis called for nonviolence to "become the hallmark of our decisions, our relationships and our actions, and indeed of political life in all its forms."[26] A broadened theology of reconciliation, I argue, provides helpful and important theological underpinning here, offering a vision of how the Church can exercise her reconciling ministry through actively nonviolent practices of loving first, resisting division, and cultivating surprising solidarities.

The final chapter explores one of the core convictions of Catholic social teaching on peace, namely, that all people desire peace. This conviction has changed shape over the course of the tradition from Augustine's view that all beings "seek their own peace," in the sense of a state of equilibrium or rest, to the belief of the post–*Pacem in terris* tradition that all people genuinely desire peace and that all conflicts are therefore resolvable by reason and dialogue. Reflecting on this shift, I argue that the post-*Pacem* account of desire for peace would benefit from a stronger account of the ways in which human sin frequently distorts both the peace we pursue and the way we pursue it. I argue that Catholic social teaching needs a stronger sense of how the pursuit of peace involves not just steady progress, but radical change, and it also needs a more strongly Christological account of the peace that all people seek. In the second half of the chapter, drawing on Augustine and a range of contemporary voices, I sketch an account of desire for peace that takes seriously the ways in which both the desire for and the pursuit of peace can be distorted by sin, giving a clearer picture of how Christ expands and transforms, as well as fulfills, our fundamental human desire. The constructive work of this chapter looks forward, suggesting themes and questions for future exploration beyond this project.

The Catholic Church is already deeply embedded in processes of peacebuilding worldwide, and its potential as a significant resource for peacebuilding can be realized still more fully. For that to happen, we need to make the Church's teaching on peace better known, to encourage it to become rooted "Church wide and parish deep," and to make it better fitted for the work of peacebuilding in the twenty-first century. These are the tasks that lie ahead.

ONE

The Early Church to Aquinas

The casual visitor wandering into the basilica of St. John Lateran from the beep and whirl of Roman traffic might well mistake it for just another baroque church in a city already replete with ecclesiastical splendor. The mistake would be forgivable: Galilei's facade, completed in 1735, soars above the square, completely obscuring the old exterior of the church, while inside the extensive remodeling by Borromini during the papacy of Innocent X (1644–55) has left little trace of the ancient basilica.

The fairly uniformly baroque appearance of the basilica as it stands now obscures its fascinating and complex history—a history of successive expansion, embellishment, catastrophe, neglect, and restoration. The original basilica was probably an adaptation of the existing hall of a Roman palace bequeathed to the Church by the emperor Constantine. In the centuries since, it has been pillaged by Goths, flattened by an earthquake, destroyed by fire, and endlessly rebuilt and remodeled. The architectural story of the basilica of St. John Lateran is laid down, layer upon layer, in strata of building and decor, the fluctuations of wealth and power, and the influences and tastes of successive popes and architects overlaid and intermixed with one another. In many ways, the story of the basilica tells the story of the Church itself during the same period, with worship and wealth, sackings and schisms all leaving their traces on the building.

This chapter and the next one narrate the Catholic Church's tradition of teaching on peace as a unity. To do so is in itself an argument for how that tradition should be read. The key question is what *kind* of unity the Church's tradition has and the reason I draw on the image of the Lateran basilica at the start of this chapter is to offer the image of a building, and the activity of building, as a way to think about the unity and development of the Catholic Church's tradition of teaching on peace.

TRADITION

The most common metaphors that shape the ways in which Church tradition is talked about and treated are associated with continuity, community, and life. Metaphors that emphasize continuity include the idea of tradition as light from a single source or a single wellspring with a continuous "flow" of tradition making its way through history. A river may change its appearance quite dramatically on its path from source to sea, and pass through different kinds of landscape, but it is nevertheless the same river. The second family of metaphors, emphasizing the community aspect of tradition, is based on the view that we stand alongside apostles and prophets as part of the one people to whom tradition belongs, receiving it from our forebears and handing it on (*tradere*) to our successors. Just as one cannot choose one's ancestry or the members of one's family, so tradition is not something we choose or identify ourselves with so much as a community of which we find ourselves inextricably a part. The third family of metaphors emphasizes tradition as something living, like a plant. These organic metaphors draw on the idea of tradition as both continuous and living, a tradition that unfolds according to its own inner principle, ours to protect and nurture but not ours to cut off.

All metaphors direct our attention to particular features of a concept, object, or experience at the same time that they obscure other aspects from view. Take the metaphor of organic growth, for example: what is handed over by Christ to the apostles, to their successors, and to the Church as a whole is like a seed, containing within it the germ that will become the full flowering of the tradition. The metaphor allows the progressive development of the tradition to be understood not as the corruption of the original deposit of faith but as its growth into maturity under the guidance of the Spirit. Here, drawing on the metaphor of successive rebuildings of the Lateran, I want to draw attention to that organic process of growth as one also involving human hands, human discernment, and human action. Someone may plant a seed, which then sprouts and grows "he knows not how," but the construction of a building involves planning, conscious decision making, and deliberate construction. To say as much is not to espouse a reductive or merely sociological view of the Church's tradition, because that process of human development also takes place under the guidance of the Spirit; it does, however, offer a change of emphasis. Those who inherited the Lateran were free to develop it but not to change its central purpose as a place of worship: they received it, faithfully reshaped it in accordance with the needs of their own time, and thus gave it to the next generation. In the same way, each generation receives Church tradition from the generation before it and, while "no-one can lay any other foundation than the one that has been laid," each generation faces the task of maintaining it, reshaping it, and handing it on to the next. "Each builder," Paul says, "must choose with care how to build on it" (1 Cor 3:10–11). The development of Church tradition is not only something we observe, as we do the growth and flowering of a plant; it is also an activity, requiring the dedicated and faithful work of many hands. Tradition is building, building is an activity, and the building up of tradition is a common task.

The metaphor of organic growth encourages us to think of the development of the Church's teaching tradition as having a certain inevitability and continuity; while the flower may not bear much resemblance to the seed, its process of germination, growth, and unfolding is gradual and smooth. The metaphor of construction encourages us to pay attention to the building process: the foundations, the progressive additions and embellishments, the seams and cracks, dilapidation and restoration, and the presence of architectural curiosities that seem a little out of kilter with the whole. The metaphor is a helpful one because the Church's tradition of teaching on peace has undergone relatively recent and quite extensive building work. Its foundations are dug deep in the just war tradition and Augustine's idea of peace as *tranquillitas ordinis*, but the bulk of the teaching was constructed as part of the development of Catholic social teaching from the late nineteenth century on, and the rapid expansion of that teaching in the post–Vatican II period. The image of building focuses attention on how more recent teaching fits with the larger, preexisting structures of Catholic doctrine and moral theology. It draws attention to the seams and points of stress within the Church's teaching on peace and to points at which the tradition may require repair or the redistribution of theological weight.

The metaphor of tradition as something living and growing directs our attention to the environment of that tradition and the conditions of its flourishing. In a different way, the image of a building draws our attention to questions of inhabitability. It is not enough for a building to be beautiful or well engineered: it must also be fit for its purpose and inhabitable. In exploring the Church's teaching on peace in the chapters that follow, I am always concerned with the inhabitability of that tradition and its fittingness for the challenges of its time and place. The metaphor of building frees us to think architecturally about what further construction work might be required in order to make Church teaching on peace fit to face the challenges of the twenty-first century.

SURVEYING THE TRADITION

Construction, repair, structural stress, inhabitability: all of the chapters in this book touch on one or more of these issues. But before launching into any constructive work, the task for this chapter and the next is something akin to a building survey, in the sense of an analytical look at the shape of Church teaching on peace as it stands. Building surveys are usually undertaken with a particular purpose in mind, whether conservation or development, and the following survey is no exception.

First, I have already stated that I want to describe Catholic teaching on peace as a single building, one that forms an inhabitable unity in spite of its various architectural oddities and structural problems. To describe the tradition as a complex whole in this way is to make an argument that it *should* be read as such rather than as a ragbag of ad hoc Christian responses to the challenge of conflict, bound together only by the label "Catholic social teaching." In one sense, the decision to read the tradition as a whole is a pragmatic one. When theologians self-consciously situate themselves in the tradition of Catholic teaching on peace, then their response to the needs of their age will also be shaped by the potentialities and limitations of the tradition as they have received it. It makes sense, therefore, to understand each development in the tradition not only in its own historical context but also in the context of the tradition as a whole, asking how it emerges from what comes before and how it reshapes it. The shape of the whole tradition as we have received it affects what we can do with it in response to the challenges of conflict in the twenty-first century. In another sense, the decision to read the tradition as a whole is a theological one—a decision to approach the Catholic tradition in a Catholic way, viewing its development as growth rather than decay and trying where possible to hold together its tensions on the principle of "both-and" rather than "either/or." This is balanced, however, by my second purpose in undertaking this building survey, which is to focus on areas of structural strain.

A word, finally, about what is obscured by the metaphor I have chosen. The survey of Catholic teaching on peace that follows is not intended as an extended encyclopedia entry, listing in chronological order everything that has ever been taught on the subject of peace. It errs on the side of less detail rather than more, focusing on giving a sense of the overall shape of the tradition and the transition between different phases of the building work rather than on the detailed features of that teaching in any given historical period. Rather like showing a tourist around the Lateran basilica, the intention is to give enough historical detail to help the reader understand the building as it stands now, without overburdening her with details that obscure the view of the whole.

The basilica of St. John Lateran occupies the site of a Roman palace and a fort that once housed the imperial cavalry bodyguard. At some point during the reign of Constantine, the buildings were gifted to the bishop of Rome, and work began to convert and extend the palace into the first basilica. If we were to excavate the foundations of the Lateran basilica as it stands today, we might find it hard to tell where these Roman remains end and the Christian building begins: at various points they are one and the same structure; at other points we would find the same materials turned to new purposes, having been reshaped, reused, and incorporated into a new structure.

The same question of where things start, and therefore where to begin, needs to be asked at the beginning of this survey of the Church's tradition of teaching on peace. As we reach further back into antiquity, we find that the earliest beginnings of Christian teaching on peace and war show evidence of the same kinds of borrowing, reshaping, and reusing, even as those borrowed materials are incorporated into a structure that receives its fundamental shape from reflection on the scriptures and the demands of Christian discipleship. This is important because it helps us to recognize from the outset that Christian ethical and theological reflection on these matters has been, from the start, pragmatic as well as systematic in character. When the early fathers of the Church considered how Christians should conduct themselves, they did so in the context of an already existing world of social obligations and structures of power, and their reflections were often occasioned by the pragmatic need to work out how to exist in this world while remaining faithful to the gospel. The beginning is messy. The point may seem self-evident, but it is worth emphasizing, lest we fall into the trap of imagining that there is a pure and homogeneous early Christian tradition, which then becomes corrupted by political realism, the fading of eschatological hope, and accommodation to empire. From its earliest beginnings, Christian thinking about peace and war is hybrid, practical, and internally plural.

The Pre-Constantinian Tradition

In the period before its adoption by Constantine as the religion of the empire, Christianity was a minority phenomenon. During this period, in a particularly acute way, early Christian communities were faced with a whole series of questions about how they were to exist in the midst of a pagan empire and how the social obligations and mores of that empire squared with their identities and duties as disciples of Christ. It was in this context that Paul wrote to the Corinthian church with guidance about the eating of meat sacrificed to idols (1 Cor 8), and it was also in this context that Christian teaching on questions of war and peace first emerged, as theologians and those with pastoral responsibility began explicitly to address the issue of military service and the extent to which participation in it was possible or desirable for Christians.

The first point to note here is that prior to the period 170–80, there seems to be no record of Christians serving in the army. That silence could mean either that military service was regarded as unproblematic or that it was generally assumed that Christians would abstain from military service and therefore the issue did not need addressing. Although there is some debate on the matter, the second of these two alternatives is, on balance, the most likely.[1] Christianity found its initial popularity among civilians in urban centers and among the lower classes, and slaves and freedmen were ineligible for military service. For those Christians eligible for military service, there were strong reasons to avoid it: it would be difficult for serving soldiers to avoid idolatry, and the Church in this early period did not readmit to communion those guilty of apostasy and bloodshed. By 173, however, there is mention of Christians serving in the "Thundering Legion" of Marcus Aurelius, and thereafter the presence of Christians in the army seems to have slowly increased, in particular on the less secure eastern frontier. This means that the earliest Christian writers on the topic are dealing not just with the general question of whether or not military service is permissible but also with an existing compromise and the more specific ethical questions attendant on it, including whether killing was outlawed for Christian soldiers and what stance Christians in the army ought to take with regard to the activities of the imperial cult, from the wearing of ceremonial laurel wreaths to taking part in victory processions.

These specific practical concerns feature prominently in the first writing we have dealing with Christians and military service, and they coexist alongside more general exhortations to peacefulness and condemnations of violence. Tertullian (ca. 160–220) writes vehemently against Christians participating in military service, highlighting the practical dangers of idolatry, violence, and lewdness, as well as making a stronger general case that "Christ in disarming Peter ungirt every soldier."[2] Origen reassures his pagan audience about Christian support for the empire and social order while at the same time discouraging Christians from participating in violence.[3] Without explicitly condemning military service, Clement of Alexandria makes clear that Christians' primary allegiance lies elsewhere: he calls Christians "a bloodless army called up by blood and the word" and exhorts them to "put on the armour of peace."[4] In a similar move, highlighting that the new standard is higher than the old, Lactantius argues that God prohibits not just murder ("brigandage") but also the kinds of killing that people regard as legal, including participation in war.[5]

These thinkers' conclusions regarding specific ethical questions about military service are of abiding significance for Christian tradition, and we will see later how contemporary thinkers draw on their sense of Christians as a socially distinct group, set apart from empire. For now, it is most helpful to note some features of the theological framework in which they came to these conclusions. The first point to note is the general consensus among the early fathers that Christianity demands pacifism. This is not a uniform, absolute, or systematically worked out position shared among the various authors, but it does amount to a common view that the gospel ideals of love of neighbor and forgiveness and the imitation of Jesus's nonviolence and refusal to retaliate against violence are the default option for Christians and are not lightly to be set aside. While acknowledging this general pre-Constantinian consensus that Christians should abstain from military service, it is important to note that there is both variation within and development during the period in question: it is not the case that there is uniform pacifism, followed by the gradual acceptance of military service after the accession of Constantine.[6] Rather, there is a strong bias against military service and toward pacifism, but the gradual increase in military service across the period both reflects and produces a range of Christian positions on the subject, such that the views of Augustine offer points of continuity and discontinuity with the tradition that precedes him.

The second point worth noting is that although the early fathers strongly discouraged participation in military service, they do not advocate a complete withdrawal from empire or public life more broadly.[7] It is certainly the case that these authors understood being a disciple of Christ to mean being in but not of the world and that they "associated displacement from the larger social order precisely with the call to Christian discipleship," but this general sense that their treasure lay elsewhere did not translate into a wholly antagonistic or separatist stance vis-à-vis the empire.[8] Rather, aware that they are writing for pagan onlookers as well as their Christian audience, these authors tended to acknowledge the legitimacy of state power and commend appropriate modes of support for it, in order to refute the charge that Christians are indifferent or hostile to the empire. Tertullian states that Christians should support the emperor by their prayers, even if they do not undertake military service, and Origen argues that Christians should "also be fighting as priests and worshippers of God, keeping their hands pure and by their prayers to God striving for those who fight in a righteous cause and for the emperor who reigns righteously, in order that everything which is opposed and hostile to those who act rightly may be destroyed."[9] Even while the case is made for Christian exemption from military service, legitimate imperial authority and the possibility of a just armed campaign are acknowledged. Christians' fundamental orientation is toward the kingdom of God rather than the world, but their pacifism does not entail wholesale sectarianism.

The third and final point worth noting is that these early authors were addressing a situation in which Christians were a minority, either with a marginal role in public life or able to exempt themselves from participating in it to any seriously compromising extent. Generally speaking, the early Christians were not, either corporately or as individuals, in positions of power, so the early fathers writing on the topic were not yet having to grapple with the large-scale questions that would emerge later regarding the use of coercive power by Christian authorities and the conditions for its rightness or wrongness. Theirs was a position analogous to the leaders of a small political party contesting a local election, able to invoke general ideas of economic fairness and commend individual virtue and small-scale local initiatives without having to solve the national pension problem. I say this not with the intent of dismissing the earliest Christian tradition as unrealistic or naive—far from it—but with the aim of reinforcing that the context of the earliest teaching on peace is distinct and that the teaching that emerged in that context cannot necessarily be applied straightforwardly to the ethical, theological, and practical problems that emerge in later periods and contexts.

In recent decades, the recovery of the early Church's tradition of pacifism has sometimes gone hand in hand with a polemic against "Constantinianism" and a reading of Christian history in which Constantine's adoption of Christianity takes on the dimensions of a fall from the pure, undiluted pacifism of the gospels and early Christianity to the checkered history of compromise, Christendom, and triumphalism that followed the Constantinian settlement. This reading of the tradition, which emerges partly from the writings of the Mennonite theologian John Howard Yoder and those influenced by his work, is often paired with an ecclesiology that highlights the importance of the Church's social distinctiveness. It is an ecclesiology that reflects something of the historical experience of Anabaptist churches, that is, an experience of being a small, socially suspect and sometimes persecuted minority. There is much to learn from this tradition and its insights about the relationship between the Christian and the state, but for a Catholic theology of peace there perhaps ought to be question marks applied to this reading of history and the kinds of ethical and theological reflection attendant on it.

The historical question mark over what might be called the "Constantinian Fall" version of events is that the evidence suggests a more complex picture. The ecclesiological question mark is that Catholics should be careful about uncritically accepting a narrative that associates the development of tradition with its corruption or weakening. This does not mean that a Catholic historiography of Church teaching on peace should smooth over discontinuities in the tradition, nor does it exempt the Church from critical reflection on its later tradition in light of the witness of the early fathers. Still less does this ecclesiological question mark mean that Catholic historiography should simplistically equate the actual historical course of Church teaching with the guidance of the Spirit: the exhortation to "test the spirits to see if they are of God" (1 Jn 4:1) applies to our reading of history as well as to our reading of the present. What it does mean is that our reading of the Church's history of teaching on this topic needs to be open to the possibility that development and discontinuity do not necessarily represent a lamentable falling away from an original pristine ideal or practice. In addition to compromise in the light of human sinfulness and frailty, such transitions may reflect the results of serious discernment under the guidance of the Spirit.

Augustine and the Two Cities

With Augustine comes the tradition's first major shift both historically, in terms of the status of Christianity, and theologically, in terms of the new questions theologians have to address and the way in which they do so.

Augustine (354–430) lived and wrote during a period of rapid change. The generation of Christians before him had witnessed the fiercest persecution yet (303–11), but scarcely had the persecution abated when Constantine's accession to imperial power resulted in the Edict of Milan (313), which offered a measure of toleration to Christians. Constantine's reign thereafter saw the gradual Christianizing of the empire: the building of churches, positions of high office for Christians, and the intervention of the emperor in ecclesiastical disputes. The Edict of Thessalonica (380), by which Christianity was made the official religion of the empire, was during Augustine's lifetime, and he, along with the other theologians and pastors of his era, faced a very different set of practical and theological questions from those of his predecessors. The overarching question facing the previous generation, concerning the proper relationship between Christians and the pagan empire, did not disappear with Constantine's conversion but morphed into a new series of theological and pastoral challenges. Augustine faced questions that arose as Christians found themselves in new positions of social responsibility and state power, he had to confront questions about the use of violent force by Christian authorities, and he also faced renewed attacks from pagan writers convinced that Christianity was the reason for the empire's decline. This changed context and the shift in theological and ethical reflection that accompanied it mark the first major structural shift in the tradition, although, as we shall see, Augustine's writings display significant points of continuity with what goes before as well as significant points of difference.

Augustine stands in the tradition of the early fathers in that his reflections on questions of the ethics of war are occasioned by specific problems or queries. Although Augustine is often cited, alongside Ambrose, as the originator of the Christian just war tradition, his "theory" of just war is unsystematic and occasional, spread across a number of different works, foremost among which are the polemic treatise *Contra Faustum Manichaeum* and two letters to Roman officials in Africa, Marcellinus (in 412) and Boniface (in 418). Briefly surveying the thinking on war that emerges from these three texts allows me to identify some of Augustine's key themes; I can then explore how these are developed more fully in his more extended treatment of peace in *City of God*.

Contra Faustum, written in about 400, critically engages a range of Manichaean beliefs, among them the idea that the God of the Old

Testament was the creator of matter and evil and was inferior to the God of the New Testament, the Father of Jesus. Dismissing this belief requires Augustine to defend the value of the Old Testament, and the morality of its various characters, and to establish the continuity of the Old and New Testaments.[10] It is in this context, as he exonerates Moses for killing the Egyptian overseer and later despoiling the Egyptians, that he has occasion to reflect on the ethics of war.[11] The first point to note here is that for Augustine war and deadly violence are not morally neutral considered in themselves.[12] As John Langan points out, these are actions "which are prima facie wrong, at least to the extent that there is some burden of justification to be carried by the person who would perform them."[13] Like his predecessors, Augustine demonstrates a fundamental presumption against killing, but, in a definite step away from the pacifism of Tertullian and Origen, he shifts the focus of moral reflection away from the rightness or wrongness of actions considered in the abstract and toward the twin questions of their justification and the interior disposition with which they are undertaken. I will take each in turn.

Commenting on Moses's killing of the Egyptian, Augustine states that eternal law forbids those with no legal authority from killing another person, even if that person is bad or an aggressor.[14] The issue of authority, then, is central to the question of whether or not a war is justified: it is not justified unless it is undertaken under the authority of a legitimate political power (a sovereign or state) or under the authority of God.[15] The authority of the former to prosecute war is, in any case, given by God, and Augustine quotes John 19:11 and Romans 13:1 in this connection: "No one can have any power against them but what is given him from above. For there is no power but of God, who either orders or permits."[16] With this emphasis on authority as God ordained comes an equal emphasis on the importance of obedience. Thus Augustine holds that a soldier is innocent who obeys the command of an unjust ruler, because obedience is his duty. This exculpation from blame applies a fortiori to those wars commanded by God: "How much more must the man be blameless who carries on war on the authority of God, of whom every one who serves him knows that he can never require what is wrong?" There would have been less harm, Augustine states, in Moses making war of his own accord than in his not doing so when commanded by God.[17]

Augustine's belief that all authority is ordained by God and that all under it are enjoined to obedience coexists with a strong emphasis on divine providence and its inscrutability. It is God who, without authoring sin, allows sinful actions their time and place; it is God who decides whether people prosper or suffer and whether they do so for their profit or to their ruin. Because these judgments are unfathomable to us, we must simply accept them without argument as divine providence. The result is that Augustine is distinctly agnostic about the significance of our experience, and particularly, in this case, our experience in the course of war.

> Who can tell whether it may be good or bad in any particular case—in time of peace, to reign or to serve, or to be at ease or to die—or in time of war, to command or to fight, or to conquer or to be killed? At the same time, it remains true, that whatever is good is so by the divine blessing, and whatever is bad is so by the divine judgement. At any rate, God's commands are to be submissively received, not to be argued against.[18]

John Langan notes that this agnosticism regarding our experience rests in part on a standard Stoic contrast between those goods within our control, virtues like humility, and those outside our control, like riches or health. In Augustine's scheme, anything that can be taken from one is a lesser good, and those spiritual goods that cannot be lost against one's will are regarded as superior.[19]

This brings us to the second characteristic emphasis of Augustine's thought on war: a focus on interiority. Augustine locates the moral problem with war less with the exercise of violence or the fact of killing—the people involved are going to die anyway, he points out—and more with the dispositions of those involved. The true evils of war, he argues, are the love of violence, vengeful cruelty, fierce and implacable enmity, wild resistance, and the lust for power.[20] It is for the punishment and restraint of such evils that war may be justly prosecuted: when war "is undertaken in obedience to God, who would rebuke, humble, or crush the pride of man, it must be allowed to be a righteous war."[21] Augustine's focus on the interior means that war cannot only be considered righteous in such circumstances, but even as loving. Writing to Boniface, he urges:

> Peace should be the object of your desire; war should be waged only as a necessity, and waged only that God may by it deliver men from the necessity and preserve them in peace. . . . Therefore, even in waging war, cherish the spirit of a peacemaker, that, by conquering those whom you attack, you may lead them back to the advantages of peace; for our Lord says: Blessed are the peacemakers; for they shall be called the children of God.[22]

Even wars undertaken for the punishment of wickedness can be loving: Augustine draws on the example of Moses punishing the Israelites for idolatry, arguing that Moses "acted as he did, not in cruelty, but in great love."[23]

Augustine's conclusion that war cannot only be rightly undertaken by Christians, but even lovingly and at the command of God, seems to put him at some considerable distance from the pacifism of the authors in the centuries preceding him, but this difference should not blind us to the significant points of continuity between them. As discussed above, Augustine is profoundly agnostic about the ultimate significance of temporal welfare and goods while at the same time being absolutely convinced of divine providence and the overriding importance of spiritual goods. This ambivalence to the world and one's fortunes within it and the radical orientation toward the kingdom, understood as otherworldly, are characteristics that Augustine shares with his pre-Constantinian predecessors; the difference is that for Augustine this standoffish relationship is lived primarily on the interior rather than the social level. The same themes receive more extended and systematic treatment in Augustine's *City of God*. His understanding of peace as *tranquillitas ordinis* and the eschatological framework in which he discusses it are both profoundly influential for the tradition that follows, and it is worth exploring them in some detail.

Peace, Augustine states, consists in the tranquillity of order, in which equal and unequal things are rightly ordered in such a way as to give each its proper place. This kind of peace is inherent in creation because creation itself is a kind of ordering: peace and created existence are, in a sense, coextensive. Thus Augustine can say that "there is no one who does not seek peace" and that even if creatures seek an unjust peace rather than God's peace "they cannot help loving peace of some kind

or other. For no vice is entirely contrary to nature so as to destroy even
the last vestiges of nature."[24] In claiming that all creatures seek peace of
some kind or other, Augustine is stating something he takes to be a general
law, like the second law of thermodynamics. Even the opposite of
peace, war, is waged because the belligerents wish "to exchange the peace
of the present for one of their own choosing"; likewise, even "robbers
wish to have peace with their fellows, if only to invade the peace of others
with greater safety." The same desire for peace extends to wild and ferocious
animals, and even to a corpse, which, left to decay, eventually "unites
with the elements of the world and, little by little, passes away into their
peace."[25] This understanding of peace as *tranquillitas ordinis* is analogical,
and the desire for peace in this sense is something robber barons can hold
in common with holy martyrs. But analogy involves difference as well as
likeness, and if Augustine unites these various senses of peace under the
concept of *tranquillitas ordinis*, he also very clearly differentiates them.
For Augustine, the difference between unjust peace and just peace, and
the difference between peace as the world gives and the eschatological
peace of heaven, is not one of scale or extent but of kind.

In order to unpack this, we need to explore the eschatological context
in which Augustine's understanding of peace unfolds. Book XIX
of *City of God* opens with what seems like an obscure engagement with
Marcus Varro on the number of schools in philosophy.[26] The discussion
is a springboard for Augustine to establish the nature of the final
good, which for Christians cannot be sought or found in earthly life.
For Christians, the final good must be eschatological, and Augustine
argues that "eternal life is the Supreme Good, and eternal death the Supreme
Evil, and that to achieve the one and avoid the other, we must live
rightly."[27] Augustine goes on to discuss the ends of the two cities whose
peace and progress he has been tracing up to this point. The end of the
heavenly city is "life eternal in peace," "a perfectly ordered and harmonious
fellowship in the enjoyment of God, and of one another in God."[28]
Included in this vision of final peace is the peace of each individual, understood
as the submission of the body to the rational soul and of the
will to God. Eternal life in peace is the perfect and happy ordering of
our existence, personal and social, in relation to the Author of all order.[29]

While Augustine acknowledges that the word *peace* is often used in
connection with merely mortal affairs, it is clear that his linking of peace

with eternal life quite radically relativizes the significance of any earthly peace. Densely put, peace as the world gives is to eschatological peace as earthly life is to eternal life. Eternal life is not our ordinary earthly life prolonged indefinitely but a qualitatively new state of being in which "there will be no animal body to press down the soul by its corruption, but a spiritual body," and we will obey God with a "delight and effort-lessness" not possible in this life.[30] In the same way, the peace of heaven is not the peace of earth intensified and undisrupted but something qualitatively different: "The Supreme Good of the City of God, then, is eternal and perfect peace. This is not the peace which mortal men pass through on their journey from birth to death. Rather, it is that peace in which they rest in immortality and suffer adversity no more."[31] For Augustine, there is no clear path of ascent between the peace that is possible in this life and the peace of the life to come.[32] The peace of robber barons and the peace of the saints are both kinds of order, but this analogy does not mean that the peace of the Roman Empire can grow into the eternal peace of the heavenly kingdom: the difference between them is of kind, not merely of degree. Between earthly peace and heavenly peace, as between earthly life and heavenly life, stands death and resurrection. This is important because, as discussed later, Augustine's thinking on this point is quite markedly different from the faith in human progress, the possibility of social transformation, and the prospects for peace on earth envisioned by *Pacem in terris* and the tradition that follows it. For Augustine, as Eugene Te Selle notes, "nothing that is physically con-structed through human effort, whether institutions, or conditions of life, can pass through the flame of death and resurrection."[33]

This discontinuity affects the relationship between the Christian and the world. Augustine does not advocate the Christian's withdrawal from the world or from involvement in its institutions: the city of God and the earthly city do not correspond to the Church and the world, and Augustine's sharp distinction between the ends and ordering loves of the two cities do not translate into sectarianism on the political or ecclesiological level. Moreover, he recognizes the peace afforded by the sphere of earthly and mortal affairs as a great good, not to be despised.[34] Here, the analogical character of peace as the tranquillity of order seems to resurface: peace is "well-ordered concord" and while the two cities may have separate origins and ends, what their citizens have in common are those relationships of order that structure this present life, such as those within the household between masters and slaves and fathers and children and the civic peace preserved or restored by just war.[35] Christians also participate in these relationships, ordering them to the love of God by undertaking them with dutiful concern for others and a love of mercy.[36] Temporal peace also allows Christians to concentrate on their struggle toward that peace of obedience to God in which the mind will rule the body and reason the vices, a peace that will only finally be theirs when they are freed from their mortal bodies and "healed by immortality and incorruption."[37] In this way, Augustine says, the heavenly city "makes use of earthly peace during her pilgrimage. . . . Indeed, she directs that earthly peace towards heavenly peace: toward the peace which is so truly such that—at least so far as rational creatures are concerned— only it can really be held to be peace and called such."[38]

It is worth noting here just how limited, how small-scale, is Augustine's understanding of the role of Christians in maintaining, promoting, or transforming earthly peace. Referencing Jeremiah's instruction to the exiles to seek the peace of the city because "in the peace thereof shall ye find peace" (Jer 29:7), Augustine exhorts Christians to "make use of the peace of Babylon," and earlier in Book XIX he states that the heavenly city "desires and maintains the cooperation of men's wills in attaining those things which belong to the mortal nature of man, insofar as this may be allowed without prejudice to true godliness and religion."[39] But, as Oliver O'Donovan points out, Augustine simply does not have large-scale social transformation in view, neither as a possible intermediate stage between earthly peace and heavenly peace nor as an obligation for Christians seeking to make good use of earthly peace.[40] The example Augustine gives of Christians making good use of earthly peace is domestic: fathers are to seek the spiritual, as well as physical, welfare of their household, treating all its members as though they were children.[41] Although Augustine notes that domestic peace has reference to civic peace, "the authority-structure of the householder will not change before the coming of Christ's kingdom. What the Christian householder achieves is to superimpose another meaning on the relationships that arise within it, very much as the Christian emperor superimposes the righteousness of his conduct upon the tasks of dominion. They are signs of God's purpose to restore created innocence, but not the substance of it."[42]

In this life, all that citizens of both the earthly and heavenly cities can attain is piecemeal peace, which is inevitably short-lived, struggled for, and incomplete. What marks Christians out is their *use* of this piecemeal peace to its proper end—the ordering of all things in obedience to God—and their vivid hope for a peace beyond the death of their mortal bodies that will be pure and eternal. They therefore make practical use of the world's peace but do not invest the presence or lack of it with much theological significance, or exert themselves in order to transform the structural conditions of the world's peace.[43] Christians are just pilgrims, passing through.[44]

Augustine is sometimes characterized as a pessimist but the label, at least in relation to his political thought, is not a helpful one: his thought is shot through with a radical eschatological hope, even as it offers a fairly bleak assessment of the possibility of earthly progress. It might be more helpful to think of Augustine's theology as being characterized by relationships of discontinuity. Even as Augustine employs the overarching concept of *tranquillitas ordinis*, the image of the two cities, and his discussion of peace in the context of their respective ends, results in a strong discontinuity between the peace of the world, an order without justice, and the peace of eternal life, in which all is rightly ordered in easy obedience to God. The same distinction produces a discontinuity between present and future, earthly and heavenly, and to the extent that the lives of Christians and pagans are concretely shaped by their respective loves, there exists a potential discontinuity between Church and world.

I have already noted that Church teaching on peace in the post–Vatican II era offers a striking contrast. Where Augustine is criticized for being overly pessimistic, postconciliar teaching on peace is criticized for being overly optimistic, even utopian, in its belief in the possibility of transforming national and international institutions to create a just peace. Where Augustine's thinking about peace is characterized by relationships of discontinuity, postconciliar teaching is generally marked by relationships of continuity: continuity between present possibility and eschatological promise, between earth and heaven, and between Church and world. Historical context accounts for some of the difference, but in order to understand how we get from one to the other, we also need to explore some of the theological shifts that take place across the same period. This means engaging with Thomas Aquinas and the way in which he reshapes and hands on what he receives from Augustine.

The Medieval Period

Augustine's understanding of peace as tranquil order within states, and in relationships between states, still informs Catholic thinking on international relations. It is his thinking on just war, however, which is most influential in the period that immediately follows him. Augustine is sometimes cited as the originator of just war doctrine, but the attribution is something of an anachronism. As we have seen, just war thinking is peripheral to Augustine's thinking taken as a whole, and his writings on the subject are occasional and unsystematic, worked out by way of riposte to Manicheism, and in response to the needs and situations of individuals like Marcellinus and Boniface. It is not until the medieval period that the just war doctrine takes on its classic shape.

Augustine's understanding of a just war as one declared by a right authority with the intention of punishment is included in Gratian's *Decretals* (ca. 1140), and this canon law context is important for how his thinking is mediated to the later tradition. Canon lawyers in this period draw not only on scripture and Christian thinkers but also on Roman law and the chivalric code as they adapt and develop Augustine's understanding of just war for the needs of their own period, in which secular and ecclesiastical power interact and overlap in complex ways: the task of the canonists, very often, is to distinguish and clarify what is in practice confused and in flux. It is a period in which the Church wields considerable power: the early Middle Ages see attempts to limit warfare between Christian nobles by banning fighting on certain feasts and days of the week and proscribing certain weapons, as well as exhortations to holy war in the crusades. Perhaps the key development in this period, however, is the growing power of the prince, which is reflected in the canonical and theological tradition by an increasing emphasis on the *ius gentium*. Although Augustine's conception of just war is still fundamental, the idea of the magistrate wielding God's sword in punishment begins to pull apart, creating an increasingly clear distinction between secular warfare waged by the prince to defend his interests and holy warfare waged for religious reasons.[45]

Also notable in this period is the development of the tradition in the direction of *jus in bello*, which is not really in view for Augustine. The chivalric code, in particular, was influential in producing a growing consensus about noncombatant immunity, which extended to those unable to bear arms, including women and children, those who did not belong to the fighting classes, like land-tilling peasants, and clergy, also on the grounds that they could not bear arms as their occupation was spiritual rather than temporal. The flipside of this clerical immunity from combat was the insistence that—excepting holy war against Saracens or heretics—the Church did not have the authority to wage war: quite simply, it was not the Church's business.[46]

Aquinas and the One Body

Aquinas's theology of peace follows Augustine fairly closely, but his distinctive historical context and theological framework also mean that his points of emphasis shift in ways that significantly affect the subsequent tradition.

We have seen how Augustine's thought on peace is structured by the analogy of the two cities and by consideration of their respective ends. The existence of the two cities, their paths through history, and the destinies that await them are made known by revelation, but there is also a strong sense that God's order and providence are only foggily knowable by human beings in the midst of a fallen creation. In Augustine's scheme, the momentum is heavenward, toward the certainty of spiritual goods and the happily ordered peace of eternal life. Aquinas's understanding of order stands in contrast to this picture in several respects. His Aristotelian borrowings mean that in his discussion of peace he is principally interested in God's order as it is revealed in nature rather than in the narrative of scripture. As Joseph Pieper puts it, creation for Aquinas is "'in itself' light, radiant and self-revealing, *precisely because it is.*"[47] Although this sense of creation as synonymous with order is something he shares with Augustine, in Thomas it is joined to a theological anthropology that gives a positive account of humans' ability to perceive the order of nature and act according to its precepts.[48]

Aquinas's thought about peace takes place against this background and in the context of an analogy between the individual person and the social body. The last end of the individual person, according to Aquinas, is happiness, and virtue is action undertaken toward that end.[49] Human happiness is twofold: we can attain a happiness in accordance with our nature simple and a happiness in accordance with our nature as it is called to participation in God's life.[50] The last end of a human being, properly speaking, is God, and we attain to this last end by knowing and loving God.[51] Natural human happiness is attainable, with help from God, by means of our natural principles; the end of our more than natural happiness, participation in God's life, is attained through the theological virtues of faith, hope, and love, which are supernatural gifts.[52] Aquinas's understanding of the body politic follows this account of individual happiness quite closely. He writes in *De Regno*, "Since society must have the same end as the individual man, it is not the ultimate end of an assembled multitude to live virtuously, but through virtuous living to attain to the possession of God."[53] The last end of human society is also the possession of God, but, as with the last end of the individual, this cannot be attained by our natural powers alone. To the king, therefore, is given the ministry of human government and the duty of directing society according to the cardinal virtues; to priests is given the ministry of directing the people—including the king—to their supernatural end, participation in God.[54]

This movement from the individual to the multitude is replicated in Aquinas's thinking about peace in the *Summa*. There, he defines peace as the unity of desire in individuals and between individuals.[55] Thus he agrees with Augustine that all people desire peace, insofar as they desire to attain what they want unhindered either interiorly, through dissension between the appetites, or exteriorly, through the dissension and opposition of others. People break peace and make war, Aquinas argues, only in order to get what they want, namely, a peace more to their liking.[56] Here, Thomas sounds closer to Augustine than perhaps he really is. Augustine's account of desiring peace is deeply ambivalent, applying even to dead bodies and robber barons, but in Aquinas's scheme, in the context of an optimistic account of the human capacity to know and do the good, the same idea of naturally desiring peace becomes much less ambivalent and much more positive.

Aquinas's account of law in the *Summa* takes us further, linking the pursuit of peace with the king's pursuit of the common good. Here, too, we see his strikingly positive assessment of the human capacity to know and participate in the eternal law, through the natural law, by which we naturally apprehend what is good for us and incline toward it, and through human positive law, which, when it is just, is a reflection of and participation in the eternal law.[57] The eternal law is written into our natures: the more virtuous we are, the more we know and correspond to it; and, according to Aquinas, we have a natural knack for virtue.[58] His discussion of divine law, comprising the old law and the new, ties in to his political thought. In discussing the question, "whether the Old Law was good," Aquinas compares the relationship between the old law and the new law to the relationship between human and divine law. The end of human law, he states, is "the temporal tranquillity of the state, which end law effects by directing external action, as regards those evils which might disturb the peaceful conditions of the state."[59] The end of divine law is to bring human beings to "that end which is everlasting happiness," which is hindered by any sin, interior or exterior. The old law, he goes on to argue, concerns the prohibition and punishment of sin, but this suffices only for the perfection of human law; the perfection of divine law requires charity, which comes only with the new law of Christ.

This distinction between old and new law, mapped onto the distinction between human and divine law, also maps onto the distinction between peace as the work of justice and peace as the work of charity: "Peace is the 'work of justice' indirectly, in so far as justice removes the obstacles to peace: but it is the work of charity directly, since charity, according to its very nature, causes peace. For love is 'a unitive force' as Dionysius says (*Div. Nom.* Iv): and peace is the union of the appetite's inclinations."[60] We can see more clearly here how much Aquinas's sense of the relationship between earthly peace and the peace of our last end differs in feel from Augustine. Like Augustine, Aquinas makes the link between peace and charity, and it is clear from this passage that peace is not just the product of a human law regulating exterior actions but also the work of charity in producing an interior disposition. Like Augustine, too, Aquinas is clear that the peace of this world is imperfect and that perfect peace is found only "in the perfect enjoyment of the sovereign good," that beatific vision in which all one's desires are united and laid to rest in one object: God.[61] But Aquinas is prepared to call imperfect peace a sort of *true* peace, and in his scheme the relationship between earthly peace and the peace of our last end is one of grace completing nature, gospel perfecting law, and charity perfecting justice.[62]

Aquinas's thinking on just war, which occupies only four short articles of the *Summa*, must be set in the context of this overarching theology of peace.[63] Although he quotes Augustine's definition of a just war as "one that avenges wrongs," his basic understanding of war is not punitive. Instead, Aquinas justifies war in the context of the pursuit of the common good of a *res publica*: a war is justified when those in authority need to defend the common weal against external enemies, just as they defend their people against internal dissension.[64] Although Aquinas discusses war in the context of the virtue of charity, as one of a series of vices contrary to peace (discord, contention, schism, strife, and sedition), his understanding of the positive function of war is as a tool for justice. The role of justice, as we have seen, is to "remove the obstacles to peace." For Aquinas, just war has a limited role: it removes obstacles to peace in the context of a much broader pursuit of the peace and well-being of the multitude.

This positive assessment of political authority and the possibility of a virtuous social life represents a significant shift from Augustine's position in *City of God*. Augustine holds that human beings are naturally social, but he regards political authority as a result of the Fall, existing only because human beings need to be restrained by the threat of force and by coercion. He understands that political authorities are established by the providence of God, but he understands their function rather more in terms of restraining evil than promoting a virtuous social life—hence, for Augustine, the focus on restraint of the wicked as a motive for engaging in just warfare. Aquinas also maintains that human beings are naturally social animals, but, by contrast, he argues that a social order of command and obedience could have existed even in the state of innocence.[65] In Aquinas's scheme, the virtuous king has rather more to do than Augustine's paterfamilias, who exercises his mastery as best he can in accordance with Christian charity. For Thomas, the virtuous king must strive "first of all, to establish a virtuous life in the multitude subject to him; second, to preserve it once established; and third, having preserved it, to promote its greater perfection."[66] The unity of the multitude, Aquinas states, "which we call peace, must be procured through the effort of the ruler."[67]

For Augustine, the peace of the earthly city is welcome, certainly, but it is temporal and piecemeal, not to be loved for its own sake, but to be made use of while hoping for the peace to come. Aquinas's positive understanding of political life and his optimistic take on the human ability to perceive the demands of natural law and act accordingly leave us with a different picture of both the possibility and the significance of earthly peace. Augustine's *peregrini* make use of the "peace of Babylon" while hoping for the peace to come, but Aquinas's analogy between the individual person and the social body makes the path of ascent toward the last end slightly smoother, less utterly discontinuous with the life of the present.[68] Aquinas is no utopian, nor is he focused on social change or progress as we might understand them, but he is very much interested in the possibility of growth toward a virtuous common life, in which political and religious authority both play their parts. Perhaps it is significant in this respect that Aquinas uses the word *viator* rather than *peregrinus*: a *viator* is a wayfarer, whereas *peregrinus* carries a stronger sense of "sojourner," "guest," or even "stranger": a *peregrinus* is away from his homeland; a *viator* is on his way there.

TWO

The New World to the Present

Aquinas is a theologian of medieval Christendom, and his theology reflects the complex relationship between church and state during this period, both in terms of their integration on a theoretical level and in terms of their various interrelations and tensions on a practical level. Aquinas's theological synthesis reflects the religio-political unity of his age, but he also bequeaths to later tradition a series of important distinctions within that overall framework of unity. His overlapping pairings of old law and new law, human law and divine law, justice and charity, the political and the spiritual—even laity and clergy—pass into the Church's teaching on peace and continue to exert a considerable influence on it, even into the contemporary period. But between Aquinas's day and our own lies the early modern period, in which the pairs he is able to hold together as part of his unified theological vision begin to pull apart and from which the rational, ethical human agent emerges still more clearly.

RELIGION AND THE SECULAR

As discussed earlier, Aquinas argues that the sovereign, an authority appointed by God, has the duty to defend the people against external enemies, just as he has a duty to defend them against internal strife. He justifies this by referring to Romans 13:4, "He beareth not the sword in vain, for he is God's minister, an avenger to execute wrath upon him that doth evil."[1] Yet, as the power of the prince grows across the medieval period, the two ideas that Aquinas is able to hold together here—the sovereign as God's minister and the sovereign as defending the people—begin to drift apart. Partly as a result of burgeoning secular power and partly as a result of the influence of Roman law and the chivalric code, *ius gentium*, which Aquinas understands as part of the divine dispensation, comes to be understood more as a body of custom. The power of the sovereign is increasingly understood not as coming from above, from God, but as coming from below, from the people. Correspondingly, there is a shift in the meaning of just war doctrine, "making it not primarily an assertion of God's judgement against evildoers, but a description of the right of princes to retaliate against troublers of their own domains."[2] Instead of "exalting the presence of God behind the magistrate . . . tradition after the thirteenth century increasingly separates God and the magistrate as motive forces for just warfare."[3] The sovereign's right to defend his people against external enemies and "holy war" undertaken to defend God's honor separate out.

James T. Johnson argues that the Protestant Reformation and the European "wars of religion" that ensue cement this distinction between the motives and the authorities for just warfare. Up to this point "religion," "Christianity," and "the Roman Church" had been synonymous in Europe, and it is only with the Reformation that "religion" first begins to emerge as a category.[4] This period is often thought of in terms of warfare between existing religious bodies—Catholics and Protestants—who understood themselves as such and pursued war against one another on explicitly religious grounds, until the rise of the secular state delivered Europe from a religious bloodbath and thereafter assumed, once and for all, sole authority to declare and prosecute war.[5] William Cavanaugh has disputed this conventional reading of the period, arguing that such an account is part of the creation myth of the modern nation-state. The conflicts of the wars of religion, he points out, routinely fracture along nonconfessional lines, with Catholic powers fighting one another, strategic alliances between Protestant and Catholic princes, and Protestant mercenaries fighting for Catholic princes and vice versa.[6] It is not always clear that religious differences are the motive *ad bellum*; what is clearer is that religious differences are used by secular authorities as a way of bolstering their own power.[7] What is occurring during this period, Cavanaugh argues, and indeed what causes the conflicts, is the transfer of power from the church to the state as the medieval order breaks down.[8] The distinction between religion and the secular, or religion and politics, emerges during the early modern period as part of this realignment: "The modern idea of religion as a realm of human activity inherently separate from politics and other secular matters depended upon a new configuration of Christian societies in which many legislative and jurisdictional powers and claims to power—as well as claims to the devotion and allegiance of the people—were passing from the church to the new sovereign state."[9] We will see later on that Aquinas's distinction between the spiritual and political spheres of authority, mapped onto this modern distinction between church and state, continues to influence contemporary Catholic social teaching on peace.

NATURAL LAW AND THE NEW WORLD

On the home front in Europe, then, the late medieval and early modern period sees the growing power of princes over against church authorities and the emergence of the nation-state. The religious and the secular, united by Aquinas in *De Regno*, have begun to emerge more clearly as separate and drift apart. The unity of divine law, natural law, human positive law, and the *ius gentium* also begins to pull apart. These cultural shifts are reflected in the changing shape of just war doctrine over the same period. The shift to a natural law framework is already present in Aquinas: after Aquinas, as Cahill puts it, "the commitment to a reasonable moral order, knowable in principle by all human beings and forming the basis of a common morality, moves to center stage."[10]

The movement of natural law to center stage happens over the course of centuries and, in addition to owing something to cultural shifts in Europe, it owes much to the discovery of the New World. Here, for the first time, theologians are discussing just war and *jus ad bellum* not in the context of Europe, and a theoretical separation of powers, but in the context of new lands and indigenous peoples over whom neither pope nor prince can claim authority. The work of the Dominicans Thomas Cajetan (1469–1534) and Francisco de Vitoria (1483–1546) was particularly important in this context. De Vitoria argues that the emperor is not the lord of the world, as "no one by natural law has dominion over the whole world," and that even if he were "that would not entitle him to seize the provinces of the Indian aborigines and to erect new lords and put down the former lords or to levy taxes."[11] The pope, likewise, has no temporal authority over the whole world, "for no lordship can come to him save either by natural law or by divine law or by human law. Now, it is certain that none comes to him by natural or by human law, and none is shown to come to him by divine law."[12] The rights of the indigenous population to property and government can be established by natural law, and de Vitoria dismisses all claims to override these rights on the basis of indigenous peoples being "naturally slaves," unbelievers, or unsound of mind. In the subsequent generation, the Jesuit natural law jurist Francisco Suárez (1548–1617) followed de Vitoria's lead, arguing that "there is no ground for war so exclusively reserved to Christian princes that it has not some basis in, or at least some due relation to, natural law, being therefore also applicable to princes who are unbelievers."[13]

The justice of war is now being assessed on solidly natural law ground, and the foundations of what will become the modern human rights tradition have been laid. This rights tradition will continue to develop, eventually resurfacing in papal teaching—after a long exile during the Enlightenment period—in *Pacem in terris*.[14] This shift to natural law is an important one not only for the substance of Catholic social teaching but also for its style. Aquinas, while a prolific commenter on scripture, tends to use scripture in the *Summa* and in his political theology as illustrative and ancillary rather than as a point of departure. The post–*Rerum novarum* Catholic moral and social teaching tradition follows his lead, tending to use scripture homiletically or in proof text fashion rather than beginning from engagement with scriptural texts.[15] The shift to natural law also eventually affects the assumed audience of Catholic social teaching. Though Aquinas is writing for medieval Christendom and de Vitoria and Suárez for early modern Christian Europe, their natural law reasoning is in principle accessible to those outside the Catholic Church or without specifically Christian faith. This "in principle" eventually becomes practice, and the documents of the Catholic social teaching tradition from the nineteenth century on are aimed as much at the public sphere as the specifically ecclesial community. This practice has persisted as the international community has become increasingly secular and multifaith. The shift in audience does not begin with Aquinas, but it is his decisive move toward a natural law paradigm that eventually makes it possible. The significance of these shifts in style will become clearer as I explore how Church teaching develops over the course of the twentieth century. Before this, however, I want to explore how Aquinas's distinction between the two ends of the human person, natural and supernatural, is mediated by the later tradition in a way that significantly affects Church teaching on peace over the subsequent centuries.

NATURE AND GRACE

Aquinas gives two ends for the human being: the natural happiness that belongs to our nature and the supernatural happiness that is the fulfillment of our vocation to life with God. The desire to see God is in us by nature, he says, but that natural desire can be fulfilled only by grace.[16] The challenge for Aquinas is to show grace as completing and perfecting nature but also as grace, that is, a free gift of God not demanded by our nature. Yet the idea of human nature without the gift of grace is hardly more than a thought experiment for Thomas, a theoretical possibility: he cannot really bracket out the concrete history of grace to address the idea of "pure nature," and he does so only to demonstrate that human nature, while compatible with grace, does not require it in a strict sense. His insistence that human beings have a natural desire to see God and that human nature is sufficient to achieve its end is intended to show that the frustration of our desire is not "built in." Rather, we are unable to attain our end because we are fallen, and thus we cannot attain our natural end without the help of God. Nor, importantly, can we *know* the inability of our nature to attain its own ends without the help of grace.[17] Only by grace can we know our need—a need that God, in Christ, has already fulfilled and surpassed. In Aquinas, we see our human nature as though at a distance, with the whole landscape of salvation history lying between it and ourselves as we are now, travelers called, fallen, redeemed, and irreversibly changed by the journey.

The generation of scholars that cement Aquinas's importance for Catholic theology by replacing Peter Lombard's *Sentences* with the *Summa Theologica* as the standard textbook for university teaching return to his treatment of nature and grace and, in interpreting it, rework it in ways that have a significant impact. Henri de Lubac's *Surnaturel* and *The Mystery of the Supernatural* traced the malaise of early twentieth-century theology to the work of Cajetan and Suárez, but it should be noted that the changing understanding of the relationship between nature and grace evident in their work was part of a wider cultural shift.[18] In different ways, the work of Cajetan and Suárez reflects that cultural shift and pushes nature and grace farther apart.

Cajetan seeks to clarify what Aquinas means by our *natural* desire to see God. A natural desire to see God, he argues, makes sense only in retrospect, looking back down the path of salvation history as I have described it above. We can speak of a natural desire for God only in the context of our knowledge of our *supernatural* vocation; take this away, he argues, and there is no desire for God intrinsic to our human nature, considered in isolation. Cajetan therefore proposes

> a hypothetical state of nature that in the absence of supernatural grace or the knowledge of revelation would have its own proper end obtainable by natural powers, i.e. the natural contemplation of God. Since Cajetan's schema envisions nature as a self-contained, autonomous system with its own end we have here the idea of the *duplex ordo*, an order of grace with a supernatural end, and an order of nature with a natural end.[19]

This state of "pure nature" is hypothetical, because God has chosen to give us a supernatural end, but it is important: without it, Cajetan believed, grace would no longer be grace because our nature would require it. We can see this *duplex ordo* at work in Suárez's consideration of natural law. We have seen Aquinas's confidence in human beings' ability to know and do good through the law written into our natures, even though he insists that we need the help of grace. In Suárez, that confidence in natural law remains, but grace is no longer so integral to the picture: the natural law is completely known to us by nature and can be followed using our natural powers alone.[20]

Henri de Lubac, engaging in the 1930s with these sixteenth- and seventeenth-century interpreters of Thomas, was motivated in part by what he described as a "cultural alienation" of the Church— an alienation that, in part, he saw as the product of their theologies of nature and grace.[21] The idea of a purely natural human beatitude attainable without the need for grace leads us, he says, "to suppose a being similar to that so often presented by rationalist philosophies—both ancient and modern: a being sufficient unto himself, and wishing to be so; a being who does not pray, who expects no graces, who relies on no Providence."[22] Whether it is quite fair to lay this at the feet of Cajetan and Suárez is debatable; what is clear is that "Enlightenment man," master of his own life and social destiny, is not just the product of the increasing separation of religion and the secular that we explored above but also the product of theological forces at work in the same period. The confident account of human reason and abilities characteristic of political liberalism owes something to the idea of "pure nature" as it emerges from Thomas's interpreters.[23] Later on, I explore how these sixteenth- and seventeenth-century interpretations of Aquinas emerge in the natural law optimism of Pope John XXIII's *Pacem in terris*; I also show how the twentieth-century debates over these same interpretations of Thomas would result in a new understanding of the relationship between nature and grace at the Second Vatican Council. First, however, let us explore how the natural law paradigm shaped the early beginnings of the Catholic social teaching tradition as it emerged at the end of the nineteenth century.

CATHOLIC SOCIAL TEACHING BEFORE 1950

Tadolini's statue of Pope Leo XIII in the Lateran basilica towers over the viewer, its arm upraised in a gesture of blessing that is anything but static. This is a pope who, marble foot protruding over the edge of the base on which he stands, has just risen to his feet and raised an arm for attention. The pose is a fitting one: it was Leo XIII's 1891 encyclical, *Rerum novarum*, with its call for the protection of the rights of workers in rapidly industrializing Europe, that inaugurated the modern tradition of Catholic social teaching. While *Rerum novarum* itself has little to say on the subject of peace beyond a general concern for tranquility in industrial relations, its robust natural law framework, combined with its consideration of what Vatican II would christen "the signs of the times" and its basic assumption that a just social, political, and economic order is the Church's proper concern, laid the foundations for a new mode of Church engagement with political, economic, and social life.[24]

The idea of a divinely established natural order, which human beings can perceive and obey, is basic to *Rerum novarum.* The reflection on the conditions of the working classes with which the encyclical opens simply states the manifest injustice of the situation. The encyclical then dismisses the socialist response to this injustice, and it is here that the natural law reasoning of the encyclical can be seen most clearly. After some extended reflection on human nature, Leo XIII defends the ownership of private property as a natural right and goes on to defend the rights of the family as a unity "founded more immediately in nature" against state interference.[25] The natural law foundation means that the encyclical, notwithstanding its critique of social injustice, appears socially conservative by today's standards. Leo XIII states emphatically that "it is impossible to reduce civil society to one dead level" and that efforts to do so are "striving against nature."[26] Human society is naturally unequal, but this does not mean that its fundamental state is conflictual.[27] Rather, the inequality of societies is to the advantage of both individuals and the community, and classes "should dwell in harmony and agreement, so as to maintain the balance of the body politic."[28] What Leo XIII advocates is not the upending of the natural order but its perfection through charity.[29] In this respect, the encyclical has an Augustinian streak: major social change is simply not within view, and attempts to foment it are strongly criticized. Instead, alongside exhortations to industrialists to treat their workers with justice, there is an exhortation to endure the pain and hardships that are an inevitable part of earthly life and to hope for heaven.[30]

This natural law framework, with an Augustinian accent, also characterizes two important documents on peace that emerge between *Rerum novarum* in 1891 and the watershed document, Pope John XXIII's *Pacem in terris* (1963). These are Benedict XV's *Ad beatissimi apostolorum* (1914) and Pius XI's *Ubi arcano Dei consilio* (1922). The dates of these two encyclicals should alert us to their context: the outbreak of World War I and its aftermath. Briefly exploring both will enable us to identify some of the key emphases in Catholic social teaching on peace as it develops during this period.

Benedict XV's *Ad beatissimi apostolorum* was written in 1914 as fighting on the Western Front ground to a stalemate.[31] The encyclical is remarkably Augustinian in feel. Benedict holds that the present "sanguinary strife" is caused by an evil "raging in the very inmost heart of human society": the abandoning of Christian wisdom in the ruling of states, the absence of mutual love between peoples, contempt for rulers, and, underpinning all these, pride and self-love. The cause of the war, as well as of the social breakdown in the states and the family, is the same self-destructive love that characterizes the earthly city.[32] If Benedict's diagnosis of the causes of conflict is Augustinian, his proposed remedies for it are equally so: he focuses on the interior life and the life to come and argues that "what are called the goods of this mortal life have indeed the appearance of good, but not the reality[;] . . . therefore it is not in the enjoyment of them that man can be happy."[33] Rather, by bearing suffering and sorrows patiently, we are "to enter into possession of those true and imperishable goods which 'God hath prepared for them that love Him.'"[34] In Benedict XV's view, peace will be attained by the proper ordering of love, and it is therefore necessary to revive hope for eternal happiness in the hearts of all, "for in no other way can individuals and nations attain to peace." He continues, "Let us, then, bid those who are undergoing distress of whatever kind, not to cast their eyes down to the earth in which we are as pilgrims, but to raise them to Heaven to which we are going: 'For here we have not a lasting city, but we seek the one that is to come.'"[35] The emphasis is markedly Augustinian, even down to the quotation of one of Augustine's favorite passages, Hebrews 13:14.

In spite of this emphasis on interior peace and the peace of eternal life, Benedict XV is by no means suggesting that Christians need take no interest in earthly peace, and his own unsuccessful efforts to resolve the conflict through diplomacy in 1916 and again in 1917 bear witness to his determination to seek the peace of the earthly city.[36] Peace is necessary, he writes, "for the sake of human society and for the sake of the Church; for human society, so that when peace shall have been concluded, it may go forward in every form of true progress; for the Church of Jesus Christ, that freed at length from all impediments it may go forth and bring comfort and salvation even to the remote parts of the earth."[37] There is a more Thomist strain here, in the reference to the progress of human society and its relationship to the ministrations of the Church, but here, too, without undermining the need to strive for earthly peace, emphasis falls on the Augustinian idea that such peace allows the Church to go about its tasks freely. On this point, the Augustinian tone of the encyclical reflects the position of the Vatican during this period. The century leading up to 1915 had seen the Catholic Church's position seriously challenged by new political arrangements in France, Spain, and Italy, with the result that the Vatican had largely withdrawn from the international stage, with the occasional exception of interventions to strenuously defend the rights of the Church.[38]

These themes—the importance of God's order, the need for right ordering of love and hope of heaven—are present in even greater measure in Pius XI's 1922 encyclical, *Ubi arcano Dei consilio* (On the Peace of Christ in the Kingdom of Christ). Eclipsed by *Pacem in terris* and remembered more for its statements about the laity than its treatment of peace, *Ubi arcano* is nevertheless worth exploring, as it is the first modern encyclical to reflect more systematically on the theme of peace. While deeply traditional in its sources and emphases, when viewed from the other end of the century that would produce *Pacem in terris*, *Ubi arcano* appears both prescient and innovative.

The encyclical, broadly speaking, is Augustinian in its diagnosis and Thomist in its treatment. Pius XI's review of the signs of the times takes the form of a catalog of evils, described in terms of disorder: first of all the disorder affecting relationships between nations—here he notes persistent and growing tensions, "a dense fog of mutual hatreds and grievances"—and then disorder affecting nations, domestic politics, and the family.[39] The list culminates in a consideration of the spiritual evils afflicting the world.[40] The Augustinian character of the analysis is particularly evident as he considers the root of all these evils, naming them as concupiscence, pride of life, inordinate desire for material possessions, and the "inordinate desire to rule or domineer over others." The list is taken almost verbatim from Augustine's list of the evils of war in his letter to Marcellinus. The influence of the *City of God* is evident later on, as Pius XI makes clear the connection between justice and peace: disorder reigns because people have forsaken God, and without recognition of God and his law there can be no justice.[41] But while Pius

XI's analysis of the conflict draws on classic Augustinian ideas of concupiscence and the *libido dominandi*, he does not completely spiritualize or interiorize its causes: he names as a specific cause the persistent "old rivalries" and their pervasive presence in political and cultural life and the tensions and grievances arising from the punitive settlements of World War I.[42] His diagnosis of the causes of conflict engages in sociopolitical, as well as theological, analysis.

Pius XI's positive proposals for peace take their shape from these Augustinian foundations, using recognizably Thomist building materials. If the root cause of war is the forsaking of God and his law, the remedy is for people and governments to recognize God's sovereignty once more: "True peace, the peace of Christ, is impossible unless we are willing and ready to accept the fundamental principles of Christianity, unless we are willing to observe the teachings and obey the law of Christ, both in public and private life."[43] Recognition and observance of God's law will result in acceptance "of the divine origin and control of all social forces" and the proper recognition of political authority.[44] This means, too, accepting the authority of the Church as the divinely instituted "teacher and guide of every other society whatsoever," though Pius is careful to add, "not of course in the sense that she should abstract in the least from their authority, each in its own sphere supreme, but that she should really perfect their authority, just as divine grace perfects human nature."[45] *De Regno* is in the background here, as well as Thomas's synthesis of divine law, natural law, and human law under the canopy of eternal law; present, too, is Thomas's insistence that peace is the work of charity as well as justice.[46]

Ubi arcano reflects the mixed influences of the tradition as I have surveyed it so far, and it shows nicely how the characteristic themes of Augustine end up mediated through Aquinas's natural law framework, itself mediated through his sixteenth- and seventeenth-century interpreters. But Pius XI advances the tradition, as well as reflecting it, and he bequeaths some important principles to subsequent teaching. The first is the emphasis in the encyclical on the peacebuilding role of the Catholic Church, a point Pius XI makes repeatedly. "There is no one," he states, "who cannot clearly see what a singularly important role the Catholic Church is able to play, and is even called upon to assume, in providing a remedy for the ills which afflict the world today and in leading mankind toward a universal peace."[47] This is no mere offer of the Church's assistance, and he claims a few paragraphs later that the Church can not only bring about "at the present hour a peace that is truly the peace of Christ, but can, better than any other agency which We know of, contribute greatly to the securing of the same peace for the future, to the making impossible of war in the future."[48] This emphasis on the peacebuilding role of the Church, and in particular the papacy, is new, and it becomes an abiding feature of Catholic social teaching on peace thereafter. This development reflects the Vatican's recent emergence from diplomatic isolation but is, in larger part, a reaction against the establishment of the League of Nations: Pius XI is explicitly looking back to the medieval period and the religio-political integration of Christendom rather than forward, and it is worth noting that only Europe is really in view here.[49] There is not yet a sense of what role the Holy See might play in peacebuilding in a multifaith or secular context, yet this strengthened understanding of the peacebuilding ministry of the Catholic Church is in itself an important step forward.[50]

The second point worth noting is that this peacebuilding ministry of the Church is not confined to the activities of the Holy See or the Church hierarchy: *Ubi arcano* explicitly mentions the activity of the laity in "bringing about world peace because they work for the restoration and spread of the Kingdom of Christ."[51] With this broad understanding of peacebuilding agents comes a broad understanding of the tasks of peacebuilding. Pius XI talks about the importance of education in "laying a solid groundwork for peace," the need for postconflict solutions that aim at reconciliation rather than "hard inflexible justice," and the need to avoid "a state of armed peace which is scarcely better than war itself."[52] In practical terms, Pius XI understands peacebuilding largely as a matter of re-Christianizing Europe, but these themes of education, reconciliation, justice, and "armed peace" are important and are developed further by later papal messages and encyclicals on peace. Pius XI's closing comments demonstrate a shift in the Church's attitude toward the world's peace—one that anticipates the relationship between the two that will emerge following *Pacem in terris* and the Second Vatican Council. He writes, "It is, therefore, a fact which cannot be questioned that the true peace of Christ can only exist in the Kingdom of Christ—'the peace of Christ in the kingdom of Christ'. It is no less unquestionable that, in doing all we can to bring about the re-establishment of Christ's kingdom, we will be working most effectively towards a lasting world peace."[53]

PACEM IN TERRIS (1963)

John XXIII's *Pacem in terris* marks a watershed in Catholic social teaching on peace. Like *Ad beatissimi* and *Ubi arcano*, the encyclical was written in the shadow of war, in this case the tensions of the Cold War and the very real possibility of nuclear warfare, which had been narrowly avoided in the Cuban Missile Crisis barely months before. Strikingly, however, the document shows few signs of having been written in such a fraught context, and it is confident rather than apocalyptic in tone. Though nuclear issues are discussed (§109–§116), the encyclical as a whole is more programmatic than occasionalist, as John XXIII offers a fairly serene set of reflections on the ideal political conditions for world peace. *Pacem in terris* is in some respects profoundly innovative but in other significant ways deeply rooted in, and continuous with, the tradition before it. It is the combination—the old building materials combined with the new—that will have such an important impact on subsequent Church teaching on peace.

Natural law is the backbone of the encyclical, and its importance is evident from the opening words: "Peace on earth—which man throughout the ages has so longed for and sought after—can never be established, never guaranteed, except by the diligent observance of the divinely established order."[54]

In part, owing to its open, optimistic tone, *Pacem in terris* is often lumped together with the Vatican II documents, but this is not quite accurate. *Gaudium et spes*, as I discuss shortly, displays an understanding of the relationship between grace and nature that owes much to *la nouvelle théologie*; *Pacem in terris*, on the other hand, displays an understanding of nature and grace that is broadly neo-scholastic. The understanding of natural law in the document is one that flows from Thomas's interpreters—Suárez in particular—and the concept of pure nature explored above. Consequently, John XXIII presents a confident picture of the human ability to discern the order that God has placed in the world and to act according to its strictures. It is only at the end of the encyclical, in exhortative mode, that the role of grace is mentioned.[55] This reliance on natural law reflects the audience of the encyclical, which for the first time includes not only the Catholic hierarchy, clergy, and laity, but "all men of good will." But at the same time that John XXIII stands in the neo-scholastic natural law tradition, he also makes significant innovations in it. As Drew Christiansen points out, rather than foreground nature and the moral order abstractly considered, John XXIII places *human* nature at the heart of the encyclical; consequently, the encyclical moves toward employing the language of virtue, as well as the more customary language of moral principle.[56] In addition to anticipating the personalism that will characterize the moral reflection of Vatican II, the move has an impact on the subsequent tradition of Catholic social teaching, which takes up his renewed emphasis on the dignity of the human person and enshrines it as a core principle.[57]

John XXIII's placing of the human being at the center in this way is not just the result of his particular interpretation of the natural law tradition. In adopting rights language, he is drawing into the Catholic social teaching tradition the kind of rights talk against which Pius IX had fulminated in the *Syllabus of Errors* scarcely a hundred years before.[58] The human rights tradition has its roots in the early modern period and theological discussions of the rights of indigenous peoples in the Americas, but it fell out of favor with Enlightenment popes whose temporal and spiritual authority was increasingly being challenged by political liberalism. In a break with this anathematizing streak, John XXIII affirms political and religious freedom and individual rights but does so in a distinctively Catholic key, pairing rights with responsibilities and expecting individual rights to balance and adjust one another in the overarching context of the common good. The encyclical thus marks a certain rapprochement with political liberalism but not a wholesale adoption of its assumptions and priorities.[59]

The emphasis on pride and lack of charity as the cause of war, so characteristic of his predecessors, is absent; John XXIII seems to assume that conflicts are caused by misunderstanding and fear and can be resolved by mutual trust and reasonable dialogue.[60] Matthew Shadle makes the case that John XXIII's optimistic account of human reason in this respect owes something to "the liberal belief, characteristic of Locke, Kant and Bentham, that individuals will act in a moral and rational manner once they have established political institutions that will overcome their shortcomings as individuals."[61] Direct lines of influence are hard to establish here—popes are not great users of footnotes—but it is worth noting that contemporary commentators made the same connection. Reinhold Niebuhr wrote, "The difficulty with this impressive document is that the Church absorbs some of the voluntarism of the social contract theory, which underlies modern liberalism, and speaks as if it were a simple matter to construct and reconstruct communities, not by the organic processes of history but by an application of 'the sense of justice and mutual love.'"[62]

The connection with political liberalism can be overstated. *Pacem in terris* is not a Trojan horse encyclical, ostensibly Catholic on the outside but packed full of liberal political philosophers within. John XXIII is both critical and creative in his use of that tradition, and the encyclical's confidence in human reason and the possibility of peaceful political cooperation owes much to Aquinas and his belief in the possibility of a virtuous commonwealth.[63] It also owes not a little to John XXIII's personal disposition and his tendency to believe in the basic goodness of ordinary people.

In this context, his belief in the capacity of international institutions to establish peace is understandable, and on this point, too, the encyclical marks a departure from the position of his early twentieth-century predecessors. Where *Pacem in terris* urges support for the United Nations, Pius XI was skeptical of the League of Nations and held up the Church as the original and most effective league of nations. John XXIII's belief in the importance of international institutions has stuck, however, and subsequent Church teaching on peace has strongly supported existing international political bodies and, in more recent years, called for their strengthening. Recently, it has called for the creation of new international political bodies to oversee the economic and environmental dimensions of the common good in an increasingly globalized and interdependent world.[64]

New, too, was the encyclical's emphasis on cooperation, with John XXIII recognizing that enacting the principles set out in his encyclical will require "extensive co-operation between Catholics and those Christians who are separated from this Apostolic See. It even involves the co-operation of Catholics with men who may not be Christians but who nevertheless are reasonable men, and men of natural moral integrity."[65]

This position reflects John XXIII's own pragmatic approach to some of the more difficult political relationships facing him, in particular his more conciliatory approach to the Soviet bloc. Again, too, it reflects the marriage of neo-scholastic Thomism with certain strands drawn from liberal political philosophies. The distinction between spiritual and political realms is as old as Aquinas, and it is seen here refracted through the neo-scholastic discontinuity between the natural and supernatural orders. What was a thought experiment for Aquinas's seventeenth-century interpreters—a natural order that is complete and self-contained—had by the mid-twentieth century taken shape as a political reality, in the form of a secular sphere occupied by people of differing beliefs who exercised natural virtues without directing them to the same supernatural end.[66] But, faced with this reality, John XXIII moves away from the calls for integralism characteristic of his early twentieth-century predecessors and instead sets out a vision in which people of differing ideological, political, and religious stripes can collaborate in the pursuit of commonly acknowledged political goods.

With its open tone and conciliatory spirit, and its faith in human reason and in the possibility of cooperation and progress, *Pacem in terris* marked a significant development in Catholic social teaching on peace. Yet among the many voices welcoming the positive and constructive tone of the encyclical were voices of caution regarding its thoroughgoing optimism. The concerns were twofold. Most people found little to object to in the ideals of *Pacem in terris*; the difficulty was that the encyclical *was* so idealistic: it seemed not to take into account the concrete conditions affecting policies of nuclear deterrence, the issue of disarmament, and the problems affecting international organizations. In his faith in human reason and goodwill, John XXIII seemed to have overlooked practical questions of power and ideology.[67] Some commentators felt that the idealism of the encyclical undercut its ability to speak effectively to those in political power. Paul Ramsey noted "the degree to which the pontiff's powerful expression of the aspirations of the whole of mankind . . . becomes a non-political statement in the arena of the actual practice of politics," and Reinhold Niebuhr suggested that the encyclical would be heeded more by idealists than by statesmen.[68]

For others, the difficulties were not just practical, but theological. Some commentators felt that John XXIII's positive assessment of the human ability to discern the divinely established order and enact its requirements was theologically problematic, because it underemphasized both the sinful aspects of human nature and the power of sin in the world. Paul Tillich thought that John XXIII's appeals to "all men of good will" rather overestimated goodwill and underestimated the ambiguity of human nature and action, and Niebuhr argued that the encyclical "is thoroughly modern in many ways, but particularly in breathing a Pelagian, rather than an Augustinian, spirit."[69] In addition to questions about the relationship between what the journalist Giancarlo Zizola called "the utopia of Pope John XXIII" and the realities of Cold War politics, there were questions about the relationship between his vision of a just world order and the kingdom of God. Paul Tillich argued that the encyclical needed to distinguish genuine hope, which has some foothold in the present, from utopian expectation, which does not.[70] While there were some signs of progress, Tillich insisted that peace is ultimately something that must be hoped for.

> There is no hope for a final stage of history in which peace and justice rule. History is not fulfilled at its empirical end; but history is fulfilled in the great moments in which ... the Kingdom of God breaks into history conquering destructive structures of existence, one of the greatest of which is war. This means we cannot hope for a final stage of justice and peace within history; but we can hope for partial victories over the forces of evil in a particular moment in time.[71]

Both Tillich and Niebuhr inhabit a thoroughly Augustinian political landscape rather than the Thomist one inhabited by John XXIII and Catholic social teaching more generally, but their criticisms nevertheless raise some important questions about the relationship between earthly progress and the peace of the kingdom.[72] John XXIII's neo-scholastic framework, in combination with his borrowings from liberal political philosophy and his own hopeful outlook, results in an encyclical that is markedly optimistic and confident in the ability of human beings to construct the rule of peace and justice in history. One of the questions raised is where sin fits into this picture: Christiansen argues that although John XXIII's appeals to goodwill did ease Cold War tensions, overall the encyclical "tended to understate the force of sin in political life" and failed to integrate a theory of conflict into its communitarian vision.[73] A second question concerns grace and whether, given the encyclical's neo-scholastic framework, the peace that is the gift of the risen Christ, alluded to at the end of the encyclical, is really integral to its proposals. *Pacem in terris* leaves Catholic social teaching with a strongly positive sense of the possibility of peace, but it also leaves it with the question of how the "peace that the world cannot give" (John 14:27) enters the frame.

GAUDIUM ET SPES (1965)

The question of whether the optimism of *Pacem in terris* was theologically warranted and practically helpful would recur in discussions on the council floor of what eventually became the pastoral constitution *Gaudium et spes*, as well as in the debates over the interpretation and legacy of that document in the years following Vatican II. At its opening in October 1962, John XXIII had stated that the council "wants to show the world how to put into practice the doctrine of its divine founder, the Prince of Peace," and when at last, in the final months of the council's last session, the fathers entered the final round of discussions on the schema *De ecclesia in mundo huius temporis*, they were conscious of the pope's intention that they make some contribution to world peace.[74] However, in carrying forward the legacy of *Pacem in terris*, they could scarcely avoid replicating some of its more problematic features, and they would add some complications of their own.

Unlike *Pacem in terris*, the council documents taken as a whole tend to reflect the renewed understanding of Thomas alluded to above. This renewed understanding emerged as theologians during the 1930s and 1940s began to question the received interpretation of Aquinas and to reach back beyond his sixteenth- and seventeenth-century interpreters in order to read his work afresh. This return to the sources resulted in a major challenge to the prevailing neo-scholastic theology and its understanding of the relationship between nature and grace. De Lubac's *Surnaturel* (1946) argued that the idea of "pure nature" was foreign to Thomas.[75] Against the "two-tiered" scholastic understanding of the natural and supernatural orders, de Lubac argued that desire for God and the vocation to participation in God's life are not an end superadded to a human life already complete in itself. Rather, he states, "we are creatures, and have been given the promise that we shall see God. The desire to see him is in us, it constitutes us, and yet it comes to us as a completely free gift."[76] For Thomas, he argued, as for Augustine and Bonaventure, nature and grace are intrinsically rather than extrinsically related. To the scholastic objection that denying "pure nature" in this way destroys the gratuity of grace, de Lubac responded that God's transcendence removed the opposition between the two. As Rahner put it, "nature" in the theological sense is therefore a "remainder concept."[77]

De Lubac initially came under suspicion and censure both from his contemporaries and from the Vatican, who suspected him and his fellow travelers in *la nouvelle théologie* of destroying the gratuity of the supernatural order, "since God, they say, cannot create intellectual beings without ordering and calling them to the beatific vision."[78] In spite of their condemnation in Pius XII's *Humani generis* (1950) it was the view of de Lubac and his contemporaries that won through at Vatican II barely twenty years later.[79] De Lubac understood his work on the relationship between nature and grace not only as a recovery of Aquinas from seventeenth-century scholasticism and its twentieth-century champions but also as an attempt to reverse the cultural alienation of Christianity that he understood as its product.[80] If nature was already graced from the beginning, then it could not be the case that the realm of grace was entirely the preserve of the Church, utterly separate from and unrelated to the world. Moreover, if grace was not extrinsic to nature, there was no need for what de Lubac called a "separated theology," unrelated to culture except by defensive apologetics. As the prevailing understanding of the relationship between nature and grace shifted over the course of the mid-twentieth century, so, too, would the relationship between theology and culture, Church and world. The impact of this shift on the Church's teaching on peace was considerable.

The opening paragraph of *Gaudium et spes* shows the degree to which the Church had moved from the fortress mentality of the nineteenth century, in which it stood unchanging and secure against the attacks and snares of the world, to being a pilgrim afoot in a world whose joys and hopes, griefs and anxieties it shared. Like *Pacem in terris*, *Gaudium et spes* addresses itself to "all people of good will," as well as to the

Church. This new openness to the world is reflected in the style of its language. In preconciliar documents, John O'Malley argues, the language tends to be one of "commanding from on high," the purpose of the documents being to define and disambiguate doctrine and practice, to anathematize unsatisfactory positions, and sometimes to exclude and punish those who hold them.[81] The language of *Gaudium et spes*, by contrast, is one of persuasion and appeal to ideals, and its positive and exhortative style is reflected in what it says about the need for cooperation and the need to strive for greater unity. This more dialogical style also extends to its analysis of the causes of, and solutions to, conflict: where *Ad beatissimi* and *Summi pontificatus* largely restrict analysis of the causes of war to moral and theological themes, *Gaudium et spes* is more clearly in dialogue with economic and political analyses of the human condition and the state of society. While remaining rooted in a theological understanding of peace, postconciliar Church teaching on the subject is open to learning from other sources of knowledge about the human person and human societies.

The open and hopeful style of the constitution was not in itself a cause for debate. With only a few exceptions, the council fathers supported a more pastoral and less juridical tone.[82] Debate focused instead on the constitution's open and optimistic stance with regard to the world and modern progress, which, like *Pacem in terris*, was contested on both practical and theological grounds.[83] This time the theological concerns came uppermost, and the schema that would become the first part of *Gaudium et spes* faced criticism from a wide spectrum of theologians during its development—criticism that often cut across the established camps of the progressive majority and the curia-led rearguard. At the heart of all these objections stood the relationship between the natural and supernatural orders, but the disagreements over this fundamental question also played out in other areas: in the attitude of the various drafts toward the world and modern culture, in the picture they sketched of the human person and the relationship between body and soul, in the proportion of natural law reasoning to theological and scriptural principles, and the structure of the schema itself. All these areas generated protracted debate and repeated drafts, and the debates themselves, as well as the not quite resolved compromise on the issues evident in *Gaudium et spes*, would prove important for the council's teaching on peace in the document itself and the Church's subsequent teaching on the subject more generally.

At issue was not only the relationship between the natural and supernatural orders—later drafts tended to eschew the terminology in favor of other terms—but the meaning or content of both those terms. De Lubac had argued that the extrinsicist view of nature and supernature had rendered the supernatural order not so much gratuitous as superfluous: man, complete in himself in the natural order, seemed to have no need of it.[84] The council fathers wanted simultaneously to affirm the intrinsic merit and significance of the natural order (and hence the lay vocation) and the idea that human beings' supernatural end is not something merely stuck on to a nature complete in itself. These desires pulled them in two different directions. Some participants wanted more emphasis on the intrinsic value of earthly realities and the natural order.[85] Other participants were more concerned that the schema was too positive regarding the natural order and "the world" and did not emphasize sufficiently the supernatural and the need for grace.[86] Some feared that the drafts were in danger of collapsing the supernatural into the natural completely, others that the supernatural no longer had an authentic role. In the discussions of Schema XIII, the disagreements fell out along linguistic lines as a division between German-speaking and French-speaking theologians, the former more influenced by interaction with Lutheran thought and hence by Augustine and the latter more influenced by Thomas and Teilhard de Chardin.[87] One of the major points of contention was the structure of one of the late drafts, known as the Ariccia text, and whether part 1 should start with a general philosophical anthropology intelligible and acceptable to those *ad extra* before moving on to speak about Christ. Ratzinger recalls the dispute.

> This was the reason for the protest against the "optimism" of the schema. . . . It was not a question of imposing a pessimistic view of man or constructing an exaggerated theology of sin. . . . The text as it stood itself prompted the question of why exactly the reasonable and perfectly free human being described in the first articles was suddenly burdened with the story of Christ. The latter might well appear to be a rather unintelligible addition to a picture that was already quite complete in itself.[88]

This particular difficulty with the Ariccia text was eventually resolved—albeit not to everyone's satisfaction, Ratzinger's included—by the inclusion of Christological themes in one of the early paragraphs, but the tensions persisted both in the final text of the pastoral constitution and its critical reception in the years following the council.[89]

Some of these cautionary voices come through in the final text of *Gaudium et spes*, but overall the encyclical is characterized by a sense of continuity between nature and grace and by a Christian humanism "based on a human nature created by God, infused with the Holy Spirit, and destined for God."[90] Despite protestations from several theological heavyweights, it also retained its positive tone in relation to the modern world and the signs of the times, with repeated references to progress, to a growing awareness of human dignity, increasing interdependence, and social development.[91] Yet in spite of the fact that, overall, *Gaudium et spes* reflects that renewed understanding of the relationship between nature and grace, its section on peace (ch. 5) displays a mixture of approaches. In some respects, it reflects John XXIII's natural law optimism and the neo-scholastic framework from which it derives; in others, it reflects the more conciliar perspective. This is, in part, a result of the complex textual history of *Gaudium et spes*. Fairly early on in the development of the document, what became part 1, covering the Church and the human vocation, was separated from part 2, which covered the "more urgent," nitty-gritty questions relating to marriage, economics, war and peace, and so on. Part 1 underwent multiple drafts, redrafts, and revisions at the hands of several different committees and under the influence of diverse theological experts, while part 2 developed along a different track and received less attention. Indeed part 2 was originally intended to be added to the end of the document as an appendix and became part of the pastoral constitution only at a late stage of the proceedings.[92] The result was a divergence in the language and theological approaches of part one and part two, only slightly allayed by the late decision to provide prologues to the sections of part two in order to bring them stylistically in line with part 1.

Part 1 displays the Christian humanism of the council, with its mixture of natural law, theological, and scriptural themes, and presents the human person and human society as coming to their true fulfillment in Christ the new Adam (§22). Part 2 displays more of the thoroughly natural law approach of *Pacem in terris*: this was a deliberate attempt,

partly under the guidance of one of the principal drafters of that encyclical, to speak in a language that would engage those outside the
Church.[93] The result was that *Gaudium et spes* as a whole, and its section
on peace in particular, evinces a mixture—sometimes slightly confused—
of different theological approaches and influences. This confusion is, in
part, what underlies Ratzinger's criticism noted above: his sense that
the optimism of the Ariccia text resulted in a picture of a human nature
complete in itself recalls de Lubac's judgment regarding the extrinsicism
of neo-scholastic approaches to nature and the supernatural. The problem is not that *Gaudium et spes* fails to move beyond neo-scholasticism
but that its strategy of moving from a general anthropology to specifically Christological material is not completely successful, partly owing
to the structural problem just noted.

What effect does this mixture of approaches have on the chapter "Fostering and Promoting the International Community"? In this
chapter, two streams—the natural law optimism of *Pacem in terris* and
the renewed understanding of nature and grace of the council—come
together, resulting in a significant shift in Catholic social teaching on
peace. The Augustinian tradition, as we have seen, maintains quite
strong distinctions between the peace of the earthly city and the peace
of heaven, between the peace possible in this present life and the peace
of the age to come, and between the inner sphere of motivations and
loves and the outer sphere of public action and justice. In the section on
peace in *Gaudium et spes*, this Augustinian context disappears. The focus
shifts from inner states—wickedness, desire to dominate— as the cause
and evil of war and personal conversion as the solution, toward a focus
on "outer" solutions to the problem of conflict, such as the "setting up
of some universal public authority," disarmament, education, and international agreements. Instead of a sense that earthly peace is necessary
so that the Church can go about its business of directing people toward
the peace of God, there is a sense that earthly peace has a deeper significance, as "a type and a result of the peace of Christ issuing from God the
Father."[94] This continuity between earthly and heavenly peace produces,
in turn, a sense of continuity between present and future.

> Insofar as men are sinners the danger of war hangs over them and
> will hang over them till the coming of Christ; but insofar as, united

in charity, they overcome sin, they overcome violence too, until the words are fulfilled "They shall beat their swords into ploughshares and their spears into pruning-hooks. Nation shall not lift up sword against nation, neither shall they learn war any more." (Is 2:4)[95]

There is an implied relationship of growth or development between the world's peace and the peace of the kingdom: though *Gaudium et spes* does not identify the growth of the former with the advent of the latter, the document sets up for subsequent Catholic social teaching a relationship of significant continuity between the "piecemeal peace" of the world and the "pure peace" that is the gift of Christ.[96]

We saw earlier that during the medieval period a further distinction crystallized between clergy and religious, on the one hand, and laypeople, on the other. Clergy and religious, belonging to the "religious" sphere and occupied with the demands of the gospel, are exempt from waging warfare, whereas laypeople, belonging to the "secular" sphere, are bound to wage war when commanded by a legitimate authority.[97] In *Gaudium et spes* this distinction, too, breaks down, and the document praises "those who renounce violence in defending their rights and use means of defence which are available to the weakest, so long as this can be done without harm to the rights and duties of others in the community."[98] This marks a clear break with Pius XII's condemnation of conscientious objection as morally indefensible in his Christmas message of 1956.[99] It also mirrors the new relationship between clergy, religious, and laity described by *Lumen gentium*, which emphasized the call to holiness common to all the baptized. Both moves owe much to the reshaped relationship between nature and grace, which meant that it was no longer the case that the laity belonged to a clearly delineated "natural" sphere, with its secular and political duties, while the clergy belonged to the sphere of the "supernatural," with its religious duties. The two parties, laity and clergy, could not be lined up neatly behind the demands of the natural law, on the one hand, and the demands of the gospel, on the other.[100]

This change in Catholic social teaching on peace is a good deal more significant than it first appears. Up to this point, the tradition of nonviolence in the Church applied largely to clergy and religious and was couched more in terms of exemption from war than in terms of a positive pacifist option. It owed at least as much to medieval chivalric codes about noncombatants as it did to the ethics of the Sermon on the Mount.[101] By commending the renunciation of violence, the council fathers integrate into mainstream Church teaching, and extend to laypeople, a positive tradition of nonviolence that, at least potentially, stands in significant tension with the just war tradition.[102] There is neither any recognition of the potential tension here nor any attempt to explain the relationship between the two approaches to conflict. Nor is there a clear sense that this approval of "renunciation of violence" is the result of a *ressourcement* return to the tradition of the early Church or even a result of engagement with scriptural texts, although subsequent Catholic peace scholarship sometimes describes the Church's move toward incorporating the pacifist tradition in these terms.[103] Rather than proceeding from engagement with scripture, the new appraisal of war in *Gaudium et spes* is prompted by the increase of "scientific weapons."[104] Nuclear weapons are clearly in the background here, and the document cites *Pacem in terris*'s statement that "in this age which boasts of its atomic power, it no longer makes sense to maintain that war is a fit instrument with which to repair the violation of justice."[105] This sense that modern weaponry and warfare demand a reappraisal of the morality of war is something that *Gaudium et spes* shares not only with John XXIII but also with Pius XI and Benedict XV, whose use of just war reasoning was also influenced by the horrors of World Wars I and II.[106] As we move into the contemporary period, much greater accent therefore falls on the criterion of last resort, and still greater emphasis on the avoidance of war and the need for trust, negotiation, and the reasonable settlement of disputes.[107] But the changed place of just war reasoning in the document is not just the result of the bloody innovations of twentieth-century warfare. It also reflects the fact that just war fits somewhat uncomfortably in the new context of continuity I described above. *Gaudium et spes* acknowledges that "peace is never achieved once for all, but has to be constantly fashioned" in the context of a wounded and sinful world and that this "calls for . . . the vigilance of lawful authority."[108] The distinction between the earthly and heavenly cities has faded somewhat, and the sense that just war has a role to play in establishing earthly justice, albeit of an imperfect kind, is weaker.[109] In Aquinas's scheme, just war had a role to play in defending the justly ordered peace of a commonwealth; in *Gaudium et spes*, war no longer makes sense as a way of seeking the peace of the international community, particularly in a nuclear age.

For all the teething problems of *Gaudium et spes* more generally, the section on peace and the avoidance of war was not hugely contentious and garnered widespread support from the council fathers. This was partly a result of their desire to honor the legacy of John XXIII and *Pacem in terris* and partly the result of a wave of enthusiasm following the speech of Paul VI at the United Nations, in which he pleaded, "No more war, war never again! It is peace that must guide the destinies of people."[110] The section, though short, has a significant impact on Catholic social teaching on peace, and the trajectories and tensions it establishes go on to shape Church teaching on peace in the postconciliar period.

POSTCONCILIAR CHURCH TEACHING

The Lateran basilica, with its ancient foundations concealed by successive renovations, is a good example of the way that later remodeling can change the way we perceive a structural whole. Taken together, *Pacem in terris* and *Gaudium et spes* constitute a comparable remodeling of the tradition of Catholic teaching on peace. The old foundations and architectural features persist, but the later structural work builds on them, reshapes them, and occasionally obscures them, changing the way that we view and describe the whole. Tracing this process of remodeling, by exploring the documents in some depth, has allowed us to get a sense of just how structurally complex the teaching tradition is by the time it reaches the late twentieth century. It has also given us a sense of some of the tensions within the tradition as it moves into the contemporary period.

The building metaphor is helpful here as we move into the postconciliar period, where divisions over the interpretation and significance of Vatican II also play out in approaches to the Church's tradition of teaching on peace. There is a temptation to resolve the tension established in *Gaudium et spes* between nonviolent approaches and just war by dismissing the validity of one or the other, either holding to Augustine as the "real tradition," and dismissing *Gaudium et spes*'s repositioning of just war reasoning within a broader vision of peacebuilding, or holding to the early Church as the "real tradition," and dismissing just war reasoning as bogus and un-Christian. Neither is satisfactory if we are to take a Catholic approach to this Catholic problem. The challenge is to approach the Church's tradition on peace as a single, albeit highly complex construction; to remain critically aware of the ways in which the tradition has been shaped in reaction to political and cultural forces but to avoid a reductive view that has no room for the Spirit; to ask what structural tensions persist and what kinds of repair and construction work—or even stripping back—may be needed.

With *Pacem in terris* and *Gaudium et spes*, we enter into a new phase of Catholic teaching on peace, in which what has historically comprised the bulk of that tradition—just war reasoning—becomes seen as one element among a much broader range of theological and practical responses to the problem of violence and the challenge of peacebuilding. It is not too much of a caricature to state that with these two documents the Catholic Church's tradition of teaching on peace shifts from grappling with the problem of war to addressing the question of peace. One of the challenges of surveying postconciliar Church teaching on peace is that, for the same reason, the tradition becomes more diffuse.

Pacem in terris and *Gaudium et spes* are the last major documents in the tradition to date. Thereafter, the theology of peace and the practice of peacebuilding are touched on in postsynodal apostolic exhortations like *Reconciliatio et paenitentia* (1984) and *Africae munus* (2011) and addressed directly in short World Day of Peace messages, released annually around the turn of the secular year. Papal teaching on peace has also developed in occasional addresses to bodies like the United Nations and as shorter sections in documents dedicated to other topics, such as development or solidarity. The collective contribution of these more recent documents is significant, but as I pick them up and discuss them in subsequent chapters, I do not attempt to synthesize or summarize here their diverse contributions to the tradition of teaching on peace. It is worth, however, spending some time with some of the more substantial documents of the postconciliar period: the Latin American bishops' comments on peace in the Medellín document (1968) and the U.S. Conference of Catholic Bishops' documents *The Challenge of Peace* (1983) and *The Harvest of Justice is Sown in Peace* (1993). In different ways, these documents pick up and carry forward some of the key themes of *Gaudium et spes*, as well as highlighting some of its limitations.

Medellín

The section on peace in the 1968 document of the Medellín conference of the Latin American bishops starts from Paul VI's statement in *Populorum progressio* that "development is the new name for peace."[111] As the concept of peace widens to include development, so the understanding of violence broadens to take into account more explicitly the kinds of structural violence that affect the Latin American continent. Augustine's concept of peace as *tranquillitas ordinis*, shaped by Aquinas into the peace of the justly ordered commonwealth, means that the Church's concept of peace has always implied just order and not merely the absence of conflict. What changes in the postconciliar period is the role of social transformation in attaining that just order. Augustine, as we have seen, does not have large-scale social transformation in view: his understanding of the peace possible in this life is largely restricted to perfecting existing relationships in love rather than reshaping them, and his focus falls on the domestic rather than the public sphere. Early Catholic social teaching tends to follow him in this focus on interiority, and even as it calls for social change, it sees this as coming about largely through personal conversion.[112] *Pacem in terris*, by contrast, emphasizes the need for just order in society, founded on due respect for human dignity, rights, and duties. The Medellín document has the same insistence on the need for just order, and social transformation in order to achieve it, but it is less optimistic about the chances of people recognizing this and striving for it. It also recognizes the ways in which appeals to the tranquillity of order can be used as a pretext for repression: some groups in society "characterize as subversive activities all attempts to change the social system which favors the permanence of their privileges"; it is "easy for them to find apparent ideological justifications (anti-communism) or practical ones (keeping "order") to give their action an honest appearance."[113] Where *Pacem in terris* displays a great faith in human nature, freedom, and our capacity to know and choose the good, the Medellín document is much more aware of the force of ideology, the possibility of pervasive moral blindness, and the willful defense and maintenance, by powerful groups, of unjust social structures that perpetuate structural violence and engender armed conflict.[114]

Populorum progressio (1967) had already widened the scope of Catholic social teaching, going beyond the Eurocentric and industrial focus of *Rerum novarum* to include consideration of global patterns of economic injustice. Medellín makes mention, too, of the "menace to peace" posed by neocolonial relationships, in which poor nations' natural resources are exploited by wealthier nations, and alludes also to the "imperialism of ideological bias," whether exercised directly or indirectly.[115] In doing so, it directs the focus of Church teaching on peace away from the European wars, which shaped Benedict XV's and Pius XI's contributions to the tradition, and away from the Cold War and the nuclear question, which formed the background to *Pacem in terris* and *Gaudium et spes*. Where those documents focus to a large extent on the role of international organizations and political leaders, Medellín asks what kinds of action for peace are necessary and legitimate in the face of political intransigence and repression. The Church's recent teaching on peace, born out of the experience of the twentieth century, focuses largely on interstate conflicts and the means for their resolution; Medellín raises some of the important issues that arise in the context of intrastate conflicts. Given that intrastate conflicts are the most common type of armed conflict in the late twentieth and early twenty-first century, the contribution of the Medellín document remains important.

The Challenge of Peace and The Harvest of Justice

The Challenge of Peace (1983) is the U.S. Conference of Catholic Bishops' (USCCB's) response to questions surrounding nuclear weapons, nuclear war, and the arms race. It thus shares the same basic context and concerns as *Pacem in terris* and *Gaudium et spes* and in large measure reflects the same shifts in style and substance that occurred with those two documents. The USCCB's document also moves beyond them in two notable respects, however, first in the way that it attempts to resolve some of the tensions we noted in those documents and second in the way it situates its specific ethical reflection within a broader and more systematic theology of peace than is found in either of the two earlier documents.[116]

I noted earlier that the interlinked questions of audience and appropriate mode of address surfaced during the conciliar debates on *Gaudium et spes* and that the finished document—partly as an accident of its process of composition—mixes the claims of natural law and Christian gospel, with the result that the intended audience is not entirely clear.

The Challenge of Peace retains the dual mode of address that characterizes *Gaudium et spes*, being addressed both to Christians in particular and the international community more generally, but is more explicit about why and how it addresses both groups.

> The conviction . . . that both the community of the faithful and the civil community should be addressed on peace and war has produced two complementary but distinct styles of teaching. The religious community shares a specific perspective of faith and can be called to live out its implications. The wider civil community, although it does not share the same vision of faith, is equally bound by certain key moral principles. For all men and women find in the depth of their consciences a law written on the human heart by God. From this law reason draws moral norms. These norms do not exhaust the gospel vision, but they speak to critical questions affecting the welfare of the human community, the role of states in international relations, and the limits of acceptable action by individuals and nations on issues of war and peace.[117]

There is in this document a clearer statement about the relationship between natural law and the gospel in Catholic teaching on peace, which goes some way toward resolving the confusion that results from the combination of John XXIII's neo-scholastic account of natural law with the *ressourcement* Thomist account that underpins *Gaudium et spes*.

The same move also results in a slightly clearer relationship between the peace of the world and the peace of the kingdom of God. We have seen that *Gaudium et spes*, while it does not identify the peace of the world with the peace of the kingdom, sets up a clear continuity between the two, to the extent that Augustine's insistence that they are qualitatively as well as quantitatively different begins to slip from view. *The Challenge of Peace*, while assuming the same continuity between the world's peace and the peace of the kingdom, again clarifies the relationship between them.

> We believe the religious vision has an objective basis and is capable of progressive realization. Christ is our peace, for he has "made us both one, and has broken down the dividing wall of hostility . . . that

he might create in himself one new man in place of the two, so making peace, and might reconcile us both to God" (Eph. 2:14–16). We also know that this peace will be achieved fully only in the kingdom of God. The realization of the kingdom, therefore, is a continuing work, progressively accomplished, precariously maintained, and needing constant effort to preserve the peace achieved and expand its scope in personal and political life.[118]

This slightly greater clarity regarding the relationship between the world's peace and the peace of the kingdom also gives a crisper picture of the Church's distinctive role in peacebuilding. The grounding of Church teaching on peace in natural law occasionally raises the question of whether Christians bear distinctive and particular obligations or tasks with regard to the pursuit of peace or whether they are—to borrow from John Webster—simply enthusiastic volunteers in a shared task.[119] The section on peace in *Gaudium et spes*—partly as a result of the uneven process of composition noted earlier—seems to lean toward the latter picture of Christians cooperating in a shared task, though *Lumen gentium*'s understanding of the Church as a sacrament of the unity of humanity is not integrated here.[120] *The Challenge of Peace* moves beyond this, and the U.S. Bishops understand the pursuit of peace as both a shared task and one in which the Church has a distinctive role.

> Building peace within and among nations is the work of many individuals and institutions; it is the fruit of ideas and decisions taken in the political, cultural, economic, social, military, and legal sectors of life. We believe that the Church, as a community of faith and social institution, has a proper, necessary, and distinctive part to play in the pursuit of peace. The distinctive contribution of the Church flows from her religious nature and ministry. The Church is called to be, in a unique way, the instrument of the kingdom of God in history. Since peace is one of the signs of that kingdom present in the world, the Church fulfills part of her essential mission by making the peace of the kingdom more visible in our time.[121]

This sense that the Church has a distinctive role to play in the pursuit of peace is reinforced by the way that document is structured. Although it is explicitly addressed to the civil community as well as the Church, the document does not foreground natural law as the basis for reflection in the same way as *Pacem in terris*. Instead, *The Challenge of Peace* situates its consideration of specific ethical questions regarding the morality of nuclear weapons within a broader theology of peace that takes a biblical account of peace as its point of departure. Peace is always the gift of God and bound up with his saving activity on behalf of Israel.[122] The Old Testament suggests that the realization of that peace lies partly within Israel's power insofar as it requires fidelity to the covenant and the pursuit of justice, understood as right relationship to God and within creation; it also lies outside Israel's power to achieve insofar as it is an eschatological gift of God and therefore an object of hope and expectation.[123] Jesus Christ fulfills that expectation, inaugurating the kingdom of God and, in his teaching and his ministry, showing the lineaments of a new way of life characterized by forgiveness, mercy, and justice. Jesus's death and resurrection accomplish and reveal the triumph of life over death, and "only in light of this, the fullest demonstration of the power of God's reign, can Jesus' gift of peace—a peace which the world cannot give (Jn. 14:27)—be understood."[124] This biblical picture of an inaugurated kingdom of peace and a victory achieved in the paschal mystery of death and resurrection, provides the context in which the document's ethical reflection unfolds. Just war reasoning still features strongly, but it finds its place within this broader scriptural and theological treatment of peace.

Ten years on from *The Challenge of Peace*, the U.S. Conference of Catholic Bishops published *The Harvest of Justice Is Sown in Peace* (1993). The document reflects on the changed geopolitical context, no longer so dominated by Cold War rivalries but marked instead by new challenges: increasing economic inequality, ethnic cleansing, conflicts over national self-determination, and religious violence.[125] Against this background, the document reiterates the importance and continuing relevance of just war reasoning and a broad-spectrum focus on human rights and development. Significantly, the document also emphasizes the importance of peaceable virtues, which are needed both for the proper application of just war reasoning and as the soil from which action for justice and peace grows.[126] The Church "must seek to foster communities where peaceable virtues can take root and be nourished," acting in this way as a counterculture to the prevailing culture of violence. Perhaps most significant is the document's emphasis on nonviolence. Quoting John Paul II's recognition of successful nonviolent movements for political change in *Centesimus annus*, the document goes on to list some of the practices of nonviolent action for peace ("dialogue, negotiations, protests, strikes, boycotts, civil disobedience and civilian resistance") and to make the case for nonviolence not just as a personal moral option, but as a public undertaking.[127]

In this shift toward nonviolence, *The Harvest of Justice* reflects and anticipates a shift in recent papal teaching toward nonviolence. In various occasional addresses, John Paul II, Benedict XVI, and Francis have each highlighted nonviolence, giving it greater prominence not just as an individual moral option, but as a public and ecclesial option, and framing it not only in terms of refraining from armed violence (the conscientious objection praised by *Gaudium et spes*), but as a positive "style of politics for peace."[128] This is not just an adaptation in light of the changing nature of modern warfare; nor is it just a tactical shift, though some of these papal statements note examples of nonviolent action being used to respond to violence and establish justice.[129] There are also signs of a deeper theological shift at work here: Benedict XVI states that "non-violence is not merely tactical behaviour but a person's way of being, the attitude of one who *is so convinced of God's love and power* that he is not afraid to tackle evil with the weapons of love and truth alone." He goes on to state that love of enemies is the "nucleus of the 'Christian revolution[,]' . . . the newness of the gospel which silently changes the world!"[130] Pope Francis's World Day of Peace message of 2017 recaps Benedict XVI's comments and states that being a true follower of Jesus today "also includes embracing his teaching about nonviolence."[131] The shift toward nonviolence in Catholic social teaching looks set to continue.

Construction and Repair

The Challenge of Peace provides a good example of the remodeling of Church teaching on peace that occurs following *Pacem in terris* and *Gaudium et spes*: the renewed understanding of nature and grace, the shift toward greater use of scripture, and the more dialogical engagement with the world. The Medellín document pushes the existing tradition further in a different way, by engaging with the realities of structural violence, and *The Harvest of Justice* identifies the important task of cultivating the spirituality and virtues of peacebuilding. The various papal interventions on nonviolence indicate the direction of travel in Catholic social teaching on peace. All of these recent documents help us identify some of the key tasks of repair and construction that lie ahead.

The survey thus far has raised a huge number of potential areas for engagement, and the explorations that follow touch on only a few of them. In the introduction, I stated that my concern in this book is with the coherence, strength, and vitality of the Catholic Church's tradition of teaching on peace. Concern for the coherence of the tradition means paying attention to points of tension and imbalance, undertaking critical work in order to uncover and understand these tensions and constructive work in order to address them. Concern for the strength of the tradition means critical and constructive work that helps Catholic social teaching on peace address the concrete realities of conflict and peacebuilding in the twenty-first century. Concern for the vitality of the tradition means asking how the Church's teaching can become better known and more deeply embedded in ordinary Catholics' lives of prayer and practice.

Each of the chapters that follow addresses a particular issue in Catholic social teaching on peace, and all of them touch in some way on the coherence, strength, and vitality of that tradition. All the chapters also share some more specific aims, which emerge from the survey of the Church's teaching tradition that I have just undertaken. Briefly noting three specific issues will set us up for the work ahead.

(i) Vitality: Scripture and spirituality

Over the course of its development, Catholic teaching on peace has engaged with scripture in different modes and to varying extents. For the early fathers, scriptural exegesis was the starting point for ethical reflection, and, in a different way, the scriptural narrative of redemption underpins Augustine's narrative of the two cities in *City of God*. With the ascendancy of the natural law paradigm, scriptural reasoning fades into the background, and biblical texts tend to be used illustratively or exhortatively rather than as the foundation or departure point for theological or ethical reflection: appeals to the content of revelation and specifically Christian faith tend to gild, rather than ground, the central principles of the tradition. The strength of this natural law–focused approach is its ability to be heard beyond the bounds of the Church: in contexts of interreligious conflict and cooperation in peacebuilding and in the secular sphere of international politics, it encourages Catholics to engage, on the basis of their faith, with common human goals and initiatives. But the weakness of the same approach is its comparative lack of a lively and well-developed connection to the faith and practice of many ordinary Catholics, which depends more directly on the language and images of scripture and the liturgy.

With the revival of Catholic biblical studies in the years leading up to the Second Vatican Council, scripture began to assume a more prominent position in the presentation of Catholic teaching on peace—a development reflected in *The Challenge of Peace* and in the more recent synthesis in the *Compendium of the Social Doctrine of the Church*. But while engagement with scripture is increasingly common and substantial, there remains much scope for scripturally deepening and enriching the Church's teaching on peace, including the concept of peace itself, as well as allied concepts like solidarity and reconciliation. Strengthening such concepts and rooting them more firmly in biblical themes will increase their capacity to enliven and motivate the Catholic faithful, encouraging them to think about the pursuit of peace not just as a moral demand incumbent upon humanity in general but also as a particular calling of their Christian faith.[132]

Spirituality, too, has a role to play in enriching the Church's teaching on peace and giving it a more vital connection to the lives of ordinary Catholics. We can think of spirituality in terms of a particular path that individuals or groups may take through the myriad doctrinal, liturgical, practical, and prayerful resources of the Catholic tradition.[133] A particular spiritual pathway has its own theological emphases and concrete shape, and it also provides a particular frame of reference or location from which the person interacts with the wider tradition. Some spiritualities—Franciscan, for example—are linked to a concrete way of life within the Church, though one does not need to be a Franciscan religious to walk that particular path; other spiritualities, like Divine Mercy or the Black Nazarene, are associated more with popular Catholicism. To recognize the importance of spirituality is to recognize that people tend to live their faith in a particular way, not a general way: they connect with particular experiences, particular images of God, particular saints or models of faith, particular kinds of prayer, and so on. If Church teaching on peace is to become more embedded in the lives of ordinary Catholics, it needs to draw on the existing resources of these particular spiritualities, as well as nurture, encourage, and explore what a "spirituality of peace" might look like.

In what follows then, I strive to draw on scripture and give it a more foundational and integral place in the theology of peace. I also aim to draw on particular spiritualities and explore their potential for rooting Catholic social teaching on peace "Church wide and parish deep."

(ii) Strength: Scale

Among the differences of style and substance that separate St. Augustine and John XXIII is a difference in their understanding of the scale of peace possible in this life. Augustine, as I discussed, focuses on the micro scale: amid the pressures of empire and the woes of this life, the citizens of the heavenly city focus on ordering their own lives and interior passions in obedience to God and on ordering their households in peace as best they can. John XXIII focuses on the macro scale and on the changes needed to the whole world order to produce a world at peace, including respect for human rights. Catholic social teaching as a whole tends to replicate this binocular focus on the micro and macro levels: on personal conversion, on the one hand, and the structural reform of international institutions, on the other. The two tend to proceed in some tension, with regular reminders that structural reform must be accompanied by conversion of heart, and the pursuit of justice with the practice of love. What has tended to fade from view—somewhat surprisingly for a tradition that produces, as John Webster puts it, "industrial strength ecclesiologies"—is much attention to the midlevel and to the cultural forms and spiritualities that are, or could be, carriers and specific cultural-historical embodiments of various aspects of the Church's teaching on peace.[134] What is missing, amid the calls to the international community and the individual, is much attention to the experience and potential of small groups and the particular challenges they face as they progress and precariously maintain what peace is possible and seek to expand its scope.[135]

Recent Catholic social teaching documents, in particular *Caritas in veritate* and *Laudato sí*, have begun to engage more explicitly with the midlevel of social transformation, but it remains for these insights to be translated into the Church's teaching on peace. In the chapters that follow, I suggest that developing this focus on the midlevel is important for both practical and theological reasons. Practically speaking, the work undertaken in situations of violent conflict by midlevel groups such as parishes, grassroots peace organizations, and religious orders is a hugely important part of the Church's peacebuilding work, notwithstanding the macro-level work of Vatican diplomacy and the micro-level work of those who quietly pursue and pray for peace in other ways. These kinds of midlevel initiatives are where Church teaching becomes practice, and it is therefore important for theologians to attend to the experience and insights emerging from them. Attention to the midlevel is also important for theological reasons. The natural law framework of much Catholic teaching on peace tends to emphasize the naturalness of peace, the naturalness of the desire for it, and the degree to which action in the pursuit of peace is working with the grain of the universe. It is less able to recognize that in a creation damaged by sin, even as the power of the resurrection is indefatigably at work in it, work for peace will be marked as much by struggle as by ease. Theological attention to the midlevel at which the pursuit of peace is worked out, with much effort and personal cost, would go a long way to making Catholic teaching more *livable* in the sense I outlined in the introduction. We need some account of the journey toward John XXIII's vision of a just and peaceful political order—an account that wrestles with *luctus et angor* as well as *gaudium et spes*. Alongside Catholic social teaching's insistence on peace as original and natural to human beings we need, as Rowan Williams puts it, some practical and concrete account of how peace in a fallen creation is "learned, negotiated, betrayed, inched forward, discerned and risked."[136] Attention to the midlevel of Catholic peacebuilding practice will help provide it.

(iii) Coherence: Struggle

The shift from Augustine to the post–*Pacem in terris* tradition is sometimes characterized, in approving tones, as a shift from "Augustinian pessimism" to "Johannine optimism"; it is also sometimes described in more critical tones, as a shift from "Augustinian realism" to "Johannine utopianism." There is some truth in both, but insofar as they encourage us to take one part of the tradition less seriously than another, these kinds of descriptions are unhelpful. In part, my determination to read the tradition as a complex whole is a determination to uphold both these aspects of the tradition and to wrestle with the relationship between them. This means upholding the Johannine conviction of Catholic social teaching that humanity is called to and capable of change, insisting on both the possibility of growth toward greater justice and peace and the necessity of the struggle. At the same time, it means holding onto the Augustinian sense of just how difficult and incomplete this progress will be in a creation still so entwined with violence and sin and the need for the eschatological transformation and completion of even our best human efforts. Only by holding these two together can we take seriously the magnitude of our vocation, both in terms of the real hope it offers and in terms of the profound transformation it demands.

In the survey above, I introduced the language of discontinuity and continuity to characterize the difference between the theology of peace in Augustine and in the post-*Pacem* tradition. Augustine emphasizes the discontinuity between piecemeal and pure peace, worldly and heavenly, present and future. The tradition after *Pacem in terris* and *Gaudium et spes* tends to emphasize continuity across all the same relationships: there is a sense of progression or growth between present and future, worldly peace and the peace of the kingdom, and so on. Some of the deep resources of the tradition also dispose us in the direction of continuity: the belief that human beings are naturally social, that harmony, not conflict, is natural, that politics is a good rather than a result of the Fall, and that a virtuous commonwealth is possible—all these contribute to a picture of peace and peacebuilding as somehow working with the grain of human nature. The key question here is how this interfaces with the experience of those engaged in peacebuilding in situations of violent conflict. Such contexts challenge peacebuilders to keep alive a hope for change but also demand that it is a real hope, capable of holding all the suffering and setback, compromise and complexity, risk, and sacrifice entailed in grassroots peacebuilding work. Talking about the gap that often opens up between the high-level political rhetoric of peace and its actualization on a local level, John Paul Lederach notes that a certain kind of pessimism is often evident among those affected by violence at the grassroots level. This kind of pessimism, he argues, is a gift, providing "a departure point for understanding the nature of change": "Constructive pessimism teaches us that distrust is needed as a reality check to assure that change is not superficial, Pollyanna-ish, or disguising other intentions. Distrust assures us that we are not dipping into and promoting a cheap hope: it keeps us authentic."[137] Translating this back into a theological context helps us name the challenge here, which is to bring together the hard realities of peacebuilding on a grassroots level with the hope for change characteristic of Catholic social teaching, in order to make sure that that hope is real, strong, and capacious enough to hold and make sense of experiences of suffering, struggle, and setback. The task here is not as simple as "rebalancing," as though Catholic social teaching on peace has become too optimistic about the possibility of social transformation, and we need to throw some more weight on the side of pessimism. Rather, the challenge is simultaneously to go deeper into the radical hope expressed by that teaching and deeper into the experiences of peacebuilders and people living with violent conflict. From there, we can ask how Catholic teaching on peace might better reflect the continuity and discontinuity that stand at the heart of the paschal mystery and hold together, side by side, the reality of death and the victory of life.

THREE

Pastoral Accompaniment and Consolation

Blessed be the God and Father of our Lord Jesus Christ,
a gentle Father and the God of all consolation,
who comforts us in all our sorrows,
so that we can offer others, in their sorrows
the consolation that we have received from God ourselves.
Indeed, as the sufferings of Christ overflow to us,
so, through Christ, does our consolation overflow.
—2 Corinthians 1:3–5

In 2018, forty missionaries were killed worldwide: thirty-five priests, one seminarian, and four laypeople. Of the priests, seven were killed in Mexico, six in Nigeria, five in the Central African Republic, three in the Democratic Republic of Congo, two in the Philippines, and one in El Salvador.[1] These numbers are not unusual. Fides, the news agency of the Congregation for the Evangelization of Peoples, recorded a similar death toll in 2017: seven lay workers, one religious sister and one religious brother, and thirteen priests. Overall, Fides estimates that 424 pastoral workers were killed worldwide between 2000 and 2016.[2] Some of them were killed in war zones, but many were killed in countries where deadly violence linked to poverty and drugs is common.[3] Not all died heroically, or for their faith, and many were the victims of armed robberies. What these numbers show, however, year after year, is that the Church remains present in situations of violence worldwide and that its lay workers, sisters, brothers, priests, and bishops are not exempt from that violence. This is the reality of pastoral accompaniment.

In the introduction, I stated that one of the concerns of this book is to encourage Catholic social teaching on peace to develop in order better to respond to the challenges of contemporary conflict and the realities of contemporary Catholic peacebuilding. The aim is to help Catholic social teaching on peace become a more effective resource for those Catholics who, in a diverse range of settings and ways, are already engaged in the tasks of peacebuilding. Sometimes this means bringing the experience of those involved in peacebuilding into conversation with the existing teaching tradition and asking how that experience might challenge the tradition to grow or change. Sometimes, however, the task is to develop theological resources that do not yet exist but need to. This chapter takes up the latter challenge, developing theological resources to support what I describe as a key practice of Catholic peacebuilding: pastoral accompaniment.

In the first part of this chapter I describe pastoral accompaniment as a practice of peacebuilding, and as a particularly Christian and Catholic practice, drawing in particular on the reflections of a prominent Catholic peacebuilder in Colombia. I then explore the significance of pastoral accompaniment in the context of twenty-first-century violent conflict, suggesting that Catholic social teaching on peace needs to develop theological resources that support this practice. The chapter then moves on to constructive theological work in this vein, first noting some of the available resources in the Catholic social teaching tradition and then exploring the concept of consolation, suggesting that it offers both a strong theological framework for pastoral accompaniment and the beginnings of a spirituality that might help to sustain those engaged in it.

PASTORAL ACCOMPANIMENT

What is pastoral accompaniment? In one sense pastoral accompaniment is the accompaniment of a Christian community by whoever fulfills the role of pastor, whether (in a specifically Catholic context) as a lay worker, religious sister or brother, priest or bishop—a definition to which I can add greater complexity and richness later on.[4] "Accompanying" means remaining with and supporting, through celebration of the sacraments and through pastoral care and availability: praying with and for, visiting, counseling, listening, leading, presence, friendship, and all the other ordinary activities that make up the life of a lay worker, brother, sister, or priest. There is also a very important sense in which pastoral accompaniment is an activity of the whole local church, a commitment to remain and to strengthen bonds of community: pastoral accompaniment also means the accompaniment of people by one another.[5] Defined in this way, pastoral accompaniment is a reality of the Church's life in all situations, but while much could be said about the practice of pastoral accompaniment more broadly, it is the practice of pastoral accompaniment in situations of direct violence that is the focus of this chapter. In such situations, I argue, pastoral accompaniment is not necessarily just an ordinary ecclesial practice caught up in an extraordinary situation. It can become an active and intentional practice of peacebuilding.

Why is pastoral accompaniment particularly important with regard to contemporary conflict and contemporary Catholic peacebuilding? Contemporary conflict has changed shape significantly from the period in which the bulk of Catholic social teaching on peace was written. In the first half of the twentieth century a high proportion of armed conflicts took place between separate nation-states, but in the mid- to late twentieth century this pattern began to shift, as Cold War tensions played out in proxy wars conducted within the boundaries of existing nation-states, between different factions armed and backed by the two superpowers. By the late twentieth century, these intrastate conflicts had become the most common kind of armed conflict, with many of them also internationalized through the involvement of regional or global organizations like the United Nations, NATO, and the African Union.

The rise of intrastate conflicts presents distinctive challenges. By contrast with interstate conflicts, in which violence may occur at some geographic distance from day-to-day civilian life, the violence of intrastate conflicts typically takes place much closer to home, as cities, towns, and villages change hands between state forces and one or more rebel groups or become the locus of ongoing insurgency. Where interstate conflicts typically involve only professional armed forces, intrastate conflicts can involve a range of armed actors of varying degrees of official standing, ranging from armed groups claiming to legitimately represent some element of the people to opportunistic criminals. The line between civilians and combatants is often blurred, and the involvement of nonprofessional soldiers, ad hoc militias, and paramilitary groups can result in greater use of nonconventional means of warfare, including hostage taking, rape, abduction, forced soldiering, and using the civilian population as a shield. The tendency for intrastate conflicts to involve such widespread human rights violations is increased by their propensity to play out along, or play into, existing ethnic, cultural, religious, or political divisions. The fact that such conflicts often directly involve protagonists' fundamental ethnic, religious, or cultural identities make them particularly deep-seated, enduring, and intractable. Widespread human rights violations by unofficial armed groups, and by government forces fighting opponents who may not "play by the rules," leave legacies of trauma and silence that can undermine faith in public institutions and the rule of law or act as reservoirs of resentment, leading to repeated or cyclical outbreaks of violence. The boundary between wartime and peace, typically clearer in interstate conflicts, is blurred, and societies affected by such conflicts may spend decades moving in and out of low-intensity but highly disruptive violence. Even when combatant groups disperse or declare an end to hostilities, violence may change shape rather than decrease, as criminal organizations grow in power and influence and occupy the vacuum often left by weakened or absent state institutions.

All of the countries I named at the start of this chapter are affected by violence or conflict of this kind, and most contemporary conflicts evince at least some of these characteristics. In these kinds of situations, the kind of peacebuilding envisaged by *Pacem in terris* and *Gaudium et spes* is harder to pursue. Both documents focus on institutions, on relationships between states, and on the role of diplomacy, international institutions, and international agreements.[6] The onus is on political leaders to pursue the resolution of disputes by peaceful and diplomatic means, and there is scant mention of the role that might be played in peacebuilding by mid-level and grassroots actors.[7] There is little sense that clashes of interest might not be resolvable through rational dialogue, or that there might be ideological, ethnic, or religious drivers of war that defy a "common-sense" approach. Yet the Church is present in contemporary conflicts of the kind I have described and, in many of them, proactively engaged in peacebuilding. Catholic social teaching on peace needs to develop in order to address the realities of contemporary conflict and to support and provide resources for the work of these Catholic peacebuilders.

Pastoral accompaniment, I want to argue, is a key practice of Catholic peacebuilding in the context of contemporary conflict. By remaining with their communities through violent conflict, pastors are not just carrying on the ordinary under extraordinary circumstances. They may also take on, by virtue of their pastoral office, distinctively peacebuilding roles: dealing with trauma, literally accompanying communities displaced by violence, recording atrocities or human rights violations, advocating or negotiating with armed actors for the safety of the community or in defense of its land rights, negotiating the release of hostages, or acting as guarantors or as channels of communication to other authorities.[8] The autonomy of priests and religious and their status as community leaders, with connections to both their local communities and higher ecclesial or civic authorities, can make them important contributors to peacebuilding processes.[9] But just as important as these roles is the fact of simply remaining present with communities caught up in violent conflict. Todd Whitmore recalls being addressed as "Father" by a Sudan People's Liberation Army (SPLA) soldier in Uganda: "The presence of clergy and religious in conflict zones—and the absence of representatives of other institutions—is so evident that the people here often assume that I am a priest."[10] The Catholic Church and other Christian churches are often the only organizations remaining in areas of protracted violent conflict when INGOs have left. This long-term, close accompaniment is a vital part of the Church's peacebuilding work.[11]

The broader sense of pastoral accompaniment, the accompaniment of people by one another, can also be an intentional practice of peacebuilding. In contexts where violent conflict threatens to displace or divide a community, the day-to-day decisions and practices that keep the Church constituted as a body, held together by relationships of belonging and mutual care, accountability and forgiveness, are practices of peacebuilding. Such ordinary practices of accompaniment cultivate resilience and are a form of resistance to violence and the damage it causes to the social fabric. To the extent that they are also able to hold open spaces of connection, encounter, dialogue, and truthfulness, such ordinary practices of pastoral accompaniment can also act as resources for civil society.

PASTORAL ACCOMPANIMENT AS PEACEBUILDING

How can we describe pastoral accompaniment as a practice of peacebuilding? Héctor Fabio Henao, director of Caritas in Colombia, has reflected in a series of articles on the practical value and theological meaning of pastoral accompaniment, which has become an important element in the peacebuilding strategies of the Church in Colombia.

Fundamentally, pastoral accompaniment means an active commitment to identifying with those suffering the effects of conflict. "The idea of accompaniment," Henao writes, "has been one of 'walking with,' of placing oneself in the situation of those who have directly suffered the atrocities and who, amid so much suffering, have established their autonomy and created alternatives for themselves and their children."[12] This intentional commitment to remain close to those who have suffered the effects of armed conflict means entering into their suffering and understanding it. Up-close knowledge of the trauma suffered by victims of violence, experience of the ways in which conflict creates fear and mistrust, and awareness of the complex damage done to the social fabric allow pastoral agents to connect with and contribute to wider peacebuilding processes. Henao states:

> The experience of pastoral agents who are in permanent contact with the hopes and suffering of communities, with social movements and with reflections on the reality that are derived from other social disciplines, allows for the construction of proposals developed along three core approaches. Firstly, deepening the understanding of the dynamics at play in social structures; secondly, recognizing alternative responses for overcoming the existing humanitarian crises; and finally, creating consensus and providing the space for working together towards the major changes required by society.[13]

Pastoral accompaniment can help strengthen community ties and community organization when these are in danger of disintegrating under the threat or reality of violence.[14] Here, accompaniment means "helping to identify principles and commitments guaranteeing the unity of the community against the threat of the conflict."[15] When the threat of violence becomes more intense, Henao states, "we have learnt that accompaniment is the ability to transmit early warnings to appropriate authorities."[16] This, in turn, can help prevent communities from becoming displaced.

Pastoral accompaniment can also be important for communities seeking reconciliation or the restoration of rights. Henao gives one example.

> When the opportunity of returning to their land was given to a community that had suffered massive displacement, Caritas Colombia had to take on the challenge of answering to those who had left and to those who had remained in spite of the presence of an illegal armed group: how were you able to have your life respected? How did you survive in spite of what happened? Were you linked to the armed actor?[17]

Accompaniment, Henao suggests, because it penetrates "to the depth of the suffering of a wounded community" and resists easy answers, can help communities answer such difficult questions and pursue reconciliation.[18]

Pastoral accompaniment can become a peacebuilding practice in this way, but it is not just a tool or strategy adopted for pragmatic reasons. Pastoral accompaniment also has symbolic and spiritual value, and it is grounded in and motivated by theological convictions. Henao argues that, above all, "it is a spiritual attitude, it is a profound choice for the victim and for the vulnerable, it is a radical option in the presence of the Lord of Life who does not abandon the poor, the orphan or the widow."[19] Identifying with the community's suffering and entering into it is an expression of faith in the God who is present with his people in their suffering, above all, in the person of Jesus: "Accompaniment discovers the presence of the Lord in the midst of the story of suffering that we live to transform it into a story of resurrection and hope."[20] The emphasis here is on accompaniment as something active and transformative, not just staying with people in their suffering, but working from within the place of suffering and death to transform it into a story of resurrection and hope. It is important, too, that the emphasis falls on "discovering the presence of the Lord." Pastoral accompaniment means communal discernment about the ways in which the Lord is present, sustaining and leading the community beyond violence and suffering and into life. This process of discovery, sustained by faith, takes time. Henao writes, "Accompaniment does not always guarantee that the accompanied will be sure of the Lord's presence or will understand the importance of walking the road. Understanding and assimilating this new presence of the Risen Christ, which breaks the paradigms of fear and trauma, takes time."[21]

In addition to drawing on the stories of the resurrection and the transformation this wrought among the disciples after the trauma of the crucifixion and death of Jesus, Henao explores the theological significance of "being with" in dialogue with the story of Ruth.[22] He reflects on the difference between Orpah, who decides to go back to her people, and Ruth, who remains with her mother-in-law, Naomi. In the case of Orpah, accompaniment has a limit, and she returns to safety and rest in her own land. Ruth decides to accompany in a way that is supportive and unlimited and is therefore able to overcome challenges and obstacles.[23] In this sense, pastoral accompaniment is an act of profound hope, requiring a prophetic vision.[24]

THE THEOLOGY OF PASTORAL ACCOMPANIMENT

Henao's reflections, though brief, provide many rich insights for developing a fuller theology of pastoral accompaniment. Here, I want to draw out just three principles, all of which are developed further in the constructive work that follows.

First, there is an incarnational dynamic at work here. The effectiveness of pastoral accompaniment as a strategy of peacebuilding comes from the closeness of pastoral agents to those suffering the effects of violence. Only by understanding that violence from within, by placing themselves within its force field, as it were, can pastoral agents truly accompany those who are suffering and effectively connect their experience, practical needs, hopes, and fears with the wider peacebuilding process.

Second, pastoral accompaniment is a response to the work of God, who is already present in conflict and suffering to console and transform. Pastoral accompaniment is not a matter of an "imitation" of Christ, in the sense of casting myself in the role of the people's savior, ready to suffer anything and lay down my life, as though Christ's presence with his people stands or falls on my heroic determination to remain. Rather, there is one flock and one shepherd, and only one who lays down his life for the salvation of his people (Jn 10:16–17): our pastoral accompaniment is a response to and a participation in Christ's. A theology of pastoral accompaniment must preserve this attitude of response, participation, and discernment, again experiencing "from the inside" the ways in which God is leading, inviting, and enabling the community. This sense of God's initiative links the theology of pastoral accompaniment with the Pauline theology of reconciliation, which is explored further below and more fully in chapter 6.

Third, pastoral accompaniment relates not just to what the Church does, but what the Church is. Pastoral accompaniment is not a task with an end date or a project with measurable outcomes. Rather, the Church's mission is her existence in places of conflict as a reconciled and reconciling body.[25] In this sense, a theology of pastoral accompaniment is not a theology of a distinct activity of the Church but a theology that helps answer the question, what does it mean to exist as the body of Christ in a situation of conflict? Again, these ecclesiological questions are explored in greater depth in chapter 6, but here I want to note how a theology of pastoral accompaniment connects with—and perhaps offers a helpful corrective nudge to—an ecclesiology of communion.

In the rest of this chapter, I want to develop a theology of pastoral accompaniment by drawing on the concept of consolation, which combines and theologically deepens the three principles noted above. The first section explores the concept of consolation in the Old Testament, beginning with an overview of its range of meaning before going on to demonstrate its centrality to the prophetic vision of Isaiah. The second section shows how this theology of consolation connects with the synoptic Gospels' presentation of the person and ministry of Jesus and his death and resurrection. The final section explores how these theological insights can support and strengthen the Church's practice of pastoral accompaniment in situations of violent conflict.

CONSOLATION

The Hebrew word usually translated as "consolation" comes from the root *nḥm*, which is used both in the context of human relationships and to describe God's relationship to individuals or to the people of Israel as a whole. In the *piel* form (denoting emphatic action), the verb most often means to comfort or console someone, in the sense of standing in solidarity with them in their suffering.[26] The word connotes pity or sympathy: thus Job's friends come to comfort him in his misfortune (Jb 2:11), and Ruth is comforted by the kindness of Boaz (Ru 2:13). In the Psalms, the word is most often used to express God's comforting of an individual, the psalmist, sometimes with the implication that God's comfort avails where human comfort is useless or sought in vain (e.g., Ps 69:20).[27] In prophetic texts, the word is more often used to express God's comforting of the people of Israel, and again, the use of *nḥm* to signify God's comforting of his people can carry the sense that only God's comfort is effective and meaningful.[28]

In the *niphal* form (passive/reflexive), *nḥm* means to relent, to regret, to feel sorrow, or to change one's mind about an attitude or course of action, and in this sense—perhaps surprisingly—it is more often used of God than of human beings.[29] The Genesis flood narrative begins with God's admission that he is sorry he has made human beings, because of their great wickedness: God sees that "every inclination of the thoughts of their hearts was only evil continually" (Gen 6:5). God's regret that he has made humankind at the beginning of the Noah narrative (Gen 6:6) is bookended by another relenting at the end of that narrative (Gen 8:21), namely, his promise, "I will never again curse the ground because of humankind, for the inclination of the heart is evil from youth, nor will I ever again destroy every living creature as I have done." Both verses make pointed mention of the continually evil inclination of human hearts, and Childs notes on this basis that God's decision not to destroy the earth or living creatures again is not the result of any improvement in human behavior; rather "he has instead fully accepted the incorrigible nature of humankind with patience and mercy. 'In view of the enduring character of human nature, [Yahweh's] patience is the only conceivable way to guarantee the ongoing existence of humankind.'"[30]

The Noah episode highlights the link between the *piel* (comfort) and *niphal* (relent) senses of the root *nḥm*: it is God taking pity on human frailty that produces the change in his course of action and the subsequent covenant promise. Even when *nḥm* is used to signify God relenting or changing his mind, then, it can still highlight his underlying and unchanging faithfulness to his creative and redeeming purpose.[31] Where *nḥm* in the sense of "relent" is negated (e.g., God will *not* relent), it highlights God's faithfulness to a course of action, usually punishment (Jer 4:28, 20:16). In this context, the word also sometimes appears in connection with prophetic intercession on behalf of the people and the capacity of a prophet pleading to make God relent and avert a threatened destruction. Thus, after the Israelites fashion the golden calf and God intends to destroy them (Ex 32:10), Moses's intercession in Exodus 32:11–13 causes God to change his mind about the disaster he has threatened (Ex 32:14).[32] Here again, however, God relenting and changing his mind also demonstrates his deeper and unswerving faithfulness to his covenant: Moses's intercession reminds God of his promises to Abraham, Isaac, and Israel (Ex 32:13).

It is worth drawing out a few theological points from this general survey. Just as *nḥm* in the sense of comforting means not mere sympathy but something effective, *nḥm* in the sense of relenting or being sorry is not a matter of mere emotion. God "being sorry" consists not in remorse or sorrowful resignation but in a concrete change of action.[33] When used in connection with God relenting from threatened destruction and the decision to comfort Israel, *nḥm* therefore approaches the sense of "having mercy on," implying both a change of attitude and a change of action—consolation that is effective.[34] Second, God relenting or changing his mind can coexist with a sense that this "relenting" is a form of faithfulness to an unswerving, deeper purpose. So although it involves a change of mind, God relenting may take the form of not actually doing anything at all, or simple patience and forbearance in the face of Israel's persistent sinfulness and rebelliousness. Third, *nḥm* used in both senses can signify setting oneself in a new relationship to the past or being determined to bring about a new situation different from the one that has gone before.

Consolation in Isaiah

These theological features are clearly evident in the second half of the book of Isaiah, in which the verb *nḥm* is used more frequently and systematically than anywhere else in the biblical canon.[35] Exploring these texts helps us connect the concept of consolation with the person and work of Christ.

The first half of the book of Isaiah deals with the prophecy of Isaiah of Jerusalem concerning Assyria, which Second and Third Isaiah consider as having come to pass with the destruction of Jerusalem at the hands of the Babylonians in 587 BC and the subsequent exile. The historical context addressed in Second and Third Isaiah is the return of the remnant of Israel from exile, so from chapter 40 on the text deals with the prophetic announcement of redemption and a new period of peace and restoration.[36] In the text, the context of this prophetic announcement appears to be the divine court, with the multiple voices present in the text understood as the speech of God with the divine attendants or with Jerusalem herself.[37] Scholarly opinion varies as to whom God is addressing with the opening injunction, "Comfort, comfort my people." Jerome held that "my people" were being addressed and instructed to comfort Jerusalem, but most modern commentators understand "my people" as the object of the verb and therefore the objects of God's comfort. The injunction to comfort is therefore addressed to some group present in the divine court. The response to this call comes from a herald who proclaims, "In the wilderness, prepare the way of the Lord" (Isa 40:3). The divine injunction is repeated in "Cry out!" (40:6), and in response to the objection of the messenger ("What shall I cry? All people are grass"), the message to be delivered is given in the following verses: grass may wither, but the word of the Lord stands firm forever (40:8): the people will see the Lord coming in victory (40:9–11).

The first point of note here is the intertextual echo between chapter 40 and the narrative of the prophetic call in Isaiah 6.[38] In chapter 6, the prophet is instructed to make the minds of the people dull, to stop their ears and shut their eyes until the Lord has allowed cities to become wastes and sent the people into exile (6:9–11). Chapter 40 is announcing new things: the herald of good tidings says, "Here is your God!" (40:9b), and "See, the Lord God comes with might!" (40:10). A few verses earlier, the heraldic voice announces that the glory of the Lord will be revealed and all peoples shall see it together (40:5). Chapter 40 thus picks up the language of divine commission in chapter 6 and reshapes it to present the new thing the Lord is doing, contrasting the earlier *not*-seeing with the coming vision of the glory and redeeming action of the Lord. The comforting of Isaiah in 40:1, then, also involves a *relenting*: "the announcement of a divine decision [in chapter 40] that now reverses the commission of judgement assigned to Isaiah [in chapter 6]."[39] Another intertextual echo may be at play between the injunction to comfort in 40:1 and the promise in 12:1 that "in that day" God's anger will be turned away and he will comfort: that day has now arrived, with the announcement that Israel's penalty has been paid (40:2). Again, this relenting bears witness to God's faithfulness and steadfast love for Israel. In the face of the people's inconstancy (40:6b–7), the word of the Lord stands firm forever (40:8).

The second point of note concerns the image of the highway in 40:3, which Second Isaiah also seems to use as a way of announcing that the redemption promised by the Lord has now come.[40] In chapter 35 the prophet declares that "a highway shall be there" (35:8), on which the "ransomed of the Lord" will return joyfully from exile. The highway is an image of the return from exile and is also connected with the hoped-for restoration of Israel, in which the desert will rejoice and bloom (35:1) and the glory of the Lord will be seen (35:2). Chapter 35 also picks up the language of healing: the deaf ears of chapter 6 will be unstopped and the eyes of the blind opened (35:5). In chapter 40, this highway image of hope is revisited again in a slightly different key: the highway of 40:3 is for the return, not of exiles, but of "our God," who will be seen coming in power to take care of his people like a shepherd (40:11). As I have already noted, the same passage takes up the language of seeing to describe this as a present reality: "*Here* is your God!" (40:9; my emphasis).

The language of comfort is central to Isaiah's proclamation of the Lord redeeming Israel. The theme of consolation announced in chapter 40 will recur throughout Second and Third Isaiah, in the assurance that the Lord will comfort Zion and turn her wilderness into a garden (51:3), or has comforted his people and redeemed Jerusalem (52:9), or will comfort Jerusalem like a mother comforts her child (66:13). This use of the language of comfort brings with it some of the features noted earlier: not just a sense of sympathy or solidarity with the suffering of Israel, but also a sense that this comfort results in a concrete change in Israel's predicament. This is in part because the passages in Second Isaiah in which the language of comfort is employed are consciously referring back to earlier uses of this language in First Isaiah, bridging the earlier themes of prophetic judgment with the subsequent announcement of salvation and the restoration of Israel. In this way, comforting language also becomes relenting language: God's comforting means his having mercy on Israel and setting her in a new relationship to her sinful past. God's relenting, his decision to withdraw Israel's punishment and redeem and restore her, bears witness to his word of steadfast love that does not change.

Christ as Consolation

How does this theology of consolation connect with the life, death, and resurrection of Jesus? The texts of consolation in Isaiah discussed above are among the most significant scriptural texts for which the synoptic Gospels writers reach as they frame their accounts of Jesus's life and establish his identity. This connection is established early on in all three synoptic Gospels by their concrete identification of John the Baptist with the figure of the herald from Isaiah 40: John the Baptist is the one crying, "Prepare in the wilderness the way of the Lord" (Mt 3:3; Mk 1:2; Lk 3:4–6). John is thus the herald of God's redemption, a confession that Luke places on the lips of John's father, Zechariah, in Luke 1:76:

> And you, child, will be called the prophet of the Most High;
> for you will go ahead of the Lord to prepare his ways,
> to give knowledge of salvation to his people
> by the forgiveness of their sins.

The subsequent accounts of John's proclamation in the desert pick up on both these themes: the coming of the Lord and the consequent need for repentance (Mt 3:2, 5–6; Mk 1:4; Lk 3:3).

This identification of the figure of John the Baptist with the herald figure of Isaiah 40 sets up from the very start of the synoptic Gospels a series of associations between the person of Jesus and the promised redemption announced by Isaiah: Jesus *is* the glory and salvation of the Lord revealed for all to see (Is 40:10; Lk 2:30–32). The synoptic Gospels writers are clearly claiming that Jesus is God's consolation of Israel. There are those who do not perceive this new thing that the Lord is doing, and this group is also understood in terms of Isaiah's prophecy in chapter 6 against the deafness and blindness of the people, which appears on the lips of Jesus in Luke 4:12 and Matthew 13:14–15. But the association being made here is not just a general one between the person of Jesus and the coming of the redemption promised by God: the gospel writers directly and explicitly associate the signs of God's consolation of Israel in Isaiah with the concrete signs of Jesus's ministry. In Luke 4, Jesus inaugurates his public ministry by reading directly from Isaiah 61:1–2 ("the Spirit of the Lord God is upon me . . . he has sent me to bring the good news to the poor") and claiming, "Today this scripture has been fulfilled in your hearing" (Lk 4:21). Jesus's answer to the question of John's disciples, "Are you the one who is to come, or are we to wait for another?," is both an allusion to Isaiah and a literal description of his own actions: the blind receive their sight, the lame walk, the lepers are cleansed, the deaf hear, and the poor have good news brought to them (Mt 11:2–4). Jesus's healings are concrete and effective signs of God's consolation of Israel. Jesus's forgiveness of sins, too, recalls Isaiah's prophecy that God's redemption of Israel will include the forgiveness of her sins (Is 1:27, 33:24). Thus the claim in Isaiah 43:25, "I, I am he who blots out your transgressions for my own sake, and I will not remember your sins," likely stands in the background of controversies over Jesus's forgiveness of sins (Mk 2:7), which are ultimately conflicts over his identity. The gospel writers' extensive use of the servant songs (Is 42, 49, 52–53) reflects the profound importance of these passages for the earliest Christian reflection on the suffering and death of Jesus.[41]

The texts in Isaiah about God's consolation of Israel are deeply bound up in the synoptic Gospels writers' understanding of the person and ministry of Jesus. In Jesus, God comes close to his people, and through Jesus's ministry of healing, forgiving sins, and announcing God's favor

God is concretely consoling and restoring Israel. There is much here that connects with the practice of pastoral accompaniment, understood as an effective coming-close to those suffering the effects of violence. Can this concept of consolation also shed light on the death and resurrection of Jesus and provide a link between the paschal mystery and the theology of pastoral accompaniment?

Earlier, I drew attention to two aspects of the root *nḥm* in its sense of "comfort": the idea of solidarity with others in their suffering and the idea that God's comfort avails where human comfort is in vain. A number of twentieth-century theologians pick up on these themes, understanding the death of Jesus in terms of his entering into and taking on the suffering of humanity or in terms of his identification with victims. These theologies are, in part, a response to the traumatic experience of the world wars, while liberation theologies that take up these themes are often responding explicitly to structural violence and repression in Latin America. Although they do not draw on the concept of consolation, they provide a useful way in to thinking about how Jesus's death relates to the landscape of human violence.

Jürgen Moltmann, writing in the wake of World War II, explores the theology of the cross along these lines.[42] Much traditional theology of the atonement proceeds on the basis that humanity is alienated from God by its sinfulness and understands the cross as God's remedy for human sin. Moltmann, rather than focusing on human sinfulness, picks up on human suffering as the cause of our alienation from God. It is our experience of suffering, and our sense that God is absent from it, that leads us to become alienated from God, rejecting and even denying God's existence.[43] In this context, the incarnation and the cross are God's demonstration of his concrete presence in and solidarity with human suffering.[44] God's coming close is a comforting that avails, even amid the meaninglessness of human comfort. Jesus "paves a way through judgement and godforsakenness, which is only passable for men in his company. . . . Christ experiences death and hell in solitude. His followers experience it in his company. That is no substitution, but a liberation."[45] But the significance of the cross is not limited to God's presence in human suffering: in the death and resurrection of Jesus, that suffering is taken up and transformed. This taking-up and transformation of suffering is, for Moltmann, an eschatological reality.

As Paul says in 1 Cor 15, only with the resurrection of the dead, the murdered and the gassed, only with the healing of those in despair who bear lifelong wounds, only with the abolition of all rule and authority, only with the annihilation of death will the Son hand over the kingdom to the Father. Then God will turn his sorrow into eternal joy. This will be the sign of the completion of the trinitarian history of God and the end of world history, the overcoming of the history of man's sorrow and the fulfilment of his history of hope.[46]

Small acts of overcoming death through liberation from poverty and injustice, from political repression, from meaninglessness and from dominative relationships with nature, are sacraments of this coming liberation.[47]

There are elements here that we can recognize from the theology of consolation, understood in the sense of comfort, as I have explored it so far. Moltmann's theology of the cross shows how God's coming close in Jesus comforts us in our experience of suffering, changing not just our inner experience of that suffering but also our concrete response to it. But before I begin to incorporate these elements into the theology of pastoral accompaniment as I have explored it so far, we need to look at how Jesus's death and resurrection also relate to consolation understood in the sense of "relenting."

In prophetic texts, God's punishment of Israel, whether actual or threatened, is often understood as a consequence of her sinfulness or folly, whether that takes the form of injustice, poor alliances with neighboring powers, or idolatry. In relenting, then, either by averting the coming destruction or choosing to cut short the disaster that Israel has brought on herself, God is actively refusing the momentum of Israel's self-destructiveness. God's relenting checks Israel's headlong slide into destruction by placing a restraining hand—his mercy—between her sins and what ought to be their natural consequences. God relents in this way out of limitless faithfulness to his covenant of love and mercy, and he does so even in the face of Israel's persistent frailty and failure. As we have seen, God's relenting, his "changing his mind," can thus manifest a deeper refusal to relent from his choosing of Israel, and from his ultimate creative and redemptive purpose. How might this affect how we see the death and resurrection of Christ? In a vein similar to Moltmann's reversal of the idea of alienation, I want to suggest that Jesus's death does not occur because God's justice is so offended that he will not or cannot relent and must therefore visit the punishment necessary for maintaining his righteousness on an innocent victim. Jesus's death is not the putting to death of *God's* hostility (Eph 1:16) in this sense. Rather, God's righteousness, his faithfulness to his creative and redeeming purpose, is manifested in his *relenting*, in the sense that through Christ's death and resurrection God refuses once and for all the ultimate consequences of human enmity and self-destructiveness.[48]

On the cross, Jesus absorbs not the hostility of God to rebellious humankind but the momentum of our own self-destructiveness, a self-destructiveness that consists not in mere indifference to God's overtures, but in active hostility to them. Jesus tells two parables to this effect: the tenants of the vineyard do not just refuse to hand over the produce, but beat and kill the slaves sent to collect it (Mt 21:34–35), and the guests do not just ignore the invitation to the son's wedding feast, but maltreat and kill the messengers (Mt 22:5–6). Matthew's placing of these parables after Jesus's entry into Jerusalem suggests that the event of Jesus's crucifixion is understood in these terms, as our decisive and ultimate rejection of God. As Paul sees it, this rebelliousness is not just our refusal of God, but our refusal of our own humanity, in the sense of our creaturely status before God (Rom 1:19–21). The result of this rebelliousness against God and our own nature is ultimately self-destructive: God "gave us up," Paul says, to our own self-destructiveness, the ultimate consequence of which is death (Rom 1:24–28, 32). In the context of our refusal of God and our refusal of our own creaturely humanity—indeed our active hostility toward both—the crucifixion of Jesus appears as both the definitive act of hostility toward God (Mt 21:37–8) and, as the destruction of a human being limitlessly obedient to God, the definitive act of hostility toward our own humanity.[49] This act of hostility is not symbolic but actual and concrete: it is the real putting to death of a human being who is also the Son of God.

Our human hostility, then, not God's, is what brings Jesus to the cross. That is not the whole picture, however: the other thing that brings Jesus to the point of crucifixion is his own faithfulness, his very concrete refusal to relent, in the face of human hostility and rejection, from his redeeming and restoring purpose.[50] Jesus's purpose is also the will of the Father to which he is obedient, and in Jesus's determination to go to Jerusalem and the Father's silence in Gethsemane we see two sides of the same coin: God's steadfast faithfulness to his purpose. This not relenting on the part of Jesus and this not relenting on the part of the Father are also a relenting insofar as they show God remaining concretely faithful to his redeeming purpose in the face of persistent human frailty and hostility. God relents not in spite of the fact that "the inclination of the human heart is evil from youth" (Gen 8:2) but because of that fact: in Paul's language, it is our utter inability to justify ourselves that necessitates God's gift in Jesus (Rom 3:23–24) and his death for us while we are still weak, still godless, and still sinners (Rom 5:6–8).[51]

In Christ on the cross, God is concretely present in the depth of human hostility toward God and the depth of human hostility toward humanity. This is, in one sense, the "putting to death" of our human hostility: its culmination in the crucifixion, in which God absorbs the full momentum of human self-destructiveness. But it is the resurrection that constitutes God's final putting to death of hostility, because Christ's resurrection is God's ultimate and absolutely concrete refusal of the final consequence of human self-destructiveness: death. From the human point of view here, we are confronted with an event of absolute discontinuity: the resurrection from death of a human being. Resurrection does not follow upon death with the inevitability of spring following winter or growth following planting. Rather than a kind of narrative continuity, resurrection is a profound discontinuity, rooted solely in the decision of the Father to raise Christ into a new kind of existence, which is not merely the resuscitation of the old, but the beginning of a new creation (Col 1:15).[52] At the same time, from the point of view of God, the resurrection also confronts us with an event of absolute continuity, because it bears witness to God's ultimate faithfulness to his purposes. God's faithfulness to his creative and redeeming purposes takes concrete shape in the resurrection as the Father's faithfulness to Christ in raising him from death. It is important here to note that God's victory over death is not mysterious and intangible, existing only in the disciples' minds or in a change of perception: it has a body that is markedly different but that is recognizable, and that can touch and be touched, eat fish and lay fires. The life that Jesus's resurrection makes possible is as human and concrete as his death.

Comforting and Relenting

When Catholic theology wants to name ways in which God's grace is manifested in concrete and dependable ways, it uses the language of sacrament. Here, perhaps we can name the practice of pastoral accompaniment as a sacrament of God's consolation. As a sacrament, it makes present and real what it signifies, in this case, God's steadfast love, his refusal to abandon his people, and his determination to restore them. We now need to unpack this, first exploring the Church as a sacrament of God's comfort and then exploring what it might mean to talk about the Church as a sacrament of God's relenting.

First, comfort: in situations of violent conflict, there are many forces—fear, suspicion, enmity, silence—that threaten to pull communities apart. In the face of such forces of destruction, the practice of pastoral accompaniment continually gathers and makes present the people whom God accompanies. In this sense, the existence and concrete presence of the community is itself a sign of God's accompanying love and its ability to overcome the centrifugal forces of violence. Simply remaining as church in such contexts and continuing the "ordinary" round of prayer and sacraments is a sign of faith in God's consolation, a sign that amid the grief, confusion, and fear of conflict God's comfort avails. Again, it is important to emphasize the *effectiveness* of that comfort. As we saw earlier, God's coming close in comfort concretely changes Israel's predicament. If it is to be genuinely sacramental of God's comforting, pastoral accompaniment must go beyond just suffering alongside people in a way that helps them feel differently about the violence they are experiencing; it must also enable people to respond differently to that violence, in a dynamic that moves from death toward resurrection. Two brief examples, highlighting how ordinary pastoral practice can become an effective sign of consolation and an effective form of peacebuilding, will help explain what I mean here.

Timothy Radcliffe, recalling a visit to Dominican sisters working in a refugee camp in a war zone in northern Rwanda, talks about celebrating the Eucharist in a context of profound suffering.

> I had visited the refugee camp with thirty thousand people and seen women trying to feed children who had just given up eating because

they could not be bothered to live. I had visited the hospital run by the sisters, and seen ward after ward of children and young people with their limbs blown off. I remember one child, eight or nine, with both his legs blown off, and an arm and an eye, and his father sitting by the bed weeping. And we went back to the sisters' house and there was nothing to say. We could not find a single word. But we could celebrate the Eucharist, we could remember that Last Supper. It was the only thing to do, and which gave those sisters the courage to stay, and to belong.[53]

That the celebration of the Eucharist brought comfort, giving words where there were none, is clear. It is also clear that this comfort was more than sympathy: it incorporated the sisters accompanying the Rwandan refugees into a story of self-gift in the face of suffering that reinforced their desire to remain. Where a community is under threat of displacement or dispersal, practices like the celebration of the Eucharist can visibly reconstitute the body of Christ in a particular place, in a way that reinforces community ties and reasserts the meaningfulness and value of ordinary life.[54]

Practices of mourning and the celebration of funerals can also be important in communities suffering from violence. Especially in situations marked by disappearances and extrajudicial executions, or atrocities that are denied by perpetrators or by the state, funerals, public mourning, and commemorations are not just opportunities for lament but also opportunities to call publicly for justice for the victims and survivors.[55] Where military or political powers use dehumanizing rhetoric or the language of "collateral damage," grieving is a way of making human victims of conflict appear as such and thereby claiming and reinforcing the value of human life.[56] It is important to recognize that practices of lament and grieving can easily become part of a cycle of violence, so that death simply leads to more death. Here, authentic pastoral accompaniment means helping a community grieve death in a way that helps it choose life. Judith Butler, writing about the swift move from national mourning to military action following the attacks of September 11, 2001, draws attention to the role that grief can play in humanizing even the enemy other: "The quick move to action is a way of foreclosing grief, refusing it, and even as it anaesthetizes one's own pain and sense of loss, it comes, in time, to anaesthetize us to the losses that we inflict upon others."[57] Giving space to grief, and to its roots in shared human vulnerability, can become a way of concretely choosing life over the temptation of vengeance.[58]

In this connection, it is worth returning to a point touched on already regarding discernment. We have seen that it is the drawing close in comfort that makes it effective: we cannot comfort others from a distance. Henao also notes that it is the closeness of pastoral agents to those experiencing the effects of violence that made them effective agents of peacebuilding: from their place within the conflict, they are able to understand its dynamics, recognize alternative responses, build consensus, and provide space for working together. Yet there is not necessarily a positive correlation between our proximity to a conflict and our understanding of it, or our positive response to it. Nor are the "ordinary" practices of pastoral accompaniment guarantees of their own authenticity: the local Church community and the sacraments can all too easily become hollowed out, replicating and reproducing ethnic and political conflict rather than reconciliation.[59] In this context, what is needed is not objectivity—with the distance that this implies from the experience of conflict and those suffering from it—so much as discernment. I suggested earlier that this was implied by Henao's insistence that pastoral accompaniment is God's initiative: it is God who accompanies, and at best our accompaniment of one another is a response to and a sign of the Lord's presence with us. We have also seen this reflected in the scriptural material on consolation, particularly in Isaiah, where the consolation and restoration of Israel is clearly God's initiative. This means that the practice of pastoral accompaniment must be discerning, attentive to the ways in which God is not just present with the community in suffering, but inviting them to take concrete steps toward life. Paul talks about "the God of all consolation, who comforts us in all our sorrows, so that we can offer others, in their sorrows the consolation that we have received from God ourselves" (2 Cor 1:3–5). This connection between consolation received and consolation extended to others—which includes even the enemy—is a key criterion of discernment, which I explore further in chapter 6.

Pastoral accompaniment is an effective sign of God's comforting his people. Is it also a sign of God's relenting? How might we understand the Church's mission of pastoral accompaniment in situations of violent conflict as a mission of relenting? At first the idea sounds strange, as though the Church's mission in areas of violent conflict consists in relenting, in the sense of not participating in violence or refraining from being drawn into the cycles of resentment and revenge. This may be true, but God's relenting, as discussed earlier, consists in something much deeper: a refusal of the consequences of human self-destructiveness, a refusal that manifests a deep fidelity to his creative and redeeming purpose. Our hostility to God and to our own humanity reaches its apex in the crucifixion of Jesus, and its natural momentum is toward the tomb. The resurrection of Jesus is God's insistence that our self-destruction shall not be the last word: God's raising Jesus to life is the putting to death of our hostility. In this context, the Church's ministry of pastoral accompaniment consists in being present in contexts of violence, both structural and direct, in ways that check the momentum and refuse the consequences of the human capacity for violence and self-destruction.[60]

This is a rich seam to explore, but let me give just two examples, one about how the Church can hold open that space of life within herself and one about how she can hold open a space of life in civil society in contexts of violent conflict.

First, then, the Church can hold open a specifically ecclesial space of life through *forbearance*. In situations of violent conflict, resisting the forces of dispersion and remaining as a community requires effort, and the fidelity demanded can be considerable and costly. Remaining alongside one another may mean cultivating a certain divine stubbornness, in the sense of a refusal to abandon the vision of a restored society, even in the face of persistent frailty and brokenness. It means an effort, continually renewed, to imitate God in not counting others' sins against them.[61] This does not mean abandoning the claims of justice but striving for what James Alison calls a "continual loosing, forgiving, of the violence of the other's relationship to the free self-giver."[62] Rather than being bound to others by relationships of suspicion, resentment, anger, or revenge, forbearance means a choice to be bound by a relationship of grace— a choice to "bear with."

In situations of long-term and complex violent conflict, forbearance, or "bearing with" others, might reflect more realistically the experience of those living in the situation than the language of communion. Catholic ecclesiology in the twentieth century has drawn heavily on the theology of communion. Its mystical language of union with God made visible in the Church's communion names an important truth but one that may struggle to connect with the reality of communities living in conflict situations. The loving communion of persons in God may, as Lisa Cahill suggests, model peacebuilding relationships, but the distance between relations of divine perichoresis and human relationships, marked as they are by sin and violence, is great.[63] In such contexts, Catholic social teaching's insistence that human beings are naturally interdependent and "built" for communion, though it also names an important truth, can seem remote: communion is not easy or mutual but hard-won, demanding sacrifice, demanding that some take the costly initiative to restore or persist in a relationship that others sabotage or abandon. Forbearance names a particular grace that is required to be Church, to accompany one another, in such circumstances. It is a grace that reflects the righteousness of God that manifests itself in forbearance and self-gift in the face of hostility (Rom 3:25).

Second, a theology of consolation can also help us notice and nurture other dimensions of the Church's pastoral accompaniment in situations of violent conflict. We noted earlier Jesus's response to John's disciples, sent to inquire whether he was the Messiah or whether they were to wait for someone else: the blind receive their sight, the lame walk, the lepers are cleansed, the deaf hear, and the poor have good news brought to them (Mt 11:2–4). These are the signs of God's consolation. Pastoral accompaniment, understood as a sacrament of God's consolation, can therefore encompass not only typically ecclesial activities like the celebration of the sacraments and meetings of base ecclesial communities, but a wider family of practices of healing, creativity, and justice, including healthcare and education. Such practices can help hold open spaces of life within civil society, allowing relationships of trust to be established or rebuilt and strengthened. They can demonstrate concretely the possibility of positive coexistence, on the minimal level of "bearing with," and toward a horizon of communion. To give just one example, in some places where state provision for the care and education of children with special needs is currently very limited or nonexistent, Catholic and other Christian organizations provide care and schooling that is open to all. In addition to bearing witness to the Catholic vision of a "culture of life," such initiatives hold open a space for encounter and relationship building.[64] They can also act as what Gaspar calls "microutopias," modeling in a concrete way the possibility of coexistence and refusing narratives that insist that peace can only be achieved through separation or by the decisive dominance of one group.[65] In Egypt, Church organizations that provide care and education for children with special needs are open to Christian and Muslim children alike, thus providing a space of mutual encounter and helping build trust between the two communities. In Israel, the L'Arche community, first in Bethany and now in Bethlehem, provides a similar space of "relenting."[66] In doing so, it models the role that David Neuhaus S.J. argues the Church is called to play in that conflict: not "stuck in the middle" of two societies tearing each other apart but deeply embedded in both and acting as leaven.[67] Where practices like these sustain life in the midst of the chaos of conflict, where they enable people to draw closer to one another, where they bear concrete witness—even in very small and fragile ways—to a vision of a reconciled and redeemed creation, they can be intentionally lived as a sacrament of "relenting" and a sign of God's consolation of his people.

Pastoral accompaniment can also enable the Church to contribute to wider political processes of relenting, by holding open space for dialogue between parties in conflict. The Church's proximity, through pastoral accompaniment, to victims of violence can enable them to play the role of advocates for their rights or represent their interests in high-level talks.[68] Likewise, the Church's pastoral accompaniment of marginalized groups on a local level can mean that armed actors associated with those groups trust Church leaders, who are then able to convene talks or act as mediators or guarantors. This is particularly important given the institutional focus of much Church teaching on peace. As I show in the next chapter, that teaching typically focuses on the work of national and international institutions and addresses political leaders: it tends not to have the grassroots, and particularly the activity of laypeople, in view. A theology of pastoral accompaniment helps broaden Catholic social teaching's vision of what peacebuilding *is*, and who does it, and helps connect the grassroots peacebuilding work of the Church with its potential contribution to higher-level political processes.

Pastoral accompaniment, Henao states, requires mysticism. To sustain the practice of pastoral accompaniment in situations of violence requires the ability not to float above reality but in some way to see "underneath" it, to the roots of action, to the significance of practice, to the situation—as far as we are able to perceive it—as it exists in God's sight. It then requires that we live out of that "underneath," not as an occasionally remembered rationale, but as a living source for fidelity, action, prayer, and discernment. In other words, the mysticism of pastoral accompaniment, a way of seeing, needs to become a spirituality, a way of proceeding.

The Church is already present in situations of armed conflict across the globe and deeply embedded in communities affected by violence. The practice of pastoral accompaniment in these areas is already a reality, and in some areas it is already a self-conscious practice of peacebuilding. What I have suggested in this chapter is that Church teaching needs to catch up with practice, offering theological resources to help support and encourage those engaged in pastoral accompaniment in situations of violent conflict and encouraging Catholics to see pastoral accompaniment as part of the Church's distinctive contribution to peacebuilding. A theology of consolation, I have argued, is one scriptural and spiritual locus to which we can turn. The theology of consolation begins with the prophets' hope of God's coming close to comfort and restore his people in their own land. It takes flesh in the person of Jesus, through his ministry of healing and consolation and self-gift among the least. It takes in the darkness of the cross, God's presence with us in the darkest place of suffering, where we are most threatened with meaninglessness and chaos, and it emerges in the light of the resurrection with God's refusal to abandon the beloved Son to death and his determination to redeem and restore all creation. Joined to the practice of pastoral accompaniment, a theology of consolation draws attention to the importance of presence with the suffering and the value of the Church's presence as a community that remains together in the face of violent division. It reinforces pastoral accompaniment as a specifically Christian and ecclesial practice, highlighting the roles not only of clergy and religious, but of the whole community. Last, a theology of consolation highlights the role that the Church can play in resisting the momentum of a community's self-destruction through violence and holding open spaces of life.

FOUR

Solidarity

I have to confess that many nights I can hardly sleep, sometimes with anger, sometimes with, and excuse me for saying this, with feelings of physically needing to vomit. But it is necessary to move toward these people as people, to build a human environment, to build trust without judgment, and to meet the guerrilla who, weapon in hand, reaches out for my rosary or my cross and asks for mass, Eucharist, and in particular, the sacrament of reconciliation. And I ask them, "How can you want this and still carry a gun or keep someone kidnapped?" And they say, "Father, it is not me, it is the organization. I am trapped, I follow orders. I want it over but I can't." So I see the evil of the pattern, the institution, and yet I see the person as a human being. This has led me to see them, sometimes with sadness, but also with a sense of sharing the pain they experience. But it leads me to build with them an environment of trust and respect and this relationship helps me to speak more directly and deeply about their responsibility. I speak as a minister of the church asking them to respect others, to understand and respect the pain of their victims. They need to move towards responsibility and reparation and truth if they are genuine about seeking personal peace. It comes with responsibility.[1]

These are the words of Fr. Darío Echeverri, a Claretian priest and head of the National Conciliation Commission of the Colombian Bishops' Conference. Over the course of more than sixty years of armed conflict in Colombia, the Catholic Church has come to play a significant role in peacebuilding efforts in diverse ways, ranging from facilitation of the national peace processes to pastoral accompaniment on a local level in communities affected by conflict. Father Echeverri's comments give us a glimpse of the tremendous emotional strain, the deeply difficult and troubling moral decisions, and the considerable personal danger faced by those who find themselves on the front line of the Church's peacebuilding efforts.

This chapter is written with peacebuilders like Father Echeverri in mind. In chapter 2, on Catholic social teaching on peace, I noted that its natural law foundation tended to give it a strong emphasis on social order and the role of institutions. On the macro level, the Church has a good deal to say about the roles and responsibilities of states and their governments and places high value on international cooperation through organizations like the United Nations. Accordingly, the Church's account of the work of peacebuilding tends to focus on statecraft and often addresses those leaders involved in negotiating peace by means of dialogue and diplomacy. This institutional focus is valuable, but it speaks to only a narrow slice of the range of activities involved in peacebuilding. In this respect, the Church's practice runs ahead of its teaching: contemporary Catholic peacebuilding consists not only of Vatican diplomacy or brokering talks between political and military leaders but also a wide range of activities undertaken by midlevel and grassroots actors, from lay organizations and local parish communities to priests and bishops. While the political and military leaders who take part in formal peace negotiations may stand at some distance from the violence they are seeking to resolve, these midlevel and grassroots actors find themselves, like Father Echeverri, personally touched by it.

My proposal here is that Catholic social teaching on solidarity represents a significant resource in this regard. Solidarity is one of the four "permanent principles" of Catholic social teaching, but it is more common to see it employed in discussions of economics than in the context of peacebuilding.[2] In what follows, I want to suggest that a theology of solidarity, theologically deepened and more closely connected to the

Church's teaching on peace, can offer an important way of addressing the activities of contemporary peacebuilding and supporting those engaged in them.

The chapter is divided into four sections. In the first section, a brief look at some of the characteristics of contemporary strategic peacebuilding offers a clearer picture of the areas Church teaching needs to address and highlights some of the ways in which it presently falls short of doing so effectively. In the second section, I explore how Church teaching on solidarity offers a potential resource. Tracing the development of Church teaching on solidarity, particularly in the work of John Paul II, enables us to see its points of connection with contemporary peacebuilding and some ways in which these points of connection with Church teaching on peace could be reinforced. This survey, in addition to highlighting the potential strengths of the concept, enables us to see some of the weak or underdeveloped points in Church teaching on solidarity. In light of this, in the third section, I consider how the concept of solidarity could be further developed in order better to support the Catholic theology and practice of peacebuilding, and I argue here that a stronger Christological emphasis would have much to offer. I suggested in the introduction that the experience and practical spirituality of Catholic peacebuilders can act as a resource for critiquing and developing the Church's teaching on peace, and in the final section I pursue this by drawing on the experience, writing, and prayer of the Jesuits killed at the University of Central America in El Salvador in 1989. Exploring their vibrant and Christological understanding of solidarity shows how Church teaching might speak more directly to and support those caught up in the risk, ambiguity, and cost of peacebuilding in situations of violent conflict.

CONTEMPORARY PEACEBUILDING

Contemporary peacebuilding has begun to diversify the modes of analysis and methods that were characteristic of classic liberal peacemaking efforts of the 1970s and 1980s. At that time, Western intervention in violent conflicts was broadly predicated on the idea that democratic societies, with an open market and a dependable rule of law, were generally peaceable and that these features could be engineered in societies affected by conflict after the conclusion of peace accords between the warring parties.[3] The limited success of such ventures, however, led to a growing recognition within the international community that moving a society from open violent conflict toward a sustainable, just peace required more than intense short-term efforts to get opposing sides to the point of a ceasefire and peace agreement, followed by accelerated economic and political reforms.[4] It was in this context that the concept of peacebuilding emerged, which includes a range of strategies and practices aimed both at reducing direct violence and at transforming the root causes of conflict and addressing its legacy.[5] As discussed in the introduction, contemporary peacebuilding recognizes that fostering a just, sustainable, and positive peace requires efforts to transform the inhumane social, political, and economic structures and destructive patterns of relating that underlie conflict; it also entails activities and practices often categorized as "postconflict," including the facilitation of truth and reconciliation processes, trauma healing, and initiatives aimed at building up civil society.

The result is a more strategic, long-term, and locally embedded form of peacebuilding, which balances an emphasis on institutional reform and nation building with an emphasis on the human impact of conflict—the personal trauma, the damage to interpersonal relationships, and the erosion of qualities like trust and hope that, in less easily quantifiable ways, also need to be rebuilt in the aftermath of violence.[6] In addition to promoting high-level peace negotiations, contemporary peacebuilding therefore engages with a wide range of stakeholders in societies affected by conflict, focusing in particular on the role of mid-level actors like academics and religious leaders and local and regional heads of NGOs.[7] These individuals are important because they have the capacity to connect elite levels of political debate and decision making with the grassroots population that is most directly affected by violence and that inherit, and to a large extent determine, the outcomes of formal peace negotiations.[8] By engaging with people at all levels of a conflict-affected society, strategic peacebuilders seek to build networks of communication, resilience, and solidarity. Contemporary peacebuilding, rather than "a temporary effort to negotiate an agreement that ends the violent expression of conflict," then becomes a comprehensive and long-term effort, focused on supporting those in conflict settings to create and sustain "a context-based, permanent, and dynamic platform capable of non-violently generating solutions to ongoing episodes of conflict, which they will experience in the ebb and flow of their social, political, and economic lives."[9]

THE MACRO-LEVEL APPROACH

In multiple conflict settings, from Mindanao to the Central African Republic and the Nineveh Plains of Iraq, Catholic organizations and individuals are already engaged in exactly the kinds of peacebuilding practices described above.[10] In this area, the Church's practice is running significantly ahead of its teaching on peace, which, I suggested in the introduction, remains focused on macro-level institutional change.

In one sense, this macro-level approach is simply a function of the teaching office itself: the pope is the leader of a global church, addressing himself to a wide range of different contexts, cultures, and issues; descending to specifics would arguably limit the usefulness of the teaching and the range of its audience. But the tendency of Catholic social teaching on peace to operate on the macro level is not just the result of a pragmatic decision to address as many people and situations as possible; it also results from the deep theological structure of the teaching tradition itself, which lends itself to a focus on the political order and the institutions that make it up. In *Pacem in terris*, John XXIII describes how relations between states should be governed by rights and duties: each state needs a ruling authority, which must then act in the relationship between states to promote the common good. This is pure Aquinas, with John XXIII simply extending the duties of the head of a commonwealth from the just and peaceful ordering of his own state to the just and peaceful ordering of the international community.[11] In the same vein, the post-*Pacem* tradition also features a heavy emphasis on the role of international political organizations, because the global common good requires a global political authority.[12] While documents on peace often include sections addressed to particular groups like families, young people, and women, they are addressed principally to heads of state and political leaders.[13]

This focus on macro-level institutional change is often paired with a micro-level emphasis on the need for interior renewal and conversion as the sine qua non of peace. Thus John XXIII, toward the close of *Pacem in terris*, states that the world "will never be the dwelling place of peace, till peace has found a home in the heart of each and every man, till every man preserves in himself the order ordained by God to be preserved."[14] The reform of institutions, by itself, will be insufficient unless it is accompanied by a change of heart. Yet this repeated emphasis on the need for conversion of heart, while important, leaves Catholic social teaching on peace with a major gap: the midlevel. Whitmore argues:

> When it [Catholic social teaching] discusses warfare, its focus is on the proper role of states or the United Nations, for instance, in forming treaties, or, when negotiation fails and as a last resort, following the just-war criteria in the use of force. In building a positive peace through development, Catholic social teaching brings attention again to international and state organizations. . . . While there is much discussion of the importance of intermediate associations, the documents describe the associations at a level of abstraction that leaves any account of their internal aims and working thin at best.[15]

Matthew Shadle, writing about *Gaudium et spes*, identifies the same gap.

> The bishops are correct to note that international institutions must play an important role in establishing peace, but other crucial pieces of the puzzle are lacking in their description of what is necessary for peace, such as any description of culture as the basis for properly functioning institutions, let alone a culture transformed by the Gospel.[16]

What is largely missing in Catholic social teaching on peace is any account of the midlevel in terms of the kinds of culture, groups, movements, virtues, and attitudes that are needed to support the creation and effective functioning of international institutions.[17] This gap means that Catholic social teaching on peace also lacks a robust account of the kinds of cultures that enable, or militate against, the kind of individual conversion for which it calls—an issue I discuss in greater depth in chapter 5.[18]

More recent Catholic social teaching has begun to recognize the limitations of international institutions, but this recognition has had a limited effect on its practical proposals. Benedict XVI's *Caritas in veritate*, for example, acknowledges the changes that have taken place since Paul VI's *Populorum progressio* in terms of the globalization of trade and finance, but its constructive recommendations nevertheless remain largely in the mold of the post–Vatican II social teaching tradition.[19] Benedict XVI recognizes that increasing economic interdependence limits state sovereignty and that it will be necessary to reevaluate the role and powers of public authorities, but his response is to call for the reform of these international authorities so that they are able to pursue and secure the global common good.[20] The situation is changed, but the answer is the same. The problem here is that the Church's calls for the reform of international institutions are often at best aspirational and at worst outright unrealistic. Discussing *Caritas in veritate*, Lisa Cahill makes exactly this criticism of Benedict XVI's calls for a world political authority capable of governing justly for the common good: it is a vision, she argues, that flies in the face "of the real roles, capacities, and limits of the United Nations; and of emerging, much more complicated, forms of global authority and control in 'the globalization era.'"[21]

The difficulty, then, is not just that Catholic social teaching on peace tends to focus on the macro level of states and international institutions but that it also tends to deal with them too abstractly. As noted in chapter 2, the post-*Pacem* tradition has a fairly optimistic view of human capabilities when it comes to pursuing peace. This owes something to influences from liberal political philosophy, I suggested, but it also owes much to the natural law framework. From its earliest beginnings, Catholic social teaching has upheld the belief that the human person is intrinsically social and that human community is therefore natural.[22] This theological belief in the essential unity of the human race in both creation and final calling underpins the theology of peace. It means not just that human beings should strive to live together in peace and mutual flourishing, but that they *can* live together in this way: it is not contrary to nature and so, with effort and with grace, it is possible. This belief in the naturalness of human community stands behind the optimism of *Pacem in terris* and *Gaudium et spes*, and even as these documents reprise the just war tradition, they display a remarkable confidence that with sufficient goodwill and the use of reasonable dialogue conflicts of interest between nations can be resolved without recourse to violence. Consequently, the emergence of conflict tends to be attributed to misunderstanding, ill will, or selfishness rather than to the genuine incompatibility of different groups' needs.[23] While this belief in human unity is fine in theory and while optimism about the possibility of peace carries one so far in practice, both leave the Church's teaching on peace with weak points. As Kenneth Himes observes, the communitarian vision of Catholic social teaching means that "conflict is viewed as more apparent than real; the organic metaphor of society, so prevalent in Catholic social teaching, induces a belief that harmony and cooperation are easier to achieve than is the case."[24]

The communitarian vision of Catholic social teaching means that it is very good at just that—providing a communitarian vision and outlining the principles that would structure a just international order—but perhaps less good at offering suggestions about how to negotiate the rough ground that lies between the reality and the vision. Again, *Pacem in terris* is a good example of this tendency: the encyclical describes peace in terms of general principles—rights and responsibilities—and offers moral exhortations, but its suggestions for how peace on earth can be established are not very pragmatic. The encyclical presumes a great deal of goodwill on behalf of individuals and authorities and underestimates the degree of struggle and conflict involved in the establishing and defense of human rights. As Drew Christiansen puts it, "John's vision of peace as a world community upholding human rights captured the end-state of a process that in lived experience would be fraught with conflict."[25] Catholic social teaching on peace tends to be strong on the end state but comparatively weak on the in-between. To the extent that Catholic social teaching on peace is weak on the in-between in this way, it is not well adapted to supporting the experience of those who, like Darío Echeverri, find themselves in between and faced with all the tragedy, compromise, uncertainty, and risk that characterize peacebuilding in practice.

In making these criticisms of the tradition of Catholic social teaching on peace as it stands, my intention is not to throw out the challenge of the gospel in the name of political realism but to raise the question of the *livability* of that teaching as I explored it in the introduction. There is a significant difference, I suggested there, between an ideal that connects with reality in all its lived complexity, and that structures and resources a response to it, and an ideal that drifts free of reality to the extent that it does not help us engage with it or change it. The lack of engagement with what I have called the in-between in post-*Pacem* Catholic social teaching on peace makes it, in some respects, too close to the second kind of idealism. So how can we encourage Catholic social teaching on peace to develop in ways that offer a stronger account of the activities of the midlevel and the experience of the in-between? It is here that Catholic social teaching on solidarity can help. While that teaching itself stands in need of some development, as we shall see, it nevertheless has the potential to offer a more robust account of the midlevel of social change and therefore has much to contribute to Church teaching on peace. In what follows, I explore the development and key themes of Church teaching on solidarity and show how these both connect with and supplement Church teaching on peace in ways that might help it engage more effectively with the realities of contemporary peacebuilding and the experience of contemporary peacebuilders.

SOLIDARITY

In *Centesimus annus*, the encyclical written to commemorate the centenary of *Rerum novarum*, John Paul II refers to "what we nowadays call solidarity" as "one of the fundamental principles of the Christian view of social and political organization" (§10). In one sense, the concept of solidarity is less well established in the tradition than his breezy announcement of the theme suggests: the term appears first in *Summi pontificatus* in 1939 and has become an explicitly central theme of Catholic social teaching—itself a relatively novel genre—only over the course of the past fifty years. Yet the roots of the concept of solidarity are sunk deep in some of the basic principles of Catholic social teaching: the intrinsically social nature of the human person and the essential unity of humanity. These themes are evident in the first mention of solidarity in *Mater et magistra*, where John XXIII states that "the solidarity which binds all men together as members of a common family . . . makes it impossible for wealthy nations to look with indifference on the hunger, misery and poverty of other nations whose citizens are unable to enjoy even elementary human rights."[26] He goes on to state that the solidarity of the human race *and* Christian brotherhood demand the elimination of inequality. The distinction between the two—the solidarity of the human race and Christian brotherhood—suggests that, in keeping with the natural law framework of John XXIII's thought more widely, solidarity is here understood as a natural law concept, distinct from particularly Christian obligations to one's neighbor. The same is true of the subsequent mention of solidarity in *Pacem in terris*, in which solidarity is invoked as one of the four organizing virtues for relationships between states.[27]

At the Second Vatican Council, the concept of solidarity is reshaped according to the council's Christian humanism. Moving beyond John XXIII's natural law minimalism, *Gaudium et spes* roots the concept of solidarity in a broad theological treatment of the community of humankind. The constitution recalls the intrinsically social nature of the human person, who "cannot find himself fully except in self-giving," and then moves on to establish the essential unity of humankind in the theology of creation.[28] God created the human race as one family and "calls us all to the same end, that is himself."[29] Changing key from faith to reason, it then makes observations in a more philosophical key about the "social character of man," noting the increasing interdependence of societies in the modern era and making general recommendations for the organization of social and political life. The section concludes by exploring how the human orientation to the social and the fact of human interdependence find their fulfillment in Christ and the Church: just as God creates human beings for social life, so God calls a people to salvation.

Gaudium et spes interleaves claims about human nature and vocation rooted in natural law, observations about the modern world, and claims about Christ and the role of the Church. The result is a wideranging and fairly loose conception of solidarity. The terms "interdependence" and "solidarity" are used more or less interchangeably to refer in turn to an observed sign of the times, a theological reality, and the human vocation. Solidarity, in the sense of the needful dependence on others, is stated as a fact of human existence but also appears as a positive value that "must be constantly increased until that day on which it will be brought to perfection."[30] *Mater et magistra*'s distinction between the demands of human solidarity and the demands of Christian brotherhood becomes cloudier. This very elastic understanding of solidarity passes into post–Vatican II Catholic social teaching. Paul VI's 1967 encyclical on development, *Populorum progressio*, is a good example: "solidarity" is sometimes used interchangeably with "interdependence" and is described as a fact emerging from the unity of the human race, a positive value toward which people must strive, and a duty they must honor.[31] There is a shift toward a clearer sense that the "solidarity" names not a morally neutral fact of modern human existence but a positive relationship that expresses and realizes the unity the human family has by creation and vocation. Nevertheless, what Christiansen calls the "polyvalent usage" of the term in the encyclical results in a continued lack of clarity: "solidarity" gets used to name the fundamental state of the human race, the duties arising from it, and the ideal toward which it should strive.[32] This interweaving of the language of facts, duties, and ideals contributes to the problem noted by Himes earlier: there is perhaps too smooth an ascent between the fact of human interdependence and the development of positive solidarity. The fact that human beings are made for solidarity does not make it straightforward to achieve.[33]

JOHN PAUL II ON SOLIDARITY

In the thought of John XXIII's *Mater et magistra* and *Pacem in terris*, in *Gaudium et spes*, and in Paul VI's *Populorum progressio*, discussions of solidarity remain largely focused on the macro level of institutions.[34] It is in John Paul II's writings that the concept of solidarity develops most significantly, in ways that are helpful for our purposes here. It is worth drawing into this discussion his earlier work of philosophy, *Osoba I Czyn* (*The Acting Person*, 1969), which reflects his experience in Poland under Communism and which clearly influences his later writings as pope.[35]

For John Paul II, growing in solidarity does not mean just creating structures or institutions, but growing in the ability to act together with others in pursuit of a common good that is consciously in view as such. This acting together with others is what produces or renews a relationship of solidarity. In *Osoba I Czyn*, Wojtyła begins with a picture of the human person as emerging in action. As we act, we experience ourselves as the originator and center of our actions. At the same time that we are aware of acting, we are reflexively aware of ourselves as acting subjects: our conscious acting includes *self*-consciousness. Being a person therefore means being capable of experiencing oneself as an agent, including a sense of one's own freedom and responsibility for one's actions. Wojtyła's understanding of community is rooted in this picture of the human person. Like the individual, the community emerges as its members act together and become aware of themselves as originators and agents of that action. This common action establishes new relations between these persons, though it does not constitute the community as a single acting subject in its own right.[36]

Catholic moral theology, with its emphasis on personal freedom and responsibility, is obviously in the background here, but so is a rejection of totalitarianism, in which appeals to "the people" are used as justification for repression. Wojtyła is trying to sketch a political middle way between individualism, driven by the need to protect the individual from the incursion of others, and what he calls totalism, in which society must be protected from the individual, with the result that the "common good" not infrequently involves coercion. His focus seems to be the grassroots: what we have here is not a call for institutional reform from the top down but a vision of communities of action shaped by a shared vision of the common good, who influence society from the grassroots up. There is a clear sense, too, that this process is effortful, particularly in Wojtyła's account of the two social values that guard against individualism and totalism, solidarity and opposition. "Solidarity" he describes as "the attitude of a community" in which there is a "constant readiness to accept and realize one's share in the community because of one's membership within that particular community."[37] "Opposition" is a constant questioning and constructive challenging of common action and the common good that arises out of deep concern for both: it is a constant impulse for renewal and authenticity, aimed at "the correct structure of communities and . . . the correct functioning of their inner systems."[38] Although Wojtyła states that the attitude of solidarity is "the natural consequence of the fact that human beings live and act together," there is a clear sense that solidarity is not something that just happens; it requires vigilance and effort and, in some cases, sacrifice.[39]

We are getting closer here, in various ways, to a stronger account of the midlevel. Wojtyła's thought helps bridge the gap in Catholic social teaching on peace between the "inner" reality of conversion and the "outer" reality of public life. He offers a picture not just of a change of individuals' inner attitudes or motivations, or simply an account of how individuals might negotiate the public sphere with as much personal morality as possible, but an account of how a group, motivated and concretely bound together by a shared vision of the common good, might work for social change.[40] We can envision this kind of midlevel group instigating and supporting macro-level institutional change, as well as critiquing it and holding it to account. These insights of Wojtyła's early work are visible in his later contributions to Catholic social teaching as Pope John Paul II, particularly in the encyclicals *Sollicitudo rei socialis* (1988) and *Centesimus annus* (1991).[41] These documents are addressed to a global audience and therefore tend toward generalization and abstraction rather more than *The Acting Person*, but they nevertheless make some important advances.

First, characteristic of John Paul II's contributions to the theology of solidarity is a greater precision in the use of language. In *Sollicitudo rei socialis*, he locates both interdependence and solidarity in the fundamental unity of humankind in creation (§§29–30) and in Christ in whom all things hold together (§31), but he also distinguishes between the two concepts: interdependence is a fact of theological anthropology and the social and political life of the modern world; solidarity is its corresponding and positive moral response (§38). The encyclical therefore speaks of the "need for a solidarity which will take up interdependence and *transfer* it to the moral plane" (§26) and states that "interdependence must be *transformed* into solidarity, based upon the principle that the goods of creation are meant for all."[42]

John Paul II's teaching on solidarity represents a step forward here because he is aware of the ways in which interdependence can become "separated from its ethical requirements" and take sinful, distorted forms.[43] Effort and commitment are required to move existing relationships of interdependence toward the good and toward true solidarity: "'Evil mechanisms' and 'structures of sin' of which we have spoken can be overcome only through the exercise of the human and Christian solidarity to which the Church calls us and which she tirelessly promotes."[44]

John Paul II does not view interdependence as a completely neutral fact, which can take either virtuous or sinful forms. Because interdependence is rooted in our creation by God, it retains a theologically positive charge, and in *Sollicitudo rei socialis* in particular John Paul II is concerned about accounts of social sin that would dissolve individual responsibility. Nevertheless, his awareness of the gap between the fact of human interdependence, so often ambivalent or distorted by sin, and the call to true solidarity is helpful.[45] Helpful, too, is the direct—though brief—connection with Catholic social teaching on peace.

> The solidarity that we propose is the path to peace and at the same time to development. For world peace is inconceivable unless the world's leaders come to recognize that interdependence in itself demands the abandonment of the politics of blocs, the sacrifice of all forms of economic military, or political imperialism, and the transformation of mutual distrust into collaboration. This is precisely the act proper to solidarity among individuals and nations.[46]

Second, *Centesimus annus* offers a more concrete account of how this "human and Christian solidarity" can restore and heal societies damaged by conflict.[47] John Paul II notes the fall of dictatorial and oppressive regimes in Latin American, African, and Asian countries and acknowledges the "difficult but productive transition towards more participatory and more just political structures," including the role played by workers in ending the Communist regime in Poland.[48] His sense of the transformation needed in these countries goes beyond the usual twin focus on macro-level institutional reform and micro-level reconciliation and draws attention to the need to transform the quality of relationships within society, which have been so badly corroded by mistrust.[49] Also explicitly in view is the contribution of midlevel groups. With reference to the fall of the Eastern bloc, John Paul II draws attention to the role played by "instruments of solidarity capable of sustaining an economic growth more respectful of the values of the person," and he names the Christian contribution to "establishing producers', consumers' and credit cooperatives, in promoting general education and professional training, in experimenting with various forms of participation in the life of the work-place and in the life of society in general."[50] Importantly for our purposes here, *Centesimus annus* also acknowledges the lived experience of midlevel actors engaged in that kind of struggle for peaceful social transformation.

> The events of 1989 are an example of the success of willingness to negotiate and of the Gospel spirit in the face of an adversary determined not to be bound by moral principles. . . . Undoubtedly, the struggle which led to the changes of 1989 called for clarity, moderation, suffering and sacrifice. In a certain sense, it was a struggle born of prayer, and it would have been unthinkable without immense trust in God, the Lord of history, who carries the human heart in his hands. It is by uniting his own sufferings for the sake of truth and freedom to the sufferings of Christ on the Cross that man is able to accomplish the miracle of peace and is in a position to discern the often narrow path between the cowardice which gives in to evil and the violence which, under the illusion of fighting evil, only makes it worse.[51]

Discernment, risk, sacrifice, ambivalence: these are the elements named earlier that need greater attention in Church teaching on peace, and they are found here in John Paul II's theology of solidarity.

Third, the way in which John Paul II distinguishes more clearly between the natural law and gospel registers of Catholic social teaching results in a stronger account of the Church's distinctive role in promoting solidarity. John Paul II's treatment of solidarity in *Sollicitudo rei socialis* moves from the interdependence of humanity as a reality rooted in theological anthropology, to solidarity as the duty and virtue corresponding with that reality, to communion as a "specifically Christian" reality. What *Sollicitudo rei socialis* does, unlike *Gaudium et spes*, is unpack more clearly what that means. It is worth quoting the document in full on this point.

> In the light of faith, solidarity seeks to go beyond itself, to take on the specifically Christian dimension of total gratuity, forgiveness and reconciliation. One's neighbor is then not only a human being with his or her own rights and a fundamental equality with everyone else, but becomes the living image of God the Father, redeemed by the blood of Jesus Christ and placed under the permanent action of

the Holy Spirit. One's neighbor must therefore be loved, even if an enemy, with the same love with which the Lord loves him or her; and for that person's sake one must be ready for sacrifice, even the ultimate one: to lay down one's life for the brethren (cf. 1 Jn 3:16).

At that point, awareness of the common fatherhood of God, of the brotherhood of all in Christ—"children in the Son"—and of the presence and life-giving action of the Holy Spirit will bring to our vision of the world a new criterion for interpreting it. Beyond human and natural bonds, already so close and strong, there is discerned in the light of faith a new model of the unity of the human race, which must ultimately inspire our solidarity. This supreme model of unity, which is a reflection of the intimate life of God, one God in three Persons, is what we Christians mean by the word "communion." This specifically Christian communion, jealously preserved, extended and enriched with the Lord's help, is the soul of the Church's vocation to be a "sacrament," in the sense already indicated.[52]

What John Paul II is describing here is solidarity transposed into the key of the gospel, and what he offers is not just a set of specifically Christian motivations for engaging in the same practice of solidarity as everyone else but also the beginnings of an account of a distinctively Christian and ecclesial practice.[53]

DEVELOPING SOLIDARITY

Catholic social teaching on peace is good at the large scale, both in terms of its tendency to address states and international bodies and in terms of its communitarian vision for how they should cooperate. It is less good, I have argued, at addressing what I have described as the midlevel and the in-between. Writing about John Milbank's presentation of the ontological peace of the City of God in his *Theology and Social Theory*, Rowan Williams makes a similar criticism: Milbank provides a compelling account of a beautiful alternative to the "ontology of violence" that structures and pervades the earthly city, but, Williams argues, in this vision "we are again confronted with something 'achieved', and left with little account of how it is learned, negotiated, betrayed, inched forward, discerned and risked."[54] I have argued that Church teaching on solidarity helps us move closer to an account of how peace is concretely learned, negotiated, inched forward, discerned, and risked. It directs our attention to those midlevel and in-between forms of peace and the networks, communities, and associations, the oases and points of leverage, in which the Church's vision of human cooperation and flourishing takes concrete shape. In John Paul II's work, in particular, we see that human interdependence can take ambivalent forms that must be wrested toward the good, and we see reflected, too, the experience of people engaged in this struggle and the need for effort, risk, self-sacrifice, and discernment. The theology of solidarity shows how the Church's teaching on peace might address the midlevel and the in-between more effectively and support better those negotiating the rough ground that lies between the complex realities of violent conflict and the Church's vision of peace. In order to fulfill this role, however, the Church's theology of solidarity needs some work.

The Church's teaching on solidarity as I have explored it so far is quite heavily philosophical. Whether it is the natural law tradition that under-pins the theology of John XXIII or the phenomenological influences of John Paul II, the content of the theology of solidarity is rooted more in general reflections on human nature than it is in reflections on scripture. This focus on general philosophical themes and theological anthropology has its strengths, particularly in collaborative contexts where not everyone in the public square will be motivated by specifically Christian themes or authorities. I have also argued, however, that this approach has draw-backs. First, in focusing on the essential unity of humanity and our voca-tion to cooperation and harmony, it arguably leaves us without adequate theological resources for addressing situations in which what ought to be has exploded into a thousand broken, violent, and suffering fragments. Postconciliar Church teaching on solidarity emphasizes that transforming interdependence into positive solidarity, like striving for peace, in some sense works with the grain of human nature. But this sense of continuity, of smooth ascent, between the fact, the duty, and the ideal does not help those engaged in the struggle of peacebuilding to make sense of the all too commonplace experiences of discontinuity, setback, and tragedy.

Second, in engaging more with natural law than with scripture and Christology, Church teaching on solidarity arguably lacks a vital connection to the practice and prayer of Catholic and other Christian peacebuilders, for whom these resources offer important motivation and support. In the Christian humanism characteristic of the post–Vatican II tradition, Christ appears as the telos of human nature and the end point or goal of human unity, but overall the theology of solidarity features scant consideration of his person and still less of his work. Arguing along similar lines, Whitmore suggests that the Church's teaching on solidarity, currently rooted in theological anthropology, needs to be more firmly rooted in Christology. Catholic social teaching bases its principles in an account of the work of God as creator and the proper balance of the natural order, but, he argues, "the focus on an underlying order, by itself, provides little ground for the kind of personal risk and sacrifice required in many instances of peacebuilding. For that, we need greater development of the Second Person— Jesus Christ— and his activity of redemption in the face of a world that is not merely imbalanced or out of order but threatening."[55] In order to engage with and support the experience of those engaged in peacebuilding work, the Church needs to speak more about Christ: about his incarnation, in which God enters into solidarity with an out-of-joint and suffering creation, and about his death and resurrection, through which God pulls redemption out of tragedy.

In the introduction, I suggested that one of the ways Catholic teaching on peace could be enriched and deepened is by paying attention to the experience of Catholic peacebuilders and the scriptural, theological, and spiritual resources that motivate and sustain their work. In the section that follows, I will make good this suggestion by drawing on the example of the Jesuit martyrs of the University of Central America, El Salvador. Their practice of solidarity was motivated by a profound and vibrant Christology, rooted in the spirituality of the *Spiritual Exercises* of Ignatius of Loyola. It allows us to draw out three insights that might help Church teaching on solidarity develop in the ways I have identified.

MAKING REDEMPTION

In the early hours of the morning of November 16, 1989, the Atlacatl battalion of the Salvadoran army stormed the residence of the Jesuit community on the UCA campus. Three members of the Jesuit community were taken out into the garden and machine-gunned. Another three Jesuits, together with their cook and her fifteen-year-old daughter, who had been staying in the house for safety, were machine-gunned in the house. The army fired grenades and rockets and machine-gunned the facade of the house, leaving over two hundred spent cartridges to try to create the appearance of an attack by the rebel Farabundo Martí National Liberation Front (FMLN). As they left, the soldiers took a cardboard sign tied to the gate notifying students that classes were canceled and wrote on the back, "FMLN executed the enemy spies. Victory or death, FMLN." The Jesuits who were killed were Ignacio Ellacuría, rector of the university and a philosopher and theologian; Ignacio Martín-Baró, a social psychologist; Segundo Montes, a sociologist; Juan Ramón Moreno, professor of theology; Joaquín López y López, director of the Fe y Alegria program; and Amando López, rector of the seminary. Their housekeeper, Elba Ramos, and her daughter, Celine, were killed because they were witnesses.[56]

By 1989, El Salvador had already suffered ten years of bloody civil war between the military-backed government and the left-wing FMLN. Government violence, which included extrajudicial killings, disappearances, torture, and massacres, was ostensibly directed against FMLN guerrillas but in reality extended to anyone who—in the words of Óscar Romero—"got in the way."[57] The Jesuits of UCA fell into this category: in the months leading up to their deaths, they were denounced in newspapers and on the radio and their names circulated on hit lists; leaflets were dropped in the streets with the slogan, "Be a patriot, kill a priest." The university itself had been bombed many times. The reason was that the Jesuits, through their university work, had sought to bear witness to what they understood to be the truth of the situation in El Salvador. They openly criticized government violence and human rights abuses, exposed fraud in the presidential elections, and argued that the government's economic and agrarian policy was causing terrible poverty and unemployment while favoring the interests of oligarchs. They criticized the Salvadoran government's dependence on U.S. economic and military support. They called for dialogue as the appropriate way to bring the civil war to an end and communicated with members of the government and military representatives, as well as leaders of the FMLN. At the same time that they criticized the abuses of the FMLN, they were not afraid to acknowledge the good done by the group. As well as university work, all of them were immersed in parish life, exposed to the immediate demands of helping those directly affected by state violence. Their way of expressing solidarity with the people of El Salvador was to tell the truth, as Jon Sobrino put it, "in a university way."[58]

My aim in drawing attention to the example of the UCA Jesuits is not to critically evaluate their particular mode of solidarity or to hold it up as an ideal; rather, I draw on their story for two broader reasons. First, like Darío Echeverri, the UCA Jesuits represent the situation of many contemporary Catholic peacebuilders who, embedded in the community affected by conflict and more or less directly exposed to the violence swirling around them, are faced with the challenge of discerning what peacebuilding or exercising solidarity means in complex and ambiguous situations where there is a moral imperative to act in some way but not necessarily a clear vision of how best to do so. As I have already noted, these are the kinds of people to whom the Church's teaching on solidarity needs to speak and whose experience it needs to support. Second, I draw on the example of the UCA Jesuits because their available writings give us some insight into the spiritual and scriptural resources they drew on as they faced their situation and the decisions it demanded of them. From these resources, we can draw out some elements for deepening the Church's teaching on solidarity theologically and strengthening its Christological dimension in the ways suggested above.

Two Meditations: The Incarnation and the Cross

Jon Sobrino S.J., a member of the UCA community, was traveling in Europe when he received news of the killings. Reflecting on their witness and the spirituality from which it emerged, Sobrino recalled the importance of two contemplations from the *Spiritual Exercises* of St. Ignatius. In the first, the meditation on the incarnation, the person making the *Exercises* is asked to picture the world and "those on the face of the earth, in such great diversity in dress and manner of acting. Some are white, some black; some at peace, and some at war; some weeping, some laughing; some well, some sick; some coming into the world, and some dying; etc."[59] Having the world in view, the exercitant is then asked to picture the Divine Persons looking at the world and to picture the Virgin Mary and the angel Gabriel. Ignatius then asks the person making the *Exercises* to "listen in" to the conversations in all three of these scenes: to the people of the earth swearing and blaspheming, to the Divine Persons declaring, "Let us work the redemption of the human race," and then to the conversation between Mary and Gabriel. Regarding the same scenes, they are then to dwell on what each of the actors is doing: the people of the earth killing and going to hell, the Divine Persons working out the incarnation, the angel delivering his message, and Our Lady humbling herself and giving thanks to the divine majesty. For the Jesuits of the UCA, Sobrino recalls, the purpose of this meditation was "to enable us to see the real world with God's own eyes—that is, a world of perdition—and to react with God's own compassion, that is, 'to make redemption.'"[60] The Jesuits' solidarity, expressed "in a university way," had its roots in their desire to see the reality of the Salvadoran situation "with God's own eyes" and to share in God's work of redemption through the incarnation.[61]

The second meditation of the *Exercises* that resonated for the UCA Jesuits, and for Ellacuría in particular, was the meditation on Christ crucified.[62] In this meditation, the exercitant is asked to imagine themselves before Christ on the cross and to speak to him, "asking how it is that though He is the Creator, He has stooped to become man and to pass from eternal life to death here in time, that thus He might die for our sins." Ignatius goes on to give the exercitant a set of questions.

> I shall also reflect upon myself and ask: "What have I done for Christ?" "What am I doing for Christ?" "What ought I to do for Christ?" As I behold Christ in this plight, nailed to the cross, I shall ponder upon what presents itself to my mind. The colloquy is made by speaking exactly as one friend speaks to another, or as a servant speaks to a master, now asking him for a favour, now blaming himself for some misdeed, now making known his affairs to him, and seeking advice in them.[63]

The three central questions of this meditation, "What have I done for Christ?," "What am I doing for Christ?," and "What ought I to do for Christ?," became for Ellacuría a meditation on the Salvadoran people, an occasion to reflect on how they were being crucified and "what we are doing about their crosses, and what we are going to do to bring them down from the cross."[64]

Twenty years before his death, in 1969, Ellacuría had proposed that the entire vice province of Central America should hold a meeting in the form of the *Spiritual Exercises*, one that took as the "subject" of the *Exercises*—the one undertaking them, that is—the vice province itself.[65] This provided an occasion for the province to reflect on its sins and to reexamine its relationship to the Salvadoran people. The path taken by the UCA Jesuits was not uncontroversial, and not unopposed; there were members of the Society of Jesus, as well as the Salvadoran episcopate, who regarded their position as extreme. Yet though the government-sponsored newspaper reports and radio tirades suggested they were motivated by communism, they understood their action in terms of the spirit of the *Exercises* and, in particular, the image of the incarnation, understood as God's determined movement toward the earth in love. The UCA Jesuits did not actively seek martyrdom. As Sobrino puts it, there was for them no "mysticism of violence."[66] There was, however, a recognition "that there can be no faith nor gospel without incarnation. And with a crucified people, there can be no incarnation without the cross."[67]

Solidarity: Making Redemption

The two meditations from the *Spiritual Exercises* offer us three insights that Church teaching on solidarity could helpfully develop. The first concerns the incarnation, understood as God's movement toward the earth in love. I noted above how the belief in the naturalness of human community that underpins Catholic teaching on peace can issue in a tendency to overestimate human goodwill and desire for harmony, on the one hand, and underestimate the reality and force of sin, on the other. I also suggested that this theological imbalance was unhelpful on a practical level. The meditation on the incarnation sets God's action, and our action in concert with God's, not in the context of an overoptimistic assessment of the condition of the world or in an overoptimistic theological anthropology but in an open-eyed and open-eared assessment of the world in all its sinfulness, chaos, and violence. At the same time that it encourages us to view unflinchingly the extent of the world's brokenness, the meditation directs our attention to the fact that God is nonetheless working in it, in contingent and historically particular ways. What might this offer to the theology of solidarity and the practice of peacebuilding? Ignatius's meditation on the incarnation shifts our understanding of what we are doing when we act in solidarity away from the idea that we are recovering a state of interdependence and community that is natural and original and toward the idea that we are aligning ourselves with God's redeeming action in a world that is seriously out of joint, one that is, as Whitmore put it, not merely out of order, but threatening.[68] God's redeeming action takes the form of solidarity with us in the incarnation, but this does not result in the restoration of human communion in an immediately obvious or straightforward way. Rather, because the restoration of broken and sinful creation takes place from within, God's redeeming action has the character of struggle with the forces of sin and death. Thus Jesus states that he has come to set sons against father and mothers against daughters (Lk 12:51–53); thus, too, Simeon's prophecy that the infant Jesus, who is the glory of Israel and the light to the Gentiles, also will be a sign of division (Lk 2:34). Jesus's solidarity with our human life, suffering, and death is the means chosen by God to overcome our division from himself and one another, but it does not necessarily issue in the tranquillity of order on the level of experience or history.

The second point concerns redemption. Acting in solidarity is our response to a realistic view of the world's brokenness, and it participates in God's work of "making redemption." In the person of Jesus, God enters into the world's brokenness, sharing the same risks and fears, hopes and fate. For Ignatius, our action in God's service unfolds in the context of colloquy rather than imitation. The exercitant is not asked to picture the world in its sinful brokenness, then asked how he might exert himself to turn the bad state of things around somehow.[69] Instead, the exercitant is placed before Christ on the cross, to contemplate the fundamental shape God's work of redemption takes, and then invited to ask himself, "What have I done for Christ? What am I doing for Christ? What ought I to do for Christ?" The work of redemption is God's, and we participate in it; it is manifested under the sign of the cross and not with any ordinary signs of victory or success.

What does this mean for the theology of solidarity? A theology of solidarity seeking to draw more fully on Christology might well want to draw parallels between God's solidarity with humanity in the incarnation and our solidarity with others; in particular, as Whitmore indicates briefly, it might want to draw parallels between Christ's identification with human suffering in his passion and death and our solidarity with the suffering, and perhaps even the death, of others.[70] Ignatius's meditation helps us see how carefulness is needed here. Our acting in solidarity is not a case of straightforwardly imitating God's action in Christ.[71] That way, at least potentially, lies the "mysticism of violence" that Sobrino eschews, or a mysticism of suffering that sees it as containing some kind of redemptive power in and of itself.[72] This temptation to think in terms of straightforward imitation should be resisted: it is Christ's death, not mine or anyone else's, that delivers from sin and death. Our acting in solidarity does not take shape as we survey the world's sin and ponder what to do about it on our own initiative and by our own lights; it takes shape as we survey the redemptive action of God already at work in the world and ask what it demands of us. As Ellacuría understood, acting in solidarity unfolds before the cross in the context of colloquy, or conversation: "What am I doing for Christ?"

The scene Ignatius paints in the *Exercises*, then, helps us remember that "making redemption" is *divine* action: it is God's coming into the world that saves us, and it is because Jesus is the Son of God that his death saves us. At the same time, the scene also draws our attention to the way in which "making redemption" is *human* action: it is because Jesus becomes human, and suffers and dies a human death, that he saves us. In a short essay written in 1966, the Scottish theologian Donald MacKinnon registered his discomfort with the propensity he observed among his theological contemporaries to drop the language of "atonement" in favor of the more triumphal "redemption." The language of redemption, borrowed from the Greco-Roman world of slavery, certainly reinforces that it is *God* who acts in Christ to free us from sin, once and for all. But what drifts from view with such a picture, MacKinnon argues, is a sense of the cross as also a *human* act. As a human act, he suggests, the cross is not devoid of "what, in literature, has long received recognition, namely the dark ambivalence of human action intended somehow to rectify an inherently false situation, and restore perception of its truth."[73] All such human action is as ambivalent as it is necessary.

No man dare, without gravest peril to himself and others, to take upon himself the task of disclosing the truth of any human situation; yet the recognition that there is often a truth that urgently demands to be disclosed, that remains obscured by lies, calculated only to perpetuate injustice, is a fundamental moral perception, such that if one makes the imaginative effort to conceive its absence from the human scene, pity itself would be imperilled, sentimentality cold in its ultimate cruelty.[74]

In choosing to face arrest and go to his death, trusting in the Father, Jesus walks a path like that of many others who, enmeshed in complex and ambiguous situations, and perhaps unable finally to discern whether their perception of their situation is true or the action they are contemplating good and right, are nonetheless possessed of the moral conviction that they must act. If Catholic social teaching sometimes makes human community sound so natural that discerning the demands of solidarity and putting them into practice appear straightforward, this emphasis on "making redemption" as human action reminds us of the equal and opposite truths, namely, that our discernment is always human discernment, afflicted by all the short-sightedness of sin, and our action in solidarity is human action, possessed of all the ambiguity and ambivalence that accompany human attempts to act from within the world's brokenness in order to heal it.[75]

Finally, and in this connection, all human action in solidarity takes place under the sign of the cross. Church teaching on solidarity has a positive view of human nature as called to and capable of unity. Post-*Pacem* Church teaching on peace is also characterized by its optimism, and by the strong relationship of continuity it envisages between the partial peace of the present and the fullness of peace in the kingdom. This "can do" theology makes Catholic teaching a valuable source of motivation and hope for those engaged in peacebuilding work, but, as I have already suggested, these theological resources need to be developed in ways that also help them hold the experiences of setback and tragedy that so often mark efforts in these areas. Peacebuilding is a long game, a very long game indeed, and the path from violent conflict to even relative stability can take many generations, far outlasting the lifetimes of those who dedicate their lives to the cause. Over the course of a year, a decade, or even a lifetime, progress toward a just and stable peace may be slender, or scarcely apparent at all, and peace may be won only in small areas or for short periods of time. The steady evolution toward peaceful and rational resolution of disputes, so characteristic of post-*Pacem* Catholic social teaching, may be more an object of faith than of experience. What does that narrative of progress offer to those who experience, for example, the repeated failure of local peacebuilding projects and the return to violent hostilities, or the disappearance and assassination of an important community leader, or the protracted and bloody intransigence of negotiating parties? If the strength of our optimistic narrative of progress means that we struggle to find a place for tragedy on a theological level, there is a danger that we will struggle to find a place for it on a spiritual, practical, and liturgical level, too. Catholic social teaching on peace needs to provide the kind of theological framework that can hold these common experiences of tragedy, failure, suffering, and grief without either discarding them as not belonging to the narrative of hopeful progress or too readily co-opting them and "making sense" out of them in a way that disregards the subjective experience of those involved.

Here, attending to the sign of the cross introduces a note of discontinuity that is valuable in both theological principle and pastoral practice. The cross is God's victory against sin, but it appears under the sign of death and failure. This is not like saying that it appeared the man on the station platform was having a heart attack, but really he was just acting, as though what occurs on the cross is one thing really and another only in appearance. God's victory does not just *look* like death and failure: Jesus's death really is the death of a concrete human being, and the resurrection does not make that death only apparent or anything less than real.[76] Jesus's death is, like any human death, "by definition the end from which he cannot return," and between this death and his resurrection "there is no common measure," no underlying continuity.[77] The absolutely discontinuous character of this death-resurrection dynamic is fundamental; both must be held together, without allowing one to cancel out or absorb the other. We cannot allow resurrection to absorb death, by describing Jesus's death as being in some sense not a real or absolute death; this might make the resurrection easier to accept but at the price of its becoming not a real resurrection at all. Nor can we allow death to absorb resurrection, by presenting it as merely a resuscitation; this might make his death easier to accept but at the price of its becoming a less than real death. In order to grasp the truth of the thing, each must be preserved in its starkness in relation to the other. To borrow a linguistic metaphor, one cannot be completely rendered in terms of the other; there will always be a remainder, something untranslatable, something that we cannot account for or make sense of.

The same point stands for any human action that, also under the sign of the cross, participates in God's redeeming action in the world. Here, one narrative temptation in particular stands out: we cannot allow the narrative of God's victory to dominate to the extent that we become unable to *hold* experiences of tragedy. I say "hold" here, rather than "make sense of," deliberately. The point is not to "make sense" of experiences of tragedy, if by that is meant their translation without remainder into the terms of the narrative of victory: it appeared that the man was having a heart attack, but really he was acting; it appeared that the lives of the campesinos were wasted, but really they were not. That way, again, lies the temptation of an uncritical mysticism of violence or suffering: too ready a willingness to collapse the experience of the tragic into the narrative of victory, and any and all sacrifice, of our own or others, becomes justifiable.[78] That way, too, lies the kind of unhelpful utopianism of which Catholic social teaching on peace is occasionally guilty. The reticence needed here about "making sense" is required not chiefly out of deference to the human experience of tragedy and suffering, but rather out of the need to preserve the discontinuity of death and resurrection that stands at the heart of God's redeeming action in the world. To return to Ignatius, when we contemplate the sinfulness and violence of the world, the redeeming action of God appears not as steady or self-propelled progress toward tranquil order but as the death of a man in humiliation and failure. When we contemplate how it is we are to respond to and participate in God's redeeming work, it is *that* image before which we place ourselves.

Attending to the sign of the cross, then, allows space for discontinuity. On a practical level, it allows us to value what Lederach calls "the gift of pessimism," which I touched on briefly at the end of chapter 2. Lederach describes how the experience of conflict engenders a certain pessimism: "We are not talking here of an attitude born of cynicism, an embittered attitude and predisposition to believe the worst of every-thing and everyone, a fault-finding par excellence. Pessimism born of cynicism is a luxurious avoidance of engagement."[79] Rather, he says, the gift of pessimism is a "well-grounded realism" born of the experience of those accustomed to living with violence.[80] It involves the suspicion of cheap promises, and the judgment of political process by their fruits and not by their rhetoric, and the desire for change coupled with suspicion of the idea that change can come easily or quickly. Lederach describes it as "the horizon of hope coupled with indifference towards the impact of violence": "Indifference does not mean that people don't care. Theirs is not the indifference of apathy. It is the indifference of the heroic but everyday journey. They keep walking the terrain in spite of the violence. This requires a selective indifference: These particular events that are out of my control will not restrict or destroy my life."[81]

Attending to the sign of the cross acknowledges the experience of those who find themselves on the way of the cross, holding together on a daily basis the horizon of hope and the reality of violence and suffer-ing. It also allows space on a theological level, helping us hold together the themes of order, progress, and continuity in Catholic social teach-ing on peace with the discontinuous dynamic of death and resurrec-tion. On a spiritual level, this space for discontinuity allows space for the common experiences of loss, frustration, anger, and grieving to be held and acknowledged. We can look upon such experiences and say more, theologically, than Paul VI's simple, "Notwithstanding . . ."[82] Without prematurely co-opting them into a narrative of progress, we can say that God's redeeming action in the world includes the cross and that the res-toration of creation is wrought by way of it and not in spite of it.

In this chapter, I have picked up some of the aims of the introduction and some of the concerns voiced in the previous chapter. The questions driving the work of this chapter have been, first, how we make Catholic social teaching on peace more responsive to the signs of the times and the particular characteristics of modern violent conflict and peacebuilding and, second, how we do so in a way that is conscious of the weaknesses of Catholic social teaching on peace as it stands. Accordingly, this chapter has focused on an issue that touches on both of these questions: how we encourage Catholic teaching to respond more effectively to the midlevel forms of peacebuilding emerging as a response to contemporary intra-state conflict and how we do so in light of that teaching's propensity to focus on institutions and macro-level social change. I have argued that Catholic social teaching on solidarity presents an important resource in this regard, albeit one that also stands in need of development. The concept of solidarity, more widely known, more closely connected to Catholic teaching on peace, and more deeply Christological in content, can help the Church address more effectively the challenge of contemporary peacebuilding work and provide resources to and support those who are engaged in it.

FIVE

Social Sin

The events of the twentieth century left the Catholic Church search-
ing for a new moral language to address the ways in which human sin
takes social shape. Episodes of terrible violence such as the Holocaust,
the genocide in Rwanda, and ethnic cleansing in the Balkans raised this
issue with particular sharpness, but the same problem was also posed by
poverty and political repression in Latin America and by the totalitarian
ideologies of the Cold War. The result was the tentative emergence, in
the years following the Second Vatican Council, of the language of social
sin. This "growing edge" of Catholic moral theology is clearly of major
significance for Church teaching on peace, insofar as it offers a language
for addressing the social dimensions of structural and direct violence. As
I show in what follows, it also presents us with a clear case of structural
stress within the tradition: the foundations of Catholic moral theology
cause cracks in the new construction work around social sin, and, in turn,
the new construction work places the foundations under stress.

The first task of this chapter is descriptive and diagnostic. Against the
backdrop of broader shifts in Catholic moral theology during the twentieth century, it traces the emergence and development of the concept of
social sin in magisterial teaching. Exploring why magisterial adoption of

the language of social sin has often been cautious and tentative will clarify the tension between the concept of social sin and the fundamental structures of Catholic moral theology. Describing this underlying structural tension will help us identify with greater precision the weakness in the concept of social sin as it stands and the ways in which it currently fails to address some of the social and systemic characteristics of structural and direct violence. Taking sectarianism in Northern Ireland as an example, the chapter goes on to suggest two ways in which the concept of social sin might develop in a way that helps the Church address more effectively the social dimensions of violent conflict.

THE CHANGING SHAPE OF MORAL THEOLOGY

The Second Vatican Council did not produce a document on moral theology. But the broader changes enacted by the council nevertheless resulted in significant changes in the Church's approach to moral theology.

Since the Council of Trent (1545–63) had laid down the norm that laypeople were to confess their sins once a year, specifying both the type of mortal sin and the number of times it had been committed, Catholic moral theology increasingly developed as a way of helping priests aid their penitents in making a good confession. This included guiding the priest carefully through questioning of the penitent, enabling him to distinguish between different kinds of sins and their varying grades of severity and properly assign the appropriate penance. By the early twentieth century, moral theology had become dominated by "manuals," comprehensive guides that systematically defined and categorized sin. These manuals, often written in Latin, were intended for use in seminaries for training priests, and by priests themselves. The preconciliar manualist tradition therefore tended to focus on sin and on particular sins: sin was always an isolatable "something" for which an individual "someone" was responsible.

In addition to focusing on the individual, the preconciliar manualist tradition tended to be act focused. The neo-scholastic tendency to treat reality as "two-tiered"—the realm of nature, complete in itself, and the realm of grace—translated into a moral theology heavily reliant on natural law. Human nature, understood as static and universal, supplied a complete set of principles for moral action: moral reasoning consisted in deducing particular moral conclusions from these eternal principles.[1] The medieval scholastics' flexibility and agnosticism regarding the content of "nature" was largely lost to view, as was the need to consider character and context.[2] It led to what Mahoney describes as "an approach to the moral life as discontinuous; 'freezing' the film in a jerky succession of individual 'stills' to be analysed, and ignoring the plot. Continuity was discounted, or at most only a 'circumstance', and the 'story' of the individual's moral vocation and exploration either unsuspected or disregarded."[3] This focus on particular acts abstracted from their context meant that the social dimensions of sin faded into the background. M. Cathleen Kaveney illustrates this tendency.

> It would be important for a manualist to clarify that giving a patient with terminal cancer narcotics would not be euthanasia, because the object of the act was to relieve pain, not to shorten the patient's life. It would be less important to reflect upon the pressures that might tempt a patient or his family members to seek euthanasia, or the social structures that would need to be in place to alleviate such temptations.[4]

The focus on sin as individual act also resulted in whole categories of sinful action fading into the background of moral theological concern. In the immediate preconciliar period, partly as a result of antimodernist anxieties, the Church had become largely focused on issues of internal Church moral order rather than on the major moral challenges facing the world. War and social problems were addressed by the popes of the early twentieth century, as we have seen, but these developments in Catholic social teaching were not reflected in the manualist tradition of moral theology. As James Keenan rather bluntly observes, "One only has to see that girls' dresses and sperm receive more attention than atomic weapons to appreciate how distant the manualists were from the world as it emerged out of the rubble of the Second World War and faced the possibility of nuclear war."[5] The period immediately following Vatican II saw Church teaching and moral theologians engage energetically with some of these neglected moral challenges, particularly with questions of war and peace.[6]

The Second Vatican Council had a major impact on Catholic moral theology. John O'Malley has described the council as a "language event," where not just *what* was said, but *how* it was said, had a transformative effect.[7] With regard to moral theology, the change of language was deeply significant. The council's tone of encouragement, persuasion, and exhortation to ideals, its call to holiness, and its concern for the whole life of Christian discipleship helped effect in moral theology a shift away from the focus on law and sin toward a focus on growth in virtue and the whole life of holiness. Where the manualist tradition, developed for use by priests, had tended to view laypeople as "incompetent moral agents," needing to be led step by step through an examination of the "nooks and shadows" of their consciences, the documents of Vatican II addressed the laity as adult Christians, engaged in the task of discerning how best to live in faithfulness to the call of God in their context.[8]

Important, too, was the council's renewed understanding of the relationship between nature and grace that I explored in chapter 2. Simply put, if grace can be experienced, then the experience of the moral agent and his or her historical and cultural context are not merely scenery, a largely irrelevant backdrop for particular moral actions, the quality of which is determined ahistorically from eternal principles; rather, historical and cultural context and the experience of the Christian are part of the basic material of moral reflection. We saw earlier how that new view of the relationship between nature and grace also emerged from and fed into a new relationship between Church and world, one characterized more by openness and dialogue than by defensive apologetics or condemnation. The period following the Second Vatican Council also saw moral theologians turning outward and engaging with topics of global concern.

THE EMERGENCE OF THE CONCEPT OF SOCIAL SIN

The above summary, albeit brief and simplistic, identifies some of the key shifts that took place in Catholic moral theology following the Second Vatican Council: a turn toward the world and its "joys and hopes, griefs and anxieties" and greater emphasis on the whole person and the social and historical context in which they live and act.[9] These changes to moral theology initiated by the council paved the way in the postconciliar period for theological exploration of the concept of social sin and the gradual and tentative adoption of the concept in magisterial teaching.[10]

The documents of Vatican II do not directly employ the language of social sin. The phrase "peccatum sociale" appeared in a draft of a conciliar document only once, but objections from the floor that the idea of "social sin" undermined personal responsibility were heeded, and the final document spoke only of the "social consequences of sin."[11] Nevertheless, in some of the sections of *Gaudium et spes* in which the council fathers sought to engage social challenges, there was a move toward moral analysis of social structures and the beginnings of an acknowledgment that social structures could form moral agents in adverse ways. *Gaudium et spes* speaks of "institutions, laws and modes of thinking and feeling . . . handed down from previous generations" (§7) and states, "When the structure of affairs is flawed by the consequences of sin, man, already born with a bent toward evil, finds there new inducements to sin, which cannot be overcome without strenuous efforts and the assistance of grace" (§25). Even as the document reinforced the Church's teaching on the dignity of the human person as made in the image of God, it also moved toward a more contextual and dynamic understanding of the human person, acknowledging that people "are often diverted from doing good and spurred towards evil by the social circumstances in which they live and are immersed from their birth."[12]

Although the documents of Vatican II do not use the phrase "social sin," they begin to move away from the individualistic, act-focused tendencies of the manualist tradition in significant ways, and lay the groundwork for the more robust account of social sin offered by the Latin American Bishops' Conferences of Medellín (1968) and Puebla (1979). In these documents, the Latin American bishops confronted the situations of social injustice and political repression affecting many of their countries and, for the first time in magisterial documents, explicitly used language of social sin to do so. Leo XIII's *Rerum novarum* recognized the social injustice caused by the Industrial Revolution, but the encyclical's diagnosis of social ills and its recommendations for reform proceed on the basis of the belief that societies are naturally unequal: for Leo, social harmony will be achieved more by individual conversion than by structural reform.[13] The documents of Medellín and Puebla, however, while acknowledging the need for personal conversion as well as structural reform, are prepared to describe certain structures and situations as sinful. Medellín speaks of serious sins "reflected in" unjust structures and is careful to call for individual conversion as well as structural reform.[14] But the bishops' final document pushes beyond the caution of *Gaudium et spes* to describe how unjust economic, political, and social structures "constitute a positive menace to the peace of our countries" (§I.1) and distinguishes between "natural causes" of misery and "sinful situations." The document recognizes that some economic, political, and social situations are neither natural nor morally neutral but positively sinful. Puebla carries the emphasis of Medellín still further and speaks of the concrete, historical situation of Latin American people as a "sinful situation on both the individual and social level" (§1032) and also of sinful economic systems (§92) and the "sinful structures" of people's personal and social lives (§281). Although it is often careful to include "individual" in the same breath as "social," the document uses the language of social sin, sinful institutions, and sinful structures straightforwardly and without justification.[15]

John Paul II, in his closing address to the assembled bishops at Puebla, also picked up the language of social sin. His willingness to echo the Episcopal Conference of Latin America's (CELAM's) language was tempered, however, by caution: he stated that one must speak about structural sin in an "analogical" sense.[16] The subsequent postsynodal apostolic exhortation, *Reconciliatio et paenitentia* (1984), reflected the same desire to engage with the language of social sin but reflected also the same caution about the danger of undermining the significance of personal sin. The section on personal and social sin begins with a caution, which is worth quoting at length, as I return to its principal points later.

> Sin, in the proper sense, is always a personal act, since it is an act of freedom on the part of an individual and not properly of a group or community. This individual may be conditioned, incited and influenced by numerous and powerful external factors. He may also be subjected to tendencies, defects and habits linked with his personal condition. In not a few cases such external and internal factors may attenuate, to a greater or lesser degree, the person's freedom and therefore his responsibility and guilt. But it is a truth of faith, also

confirmed by our experience and reason, that the human person is free. This truth cannot be disregarded in order to place the blame for individuals' sins on external factors such as structures, systems or other people. Above all, this would be to deny the person's dignity and freedom which are manifested— even though in a negative and disastrous way— also in this responsibility for sin committed.[17]

The document then goes on to discuss three permissible meanings of the phrase "social sin" and one impermissible meaning.[18] First, "social sin" refers to the fact that, by virtue of human solidarity and interdependence, each individual's sin affects others: there is a "communion of sin" that corresponds to the communion of saints, and it is as real and concrete as it is mysterious.[19] Second, social sins are those that constitute a direct attack on one's neighbor; included are sins against justice in interpersonal relationships, sins against the human person, and sins against the common good, whether of commission or omission.[20] The third sense of social sin seems to be the closest to that intended by the bishops at Medellín and Puebla and refers to "relationships between the various human communities ... not always in accordance with the plan of God." It first names class struggle and goes on to condemn obstinate opposition between blocs of nations or between groups within nations, although both are described as "social evils" rather than social sin. John Paul II writes:

> In both cases one may ask whether moral responsibility for these evils, and therefore sin, can be attributed to any person in particular. . . . [R]ealities and situations such as those described, when they become generalized and reach vast proportions as social phenomena, almost always become anonymous, just as their causes are complex and not always identifiable. Hence if one speaks of social sin here, the expression obviously has an analogical meaning.[21]

The pope qualifies this by saying that speaking analogically about social sin "should not cause us to underestimate the responsibility of the individuals involved." He then states that any definition of social sin that opposes it to personal sin in order to erode the significance of the latter and lodge blame with "some vague entity or anonymous collectivity such as the situation, the system, society, structures or institutions" is not permissible.[22] Rather, "whenever the church speaks of situations of sin or when she condemns as social sins certain situations or the collective behaviour of certain groups . . . she knows and proclaims that such cases of social sin are the result of the accumulation and concentration of many personal sins. . . . The real responsibility, then, lies with individuals."[23]

In allowing certain precise senses of social sin, *Reconciliatio et paenitentia* moves beyond the Second Vatican Council fathers' worry that mention of social sin would undermine the traditional understanding of sin as a free, knowing act for which an individual is culpable. Nevertheless, the treatment of the theme in *Reconciliatio et paenitentia* demonstrates that the same worry persists. The first two senses of social sin named by the document might more accurately be described by the term *Sacrosanctum concilium* eventually settled on, "the social consequences of sin." The examples given of the third sense of social sin—class struggle and obstinate opposition between or within nations—suggest that the definition of sin as a free, knowing individual act has been translated to the collective level. The document seems to be referring to attitudes that are consciously held and that structure concrete relationships of opposition that it calls sin only in an analogous sense.[24] The more clearly the concept becomes social, the less clearly it seems to be formal sin.

Sollicitudo rei socialis (1987), the final document I want to consider, advances a little beyond *Reconciliatio et paenitentia*. Here, as Margaret Pfeil points out, John Paul II seems more ready to acknowledge the "almost automatic" nature of the unjust social structures that ensnare the poor. This is a few steps beyond the sense in *Reconciliatio et paenitentia* that "social sins" are simply free, knowing personal sins on a mass scale.[25] John Paul II states that the situation of the contemporary world cannot be properly analyzed without reference to "structures of sin."[26] To speak of the present situation in terms of sociopolitical analysis is not enough: only by bringing in language of sin, and therefore bringing the situation into the light of the gospel, can we begin to describe both the true nature of the problem and the means of its remedy.[27] On the one hand, we have here an important recognition that sin language must be applied to social situations and not just to the acts of individuals. John Paul II writes, "I have wished to introduce this type of analysis above all in order to point out the true *nature* of the evil which faces us with respect to the development of peoples: it is a question of *moral* evil, the fruit of *many sins* which lead to 'structures of sin.'"[28] On the other hand, the shift in preference for the language of "structures of sin" rather than social sin, as well as the placing of the phrase in quotation marks, indicates that the worry about dissolving personal responsibility in the social persists.[29]

STRUCTURAL STRESS

The development of the concept of social sin presents us with a classic case of structural stress within the tradition. In the rest of this chapter I diagnose the structural problem more precisely and begin some constructive work, by starting to explore how a more strongly social sense of sin might become better integrated into Catholic moral theology and social teaching.

In traditional Catholic moral theology in the manualist tradition, the essential features of the definition of formal sin are as follows: a sin is (i) an act offensive to or contrary to the laws of God; (ii) committed with knowledge that this is the case; and (iii) committed freely in that knowledge. Sin is always *personal.* When this understanding of sin is then applied to social situations, difficulties arise. First, if sin is always personal, it can only pertain to individual persons and not to groups. Groups and structures, social bodies, and systems cannot commit sins. Second, the more an act proceeds *unconsciously* from embedded social attitudes or systems, the less it can be said to be committed in full knowledge. Third, the more an act is compelled or the more my options are constrained in choosing to undertake it, the less I can be said to be free. The difficulty is that the concept of social sin arose precisely as a means of acknowledging the way that profoundly unjust social systems can operate almost automatically or unconsciously, without the full awareness or consent of those who participate in them. Yet to the extent that my action is not fully free or not fully informed, I am not culpable for it: the objective evil stands, but the element of formal sin is attenuated. Social sin seems to be an autodestructive concept. The more social the concept becomes, that is, the more it takes account of the automatic and unwitting nature of much systemic evil and the less it resembles sin, classically conceived; the more like sin it becomes, being committed in full freedom and knowledge, the less its social and systemic dimensions remain in focus.[30]

What is more, the foundations of Catholic moral teaching in this respect cannot be significantly altered without undermining the entire structure. The freedom of the human person before God and the ability to know the good and to choose it are integral to human dignity in the Catholic social teaching tradition. Deny or undermine the capacity of the human person to make free, informed choices, and you erode the terms in which human dignity has traditionally been expressed.[31] The problem is not just theoretical. The concept of social sin has been developed in large part by those working in situations where basic human dignity is under attack from the direct violence of political repression and the structural violence of poverty precisely as a means of denouncing those systems of violence. In such contexts, to trade the basic terms of human dignity for a more strongly social concept of sin would be to saw off the branch one was sitting on.

Given these difficulties, it should be evident why Church teaching has insisted on social sin as being the result of the addition of many personal sins, on the one hand, and spoken about social sins in terms of personal sins with particularly egregious social effects, on the other. The problem is not simple intransigence but rather that the foundations of Catholic moral theology cannot support a more ambitious construction of social sin: it simply collapses. The only solution is the compromise adopted in *Reconciliatio et paenitentia* and *Sollicitudo rei socialis*, and yet this compromise, too, is beset by difficulties. Specifically, I want to suggest that the understanding of social sin put forward in magisterial teaching results in a problematic understanding of the relationship between the individual and society.[32] When John Paul II states that situations of social sin are the "result of the accumulation and concentration of many personal sins," two difficulties are lurking in the background.[33] First, the language of "accumulation and concentration" suggests that the relationship between individual and social here is understood as one of part and whole: facts about social situations of sin can be explained in terms of facts about the individuals involved.[34] If social sin is the sum of its individual parts—personal sins—then it is hard to avoid implying a broader view of the social as simply the sum of its individual parts.[35] Second, and relatedly, the language of "result" suggests that the relationship between the individual and the social is understood as one of cause and effect.[36] Put simply, in striving to avoid the view that the social straightforwardly produces individuals—a view that might lead to determinism and people failing to take responsibility for sin by blaming it on "society"—Church teaching on social sin arguably strays too far in the opposite direction, leaning toward the view that individuals straightforwardly produce the social. This social atomism results in a number of theological difficulties.[37]

First, the social is not reducible to the sum of its individual parts. If we are concerned with the social, then, as Roy Bhaskar puts it, we are "not concerned, as such, with large-scale, mass or group behaviour (conceived as the behaviour of large numbers of individuals)" but rather "with the persistent *relations* between individuals (and groups) and with the relations between these relations and nature and the products of such relations."[38] That is, facts about social situations and social structures (which I will now refer to simply as "the social") are not reducible to facts about individuals or about groups of individuals: social facts are facts about relationships.[39] So, in the same way that it is not enough to explain social groups solely in terms of facts about the individuals comprising them, it is not enough to explain socially embedded situations of structural injustice and violence solely in terms of the particular acts and attitudes of the individuals involved. The Church's position recognizes this insofar as it acknowledges that social sin involves effects and structures that outlast the life spans and outreach the intentions of those involved. Nevertheless, the Church's teaching remains focused on particular individuals and their acts—the "many personal sins"—and thus struggles to account for those aspects of structural injustice and violence that are most truly *social*: embedded unjust relationships, persistent blindness, and prejudicial assumptions. Ignacio Martín-Baró, one of the UCA Jesuits murdered by the Salvadoran security forces, wrote this about the violence engulfing the country shortly before his death.

> Fundamentally, the problem is not one of isolated individuals whether few or many; it is a problem whose nature is strictly social. The damage that has been produced is not simply in the destruction of personal lives. Harm has been done to the social structures themselves—to the norms that order the common life, to the institutions that govern the life of citizens, to the values and principles by which people are educated and through which the repression has tried to justify itself.[40]

Accounting for social sin simply in terms of the "accumulation and concentration" of many personal sins does not do justice to its truly social dimensions, because the social itself cannot be exhaustively or straightforwardly accounted for in terms of the accumulation and concentration of individuals comprising it.[41]

Second, the lurking social atomism in the doctrine of sin leaves us with what Bhaskar calls a "voluntaristic idealism with respect to our understanding of social structure."[42] Bhaskar has social scientists in his sights when he makes this criticism, but it strikes home in Catholic social teaching, too: if we build into our doctrine of sin the assumption that social sin is simply the accumulation and concentration of personal sin, then the remedy for social sin is simply personal conversion. We get rid of socially embedded injustice and violence by appealing to individuals. The logic is simply that of auricular confession, transferred to the social level. Now, on one level this is not problematic at all. The gospel *is* a call to radical, ongoing conversion on the part of every individual, and it is not wrong to call people to such conversion.[43] What is more problematic is when that call to personal conversion pushes us toward a kind of social Pelagianism, as though the eschatological renewal of creation and the wiping of tears from every cheek were within our reach if only we would put our backs into it. This kind of social Pelagianism can become a demand for an unrealistic kind of moral heroism. The point here is not that the gospel is too idealistic and that it is simply not realistic in the face of economic injustice, for example, to call everyone to the witness of a St. Francis, or in the face of political repression, to call everyone to the witness of a Franz Jägerstätter. We *are* all called to holiness, and our sinful inability to make a clear-ringing answer to that call during our earthly lives is no reason to undermine its magnitude. Rather, the problem is that the all-pervasive, social, and structural nature of the evil we face is such that it undermines our ability to hear that call to holiness and to answer it. The social evil I am called to face and overcome is not just a feature of my situation, but of my self.[44] Overcoming social sin, then, is not so much a matter of overcoming some sinful situation outside of myself in which I am only incidentally involved; it is much more like the struggles of a mental illness such as depression, in which my identity and my illness, constantly merging and separating, cannot be clearly distinguished and in which my sense of agency, which is only partially under my conscious control, can dim and brighten. Tackling complex structural sin with a call to individual conversion is like telling a depressed person that she or he has nothing objective to be sad about and ought to cheer up: there may be some truth in it, and it may well accurately name some of the objective features of the situation, but it does not get to the bottom of the problem, and it is not helpful.

Taking an example from Northern Ireland will help bring the points covered so far home to the problem of violence and the practice of peacebuilding. Writing about the embedded sectarianism that produces everything from pipe bombs and shootings to "peace walls" and benign apartheid, Joseph Liechty and Cecelia Clegg argue:

> Much thinking about sectarianism is faulty because we take a solely personal approach to a problem that is both personal and systemic. When thinking about sectarianism, we typically begin with personal attitudes and personal actions. Thus we absolve a person of responsibility, we think, when we say, "She doesn't have a sectarian bone in her body." In one sense, this concern with the personal is not only appropriate, we need more of it, not less. At the same time, however, too exclusively personal an approach fails to take seriously enough the systemic issues around sectarianism. To pose the problem another way: a sectarian system can be maintained by people who, individually, do not have a sectarian bone in their bodies.[45]

This systemic aspect is precisely what the Church's teaching on social sin as the "accumulation and concentration of many personal sins" struggles to address. The problem is not one of wrong actions undertaken unwittingly or unfreely—actions which, once the moral blindness involved in the situation is removed, can be recognized as wrong. The problem is that social relations in this context have become so persistently distorted that normal attitudes, innocent acts, and understandable choices—even *good* acts and attitudes—can maintain and perpetuate an unjust social fabric. It is thus, Liechty and Clegg suggest, that "the sectarian system born from gross violence and what most people would now see as unapologetic injustice, can now maintain itself on a diet consisting largely of our rational responses, understandable comparisons, good intentions and positive actions."[46] This is the truly social and structural face of sin. If the Catholic

Church is to engage in and support the work of social reconciliation, it needs theological resources to address situations of this kind.

CONSTRUCTION WORK

The Church's teaching on social sin is shaped by the deep structures of its moral theology and by the long tradition of individual private confession. The renewal of moral theology around and after the Second Vatican Council did much to transform the individualistic, abstract, and act-focused understanding of sin that dominated the manualist tradition of moral theology and restore a concern for the ways in which both individuals and their moral choices are shaped by their contexts, for good and for ill. Yet the subsequent search to find a language of social sin has been unable to escape the deep constraints of Catholic moral theology and the basic understanding of sin as a free, knowing, moral wrong committed by an individual. The result is an understanding of social sin as sin only by analogy. This in itself is not problematic: after all, in the Catholic tradition original sin, too, is analogical, which in no way diminishes its usefulness as a concept or its grip on the Catholic imagination.[47] The difficulty is that social sin is not left on the level of analogy but actually parsed in terms of the "accumulation and concentration of many personal sins." I have argued that this creates a lurking social atomism in the doctrine of sin, whereby the relationship between the individual and the social is implicitly treated as one of part and whole, or cause and effect. This account of social sin, and of the social itself, simply does not do justice to the characteristically social forms that sin takes in situations of structural injustice and violence.

The problem is a complex one, involving some of the most basic elements and instincts of Catholic moral theology. Arguably, it cannot be solved in the terms in which it is posed, in which the terms "social" and "sin" inevitably pull in opposite directions: redefining the social as an accumulation and concentration of individuals is not a satisfactory solution, nor is redefining sin to remove the requirement of personal responsibility. Another way forward is needed. In the rest of this chapter, I want to explore some resources that might help us develop a more adequate account of social sin, first by sketching out a better account of the relationship between the individual and the social and then by asking what this means for the Church's approach to social sin. It is important to keep this discussion on the "rough ground" of reality rather than deal with the moral question in the abstract, so I will return the discussion often to the example of sectarianism in Northern Ireland.[48] This commitment to remaining on the rough ground is important because the discussion that follows does not aim at removing the ambiguity from the concept of social sin and replacing it with satisfying precision but rather at developing resources that do justice to the intractable complexity of situations of violence and injustice.

THE INDIVIDUAL AND THE SOCIAL

Earlier, I suggested that the Church's teaching on social sin implied an understanding of the relationship between the individual and the social as part and whole, or cause and effect—a view I described as social atomism. The question we face here is, if individuals do not straightforwardly produce the social or, conversely, if the social does not straightforwardly produce individuals, then what *is* the relationship between them?

The question of the nature of the social, and how individuals relate to it, is obviously a sizable one, and my intent here is to sketch the basic lines of an answer rather than give a full and finished account. In the context of this discussion of social sin, perhaps the best place to begin is with experience: how, as individuals, do we experience the reality and force of the social, and what does this tell us about the nature of the social and how we relate to it?[49] As we act in a given social context, interpret others' actions, express our views, disagree with one another, and act on the basis of assumptions, we draw on unspoken collective understandings about all kinds of things, from what constitutes acceptable social behavior to what is likely to happen if we transgress it. These collective understandings are not fully understood, but neither are they followed blindly; they are, as Kirsten Hastrup puts it, "part of the background knowledge that makes people sense the horizon of a 'we.'"[50] Over time, these shared understandings can take on an objectified force as social "rules," but even if they "become institutionalised and outlast individual action . . . they must be constantly confirmed in practice."[51] Social forces thus exist somewhere between subjective and objective, part and whole.[52]

"The social," then, is neither a subjective attitude or conscious choice nor an objective law but something in between. Situations of structural violence or entrenched social division provide good examples. In some of these situations, the social rules about acceptable social behavior are clearly articulated, as with the "Whites only" and "Coloreds" signs of apartheid South Africa or in the anti-Tutsi propaganda of the Rwandan media in the months leading up to the 1994 genocide. In other situations, perhaps the majority, beliefs about the other may be so ingrained and objectified that we seem to experience them as features of our environment or our bodies rather than attitudes wholly under our conscious control.[53] Clegg and Liechty provide another helpful example from a group discussion.

> A woman spoke of the effects of an annual Orange parade in the neighbourhood where she grew up. As she told the story, this was not a rowdy parade, and indeed nothing dramatic ever happened. And yet that annual event, always accompanied by her family staying in their house and quietly hoping that nothing would happen, generated in her an unspoken but ever-present sense of intimidation and limitation that shaped her life: where she would go, obviously, and whom she would befriend, but more subtle and internal limitations as well; a reserve and caution that did not always show, but that always shaped those encounters she did have with Protestants. As she spoke, however, what seemed to distress her most was her sense, as a middle-aged mother of older children, that without ever intending or realising it, she had somehow passed on the same limitations to her children. In one sense little or nothing had happened, and yet the quietly destructive effects could shape a life and pass silently to a new generation.[54]

These kinds of working assumptions about the other, and about where and how it is possible or not possible to interact with them, may not be consciously held by individuals or explicitly articulated in the social context concerned: they are neither subjective attitudes nor objective laws. Nevertheless, the woman's sense of limitation in this example—for which we could easily find parallels in limitation sensed on the basis of race or social class—shaped her sense of the "horizon of a 'we'" over against a Protestant "they." Her experience was produced by, and productive of, a broader pattern of social division. While not in themselves drastically harmful, her assumptions were part of the fabric of a situation of direct and structural violence that cannot easily be broken down into particular individuals' acts or attitudes.

What goes for knowledge of particular social rules also goes for knowledge of whole social situations or societies. Societies do not exist as static, objective wholes that can be comprehensively mapped as though they were landscapes viewable from above, nor can social situations be mapped by collating the subjective views and experiences of individuals. Societies are dynamic and constantly shifting sets of relationships that can only ever be experienced from some particular point and pieced together from there. This means that when we try to describe a culture or society, our account is inevitably a construction, a temporary objectification of a constantly shifting set of relationships.[55] Societies are not discovered but told or narrated: their reality requires assembly, as it were.[56] As Hastrup puts it, the social is *emergent*: its reality is something that emerges, or becomes evident to us, as we experience social assumptions, constraints, compulsions, and so on, and begin to construct these into some temporarily objectified picture of a constantly shifting social whole.[57] The process of discovering and describing societies is like trying to describe the plot and characters of a play that is still going on, in which the roles and action is partly scripted but also open to improvisation and change and in which none of the actors has the full script.[58]

What does all this mean for social sin? First of all, it gives us a more complex view of the relationship between individuals and the social. It is not the case that the social straightforwardly produces individuals and their behavior or that individuals and their behavior straightforwardly produce the social. Rather than one being a "side effect" of the other, the two produce one another, standing in a reciprocal, mutually constitutive relationship.[59] Societies very strongly form people to perceive their reality in particular ways and to choose and behave within it accordingly. At the same time, however, societies do not absolutely determine people's perception of their situation, their choices about how to act in relation to it, or their behavior within it.[60] This leaves us with a significant gray area with regard to social sin.

Situations of complex systemic injustice and violence cannot be exhaustively explained in terms of the personal acts and attitudes of those involved—the personal sins whose accumulation and concentration the Church suggests is responsible for so-called situations of social sin. In what Puebla calls "situations of sin," there is a remainder that is left once personal acts and attitudes have been accounted for. This remainder includes things like damaging beliefs or assumptions I may have about others, which appear to me not as consciously held beliefs but as features of objective reality: stereotypes of certain races or classes as lazy or violent, for example, or beliefs that other nations or groups threaten my safety. It also includes understandable acts I might undertake in view of my understanding of reality, like not wanting my children to grow up in an unsafe area or wanting them to marry the "right" person. Liechty and Clegg note, for example, that "sectarianism feeds on Christians' religiously motivated boundary maintenance. We choose to worship, educate, and marry almost exclusively among our own. Our motivation is not to be sectarian, it is to build strong communities, but because our efforts fall within the boundaries set by sectarianism, our best pastoral efforts can end up strengthening the sectarian divide."[61] This remainder might also include things I fail to do because they seem to me to be too difficult, too risky, or even impossible. Such acts and attitudes are not wholly knowing or wholly free but not wholly unwitting or wholly compelled either. They can be undertaken with good intentions, and they are not, considered in themselves, necessarily wrong, yet they are undeniably part of an unjust social fabric. These acts and attitudes may not be formal sin, or perhaps even *material* sin, but the "situation of sin" cannot be satisfactorily explained without accounting for them or addressed without transforming them.

The more reciprocal relationship between the individual and the social that I have articulated here, which includes the assertion that the reality of the social is emergent, also leaves us with a second conclusion: social sin requires *narration* in order to emerge and be perceived as such.[62] The reality of situations of sin, like that of any social situation, requires assembly. This is not a new insight, of course. Liberation theologians have written of the need to identify, describe, and strip away the false consciousness that accompanies wealth and power and replace it with a view of the reality of social structures as they are experienced by the poor and marginalized. This kind of reasoning stands behind Himes's argument that

> the truly insidious aspect of social sin is the blindness it causes, what Daniel Maguire calls the "tissue of lies" placed before our eyes so that we fail to see reality. Social sin is an aspect of our fated condition and we are ushered into the enveloping darkness of false consciousness from the outset of our lives. Only with the removal of the ignorance which accompanies the blindness of social sin do we enter into the world of moral responsibility.[63]

On this view, the way to address social sin is to deal with the remainder—to bring the people in situations like those described in the examples above out of the foggy half-light of semi-knowing and semi-willing and semi-acting into the light of the gospel, in which the situation of sin is visible for what it is and in which our agency and the right course of action become clear to us.[64] Yet Himes's approach, albeit awake to the more characteristically social dimensions of sin, arguably remains within the generally individualistic framework of Catholic moral theology insofar as he proposes addressing situations of social sin by breaking them down into individuals' problematic attitudes and actions and what they can do about them.[65] The turning point, as in the sacrament of confession, is realizing and admitting responsibility or culpability.[66] This is hugely important, and I do not want to undermine the degree to which addressing situations of social sin *does* rest on people identifying, as clearly as they are able, the part they play in the situation and taking responsibility for it. But, as we have seen, social sin is not completely soluble, as it were: it cannot be straightforwardly or wholly broken down into the sinful acts and attitudes of individuals. I want to explore, therefore, two other possibilities opened up by the idea that the reality of social sin requires assembly or narration—possibilities that do not return our attention quite so immediately to the role and responsibility of the individual as the only way of describing and addressing situations of systemic injustice or violence.

NARRATIVE VERDICTS

The Australian philosopher Raimond Gaita writes in *A Common Humanity*:

> Nearly everyone is vulnerable to the tendency to believe that severe moral appreciation must run together with blame. But there are voices in our culture that speak of different possibilities. Sophocles' *Oedipus the King* shows how moral severity may take the form of pity. The chorus did not blame Oedipus for the evil he did on account of ignorance for which he was not culpable. It pities the evil-doer he became and that informs the quality of the pity it feels at the terrible spectacle of a man who has lost his kingdom, whose wife/mother has hanged herself, who has blinded himself and is exiled. Its severe pity holds him fast in serious moral response—it holds him *responsible* to the evil-doer he has become, insisting that he face the full meaning of it.[67]

The tradition of Catholic moral reasoning, in theory and in practice, is strongly shaped by the practice of auricular confession. Central to this tradition as it has developed in the Latin West is the requirement to establish culpability: to what degree there was grave matter, intention, knowledge, and freedom.[68] The tradition of auricular confession leaves us, as Gaita puts it, tending to think that severe moral appreciation must run together with blame. When we perceive some situation of human moral evil, we try to identify people to blame. Our moral thinking is geared to establishing culpability. Yet in the kinds of situations I am concerned with in this chapter—situations of direct violence like political repression, ethnic cleansing, torture, and genocide, or systemic violence like racism, poverty, or sexism—the task of establishing individuals' culpability may be extremely difficult. The important thing to realize here is that the difficulty of establishing culpability in complex situations of systemic injustice and violence does not leave us morally shrugging, as it were, unable to make judgments or to take action. We need not accept the strict choice suggested by Church teaching between *either* the possibility of personal responsibility, and the resulting assertion that social sin is "the accumulation and concentration of many personal sins," *or* blaming the situation on an "anonymous collectivity or group" and thereby avoiding personal responsibility altogether. Put another way, the alternative to "This person is culpable and must repent" is not "Nobody is culpable and nothing can be done." Gaita's argument in the passage quoted above is that it is possible to see and judge situations in what he calls a "severe moral light" without pursuing the question of culpability and attributing blame. There is the possibility of a narrative verdict, the primary purpose of which is not to attribute blame but to establish an understanding of what wrong has occurred and how. Narrative verdicts are not dominated by the need to identify culpable individuals, or even by the need to pronounce on the final and definitive cause of an event. Such narrative verdicts can enable those involved to recognize their responsibility and agency, even when the question of formal culpability may be hard to determine or unhelpful to pursue.[69]

This kind of severe moral description is not just possible; there may even be situations in which it is preferable. The conflict in Northern Ireland, again, provides a good example here. First, the conflict is perpetuated rather than resolved by continual attempts to establish the historical and present culpability of the various actors involved. Liechty and Clegg note that the widespread culture of blame is a "pernicious force that entrenches sectarianism."[70] Second, although calling individuals to account and bringing them to justice can be important, the question of individual culpability, if it is allowed to dominate, detracts attention from the systemic nature of sectarianism and perpetuates the myth of an innocent majority and a guilty few.[71] This does not mean that in situations like Northern Ireland the question of individual responsibility should be forsaken altogether, but it does leave us with the challenge of naming and constructively addressing the reality of sectarianism by another means. Liechty and Clegg's approach arose in the context of group discussions of people's experiences of sectarianism.

As story after story revealed the contours, complexity and sinister power of sectarianism, a numinous atmosphere settled over the group. Regrettably, however, the divinity evoked was a dark one, and the awe it inspired was enervating. Joe made some fumbling, reifying remarks about the nature of the beast we were confronting. It sparked some recognition and interest, and after the session some people asked Joe to elaborate. That night he wrote out an initial, cruder version of the reflection on sectarianism as a system . . . , and the next morning he shared it with the group. What he said met with quiet but firm assent, and the mood changed. Having evoked, recognised and named sectarianism, we could now get on, it seemed, with the business of challenging it.[72]

It is worth noting several things about this account. First, Liechty and Clegg's account of the group's reflections echoes the account I offered earlier of social reality as emergent. As individuals narrated their experiences of sectarianism, its objective power and reality emerged or became evident. Second, the reality of sectarianism needed to be narrated: its comprehensive reality required assembly, as Joe attempted to do on the night of the discussion. Third, Joe's efforts to narrate sectarianism, to reify it as a system and name it as a force "out there," met with recognition and a positive response, as the participants recognized the reality confronting them and their freedom and agency in the situation. Liechty and Clegg's aim in this group discussion, and in the definition of sectarianism as a system that proceeded from it, was not to establish culpability. Rather, they state, "the response we hoped to evoke in those we were with might be put like this: we face a problem of awesome power and subtlety; there is no hiding from it and little innocence in the face of it; it implicates us collectively and individually; let us join together to face it."[73] Their work offers an example of the potential helpfulness of narrative verdicts in contexts where it is difficult or unhelpful to pursue the question of individual culpability on a mass scale.

It is important to note the unavoidably provisional nature of such narrative verdicts. Earlier, I noted that it is impossible to gain an objective view of social situations or groups from the outside or comprehensively map them as though they were landscapes viewable from above. Social situations and groups can only be pieced together from the inside, by participating in the constantly shifting network of social relations and constructing a temporarily objectified view of the whole from there. That view will inevitably be just that—a temporary objectification and a construction.[74] Any narrative verdict based on such a construction, then, is not final and never can be. In a straightforward sense, none of us has an objective viewpoint that would allow us to produce a definitive narrative verdict. The true nature of social situations, events, and groups is very hard to establish in their own place and time and scarcely any easier at thousands of miles' and hundreds of years' remove.

This should lead us to approach with some caution, I think, approaches to social sin that lean heavily on the possibility of "dissolving" it by providing some definitive account of a social situation that enables individuals to recognize their culpability and change their behavior accordingly. The optimistic determination of this kind of approach can easily slip into a kind of naïveté, as though the principal difficulty with social sin is a pervasive blindness, which, once removed, leaves everyone clear about the truth of the situation and what should be done about it. The reality is that the moral significance of social situations is not always straightforward to ascertain or diagnose, that the process of coming to judgments about them is complex and fraught, and that the task of deciding what to do in order to ameliorate such situations is more difficult still. It is true, too, that knowledge of the sinful reality of a situation does not always lead to action: people are often inchoately or explicitly aware of the unjust nature of the systems and societies in which they participate but, because of inertia or actively selfish interest, have little interest in acting to change them. These difficulties facing the task of severe moral description do not exempt us from the need to judge and to act, but it is worth reminding ourselves of the difficulty of the task and the provisionality of our attempts to address it, lest we imagine that definitive judgments of our situation lie within our grasp or slip into the kind of social Pelagianism that acts as if the new creation could be built wholly by human hands.

The limited nature of our ability to see and judge our situation is not just a commonsense point about human limitation but also a theological point about the relationship between creature and creator. Definitive seeing of the comprehensive truth of human affairs, and definitive judgment of them, belongs only to God; the measure of human seeing is the degree to which it shares in God's vision and judgment. This is made known to us most clearly in the ways that Jesus sees and judges during his ministry, and in his death and resurrection, in which we see God's judgment at work. A great deal more might be said on this point, but it is enough to note here that our sharing in God's vision as pilgrims *in via* is always partial, intermittent, and fallible. Only in our encounter with

Christ as judge will we come to know finally the truth of our own lives as they have been in God's sight.[75]

SOCIAL CONCUPISCENCE

The point about the difficulty of "dissolving" social sin into personal sins brings me to a final constructive suggestion. I have raised throughout this chapter the problem of the "remainder" left once sinful situations have been broken down into individual acts and attitudes. In situations of social or structural sin, we are dealing not just with personal sins and with material wrongdoing that could at least potentially emerge as formal sin. We are also dealing with material that is *to one side* of the moral: bodily reactions of fear, discomfort, or anger; good choices; habits that nevertheless perpetuate and entrench bad situations; and even our concept of reality. Even when we recognize our agency in a situation of injustice, a sense of what we ought to do might elude us, as might the strength to do it. Perhaps we need, as much as social sin, something that gives us a language for this remainder—what Rahner calls the "unexpressed impulses, basic dispositions and attitudes which escape total clarification by reflexion" but which "are of more comprehensive significance for the totality of our spiritual life in certain circumstances than what is objectively recognized and expressed."[76]

At the heart of the concept of concupiscence in the Catholic tradition, Rahner argues, when all unnecessary associations are cleared away, is the idea that "man is divided against himself."[77] There is no need, Rahner states, to parse this division as the opposition of flesh to spirit, or the opposition of what is "lower" in humanity to what is "higher," although concupiscence can and does manifest itself in this way in our experience.[78] Instead, Rahner sketches out an understanding of concupiscence as a naturally spontaneous act of desire, a reflex that resists our free decision.[79] Human beings are both sensitive and spiritual by nature, and inseparably so, and so this spontaneous desire is always both sensitive and spiritual.[80] It appears in our experience as a sort of resistance, a drag on our free self-disposal, as the "solidity and impenetrability of nature," as well as a certain obscureness to ourselves.[81] Concupiscence thus understood can equally manifest itself as a natural resistance against a morally good decision, as, for example, when someone decides to be brave but trembles, or as a spontaneous response or resistance to a morally bad decision, as when someone blushes in the act of lying.[82] In concupiscence, we make experience of the truth that human beings are simply unable to be all-of-a-piece: "Man never becomes wholly absorbed either in good or in evil."[83]

We are, Rahner says, *called* to the kind of integrity we desire, that is, the ability to dispose of ourselves both freely and wholly. "The free decision," Rahner writes,

> tends to the end that man should dispose of himself as a whole before God, actively make himself into what he freely wishes to be. Thus the end to which the free decision is orientated is that everything which is in man (nature), hence the involuntary act as well, should be the expression of what man as a person wishes to be; thus that the free decision should comprehend, transfigure and transfuse the spontaneous act, so that its own reality too should no longer be purely natural but personal.[84]

We are called to be gathered up in a free disposal of our whole selves before God, and may desire it, but this kind of integrity inevitably eludes us.

> Man's concrete being is not throughout its whole extent and according to all its powers and their actualization the pure expression and the unambiguous revelation of the personal active centre which is its own master. In the course of its self-determination, the person undergoes the resistance of the nature given prior to freedom, and never wholly succeeds in making all that man is into the reality and expression of all that he comprehends himself to be in the core of his person.[85]

There is always something left out. Rahner talks about free decisions in which "a bit of the human material of free decision is left over without being refashioned, or . . . a bit of the inclination of the free decision remains without achieving anything, because it becomes stuck fast."[86] His emphasis on human freedom is bound up with a clear sense of the ways in which that freedom is shaped and even constrained by other inner forces.

The usefulness of Rahner's concept of concupiscence for our purposes here should be becoming clearer. In problematizing the idea of social or structural sin as "the accumulation and concentration of personal sins," I have referred to the difficulty of the "remainder" left when personal sin has been accounted for: acts, beliefs, and attitudes that are not personal sin but that undeniably form part of structural sin, which are in one sense blameless and in another sense nevertheless bound up in the perpetuation of systemic injustice. The example of sectarianism in Northern Ireland showed us the kinds of acts and attitudes involved and the undeniable power and persistence of this systemic "remainder."

Rahner's concept of concupiscence is nicely teleological—a feature to which I return—but it is not explicitly social. There is no reason, however, why its social dimensions could not be explored and developed. Human persons are both spiritual and sensitive by nature; they are also social, and, as we have seen, our being social touches us at the level of the spontaneous act, at the level of our premoral reflexes of perception, desire, and pursuit. Our social nature shapes our worldview and sense of reality, shapes what we perceive as goods and how we react to them, and shapes even our bodily reactions. Thus, to draw on the example of the woman from Northern Ireland given above, a kind of social dimension of concupiscence manifests itself in her reserve or fear in relation to Protestant others, which might persist alongside a conscious desire for good and peaceful relationships, or in her sense of having passed on her inhibitions to her children without ever intending so to do. A social dimension of concupiscence working in the other direction might be seen in an example Emmanuel Katongole cites, of a Hutu boy during the Rwanda genocide who "had spent so much time with Tutsis in his early childhood that he was confused. He didn't know how to draw the 'proper line' between ethnic groups. Afterward, when he returned to his village, he did not get involved in the killings. The *interahammwe* militias tried to force him to participate in the killing but eventually gave up on him because his mind was, in their words, 'clearly overwhelmed.'"[87] In this being "clearly overwhelmed," we might see how a social concupiscence can manifest itself as a spontaneous pull toward the good. Perhaps, in the light of these two examples, we might specify the social dimension of concupiscence in terms of a reflex need to be together-with-others, a basic desire not to be divided—one that can take both destructive and salutary shape and that contains the invitation to be "transfigured" and lived consciously as a free decision to be in communion with others.[88]

Concupiscence in social mode can therefore manifest itself in just the kinds of "remainder" I have been exploring, and which are characteristic of structural sin: a bodily discomfort or even visceral fear around the other that persists despite our conscious desire and best efforts to treat them as equals; habits of language and thought, social association, or consumerism, even ways of negotiating our physical environment that we sluggishly persist in and find hard to break, in spite of our awareness that they reinforce social division and perpetuate structural inequality. In this social dimension, too, concupiscence cannot be divided into "inner" and "outer," as though it always concerned an inner intention for the good held back by lack of physical courage, for even when thrown together on the "outer" level of social interaction we can retain inner borders of prejudice. In complex ways, too, this "inner" experience of resistance and being stuck can become an "outer" reality, taking concrete shape as part of a structure of sin.

Kirsten Hastrup explores how, through "ontological dumping," our habitual ways of knowing and understanding the world and simplifying and collating our experience become understood as objective realities "out there."[89] What begins as a way of understanding the other or analyzing a social problem ceases to appear as a belief about the world, or a way of looking at it, and becomes instead a feature of the world as we experience it. Thus "dumped" as a feature of objective reality, it becomes less available for critical reflection.[90] Problematic understandings of the "poor," for example, understood as objective reality, become laid down in language and thought, become reflected in official government policies or policing strategies, take shape in town planning, transport, and service provision. If we want to meet the other, we encounter resistance not just on the inner level but on this outer level also. Inner reserve becomes outer distance, and outer distance, in turn, engenders, reinforces, perpetuates, and passes on inner reserve. We could multiply any number of examples of this phenomenon. The "remainder" of which Rahner speaks, which is so hard to transform, the sense of being somehow "stuck" in spite of our decision to move in a certain direction, our obscurity even to ourselves—all these are features of our experience of the struggle for *social* transformation, as well as our experience of desire for transformation on a personal level. Concupiscence as Rahner understands it gives us a helpful language for describing and addressing this aspect of structures of sin. We are not dealing with personal sins or always with acts and attitudes that, once we understand their place in an unjust system, clearly appear to us as sin. We are dealing with a sort of social concupiscence, a premoral need-to-be-together that has the capacity either to drag us back toward a social life of sin—the mysterious "communion of sin" of which *Reconciliatio et paenitentia* speaks—or draw us forward to the communion of saints and a social life of virtue.[91]

Rahner's short chapter on the theological concept of *concupiscentia* ends with the following note.

> Concupiscentia, and death too, is not just the manifestation of sin, in Christ's order it is not just what is left over in the justified, something to be overcome eschatologically because it is in contradiction with human nature in this concrete order; it is also the form *in* which the Christian experiences Christ's sufferings and suffers them himself to the end. But of this we shall say no more here.[92]

Perhaps we can say this in the context of social transformation as well as personal transformation. We are called to overcome the "many personal sins" that feed into situations and structures of sin. We are called to grow in awareness, so that we also grow in knowledge and freedom: knowledge of the ways we are unwittingly bound up in injustice and freedom to change. And we are called, too, to gather in the "remainder," all that stubbornly resists such transformation, so that even our spontaneous desires and fears become part of our long and deliberate journey toward the communion of saints. But that "remainder" I have been addressing is not just the manifestation of sin, a leftover to be wrestled with and overcome: on a social level, too, it can become a way in which we experience the whole of creation "groaning in one great act of giving birth" (Rom 8:22) to the new creation in which will appear, finally, the freedom and glory of the children of God.

SIX

Reconciliation and Catholic Nonviolence

Since the South African Truth and Reconciliation Commission of 1994–96, over twenty countries emerging from the violence of war or a recent history of political repression have undertaken truth and reconciliation processes. In all of these processes, the language and concept of reconciliation was central; in some of them, Christian churches in general and the Catholic Church in particular have played important roles.[1]

This presents a significant opportunity. Where some of the language and concepts of Catholic social teaching struggle to gain a hearing in the political sphere, reconciliation is one area in which the Church should be able to make a strong theological and practical contribution. But if the theology of reconciliation is one of the Catholic Church's most promising resources for the theology and practice of peacebuilding, it is also one of the areas most in need of development. At present, the concept lacks the theological richness and coherence that might embed it more firmly in Catholic self-understanding, spirituality, and practice. The first challenge here is that the Church's theology of reconciliation remains quite tightly tied to the theology of the sacrament of reconciliation, particularly the way that this has taken shape in the West as the practice of individual private confession. In terms of the theology and practice of reconciliation, the Church finds it difficult—quite literally—to think outside the box. The second and related challenge is that the Church's theology of reconciliation is, at present, not well integrated with its teaching on peace and peacebuilding. Most of the magisterial teaching on reconciliation has focused on its implications for ecclesiology and sacramental theology; its implications for Catholic social teaching are far less well developed.

In this chapter I want to work toward making the concept of reconciliation both theologically richer and better integrated with the Church's teaching on peace. In particular, I want to show how a renewed theology of reconciliation can provide important support for a Catholic practice of active nonviolence. In his message for the 2017 World Day of Peace, Pope Francis described peacebuilding through active nonviolence as "the natural and necessary complement to the Church's continuing efforts to limit the use of force" and called for nonviolence to "become the hallmark of our decisions, our relationships and our actions, and indeed of political life in all its forms."[2] If this new emphasis in Catholic social teaching on peace is to flourish, and offer support to Catholic peacebuilders already engaged in nonviolent action, then we need a richer theological understanding of nonviolence. A renewed theology of reconciliation, I argue, offers helpful resources here.

Like the foregoing chapters, this chapter begins with a structural survey and diagnosis before moving on to constructive repair work. The first section explores the emergence and development of the Catholic Church's postconciliar theology of reconciliation, focusing on three key documents: John Paul II's *Reconciliatio et paenitentia* (1984), the International Theological Commission document *Memory and Reconciliation* (1999), and Benedict XVI's *Africae munus* (2007). In addition to setting out the theology of reconciliation as it stands, this critical exploration enables us to identify some of the factors that currently limit its usefulness to the theology and practice of peacebuilding. One of those factors is its relatively underdeveloped relationship to scripture, so the second section engages in some depth with Paul's theology of reconciliation. From this fuller engagement with the dynamics of reconciliation in Paul, I draw out three principles—reconciliation as God's initiative, as breaking down human division, and as having cosmic scope—and explore how they open up new theological space, broadening our understanding of the Church's ministry of reconciliation and supporting the Catholic practice of active nonviolent peacebuilding.

CHURCH TEACHING ON RECONCILIATION

If analysis were to proceed solely on the basis of a word study of the documents of Vatican II, we might be justified in concluding that the concept of reconciliation was not central to the council's vision or theology. The word *reconciliation* appears only a few times in the major conciliar documents, usually referring to reconciliation between human beings or to the sacrament of reconciliation.[3] In the conciliar documents, as in John XXIII's *Pacem in terris*, the biblical concept of reconciliation is not really in view.[4] Nevertheless, the absence of much explicit language of reconciliation should not lead us to conclude that the theme is entirely missing, because the ecclesiology of the council foregrounds several themes that bring the theme of reconciliation closer to the heart of the Church's self-understanding. *Lumen gentium* opens by describing the Church as the sacrament of union with God and the unity of the whole human race, and other images used in the document also lend themselves to an emphasis on interdependence and unity: the metaphor of the body and, particularly, the theme of the one people of God, to which all people are called and in which all, in differing degrees of belonging, participate.[5] Though the language of reconciliation is not explicitly present here, it is easy to see how John Paul II's description of the Church's mission in *Reconciliatio et paenitentia*, twenty years later, is an extrapolation of these conciliar themes of unity and interdependence: "One can therefore sum up the church's mission, rich and complex as it is, as being her central task of reconciling people: with God, with themselves, with neighbor, with the whole of creation."[6] If unity is the fundamental nature and calling of humankind, reconciliation is the means by which it is achieved.

Given the centrality of the themes of human unity and interdependence to the council, and its ecclesiological vision of the Church as the sacrament of human unity, one might have expected more emphasis on the theology of reconciliation in the years following Vatican II than has actually been evident. As it is, the theme is taken up substantively in only two comparatively low-profile papal documents, the postsynodal apostolic exhortations *Reconciliatio et paenitentia* and *Africae munus*, and in the International Theological Commission document *Memory and Reconciliation*. This is partly, as I discuss below, because Catholic theology runs more easily in other tracks: where we might expect to see mention of reconciliation, the theology of communion is often more in evidence. So the underdevelopment of the Church's theology of reconciliation is partly to do with what has *not* been said, in the sense that reconciliation has not yet been integrated as a major or explicit theme of Catholic social teaching. As I have already indicated, however, it is also to do with what *has* been said, in particular the way in which the Church's theology of reconciliation has been shaped by the paradigm of individual confession. To explain this, we need to look more carefully at *Reconciliatio et paenitentia*.

Reconciliatio et paenitentia (1984)

Reconciliatio et paenitentia opens with a general introduction to its two themes and a brief consideration of the signs of the times to which it responds: "deep and painful divisions," including assaults on the rights of the human person, violence and terrorism, poverty, and, persisting in the midst of these, a desire for reconciliation. The document then engages with the parable of the prodigal son. The departure point is the son's decision to leave the father's house and his subsequent disillusionment, shame, and decision to return. The father, having waited for the son's return, welcomes him with love; the character of the elder brother is used to highlight the ways in which the human family is divided by selfishness. Part 1 of the document states that reconciliation is primarily the gift and initiative of God and notes, briefly, Paul's conviction that Christ died for us while we were still sinners (Rom 5:8), that reconciliation has cosmic dimensions (Col 1:20), and that the message of reconciliation has been entrusted to "us," the Church (2 Cor 5:19). The document describes the Church as the sacrament of reconciliation, the effective sign of the reconciliation initiated by God and made manifest in Christ.[7] She is so by virtue of her existence as a reconciled community and by virtue of her reconciling mission, which she undertakes through preaching, attention to the word of God and to prayer, and the sacraments. Part 2 of the document deals with sin in some depth, characterizing it primarily in terms of disobedience, rupture, and exclusion of God, which leads to division "between brothers."[8] It covers the distinction between personal and social sin in some depth, arguing that sin is always personal and social only by analogy.[9] Part 3 of the document deals with the Church's means of reconciliation, covering dialogue, catechesis, and the sacraments, particularly the sacrament of reconciliation. The discussion of the Church's reconciling work in violent conflict is very brief and refers chiefly to the diplomatic work of the Holy See and bishops.[10]

What is noteworthy about the way in which the document deals with the theme of reconciliation? The introduction sets out to examine the situation of the world with "the gaze, anxious yet full of hope, of a pastor" and goes on immediately to diagnose the forms of division and alienation affecting the world.[11] This framework is typical of social teaching, but, together with the framework provided by the story of the prodigal son, it means that in spite of the document's emphasis on reconciliation as God's initiative, it actually begins with the fact of estrangement and the recognition of sin. Indeed, the document explicitly states that recognition of one's own sin is the first step in returning to God.[12] The document emphasizes the priority of "vertical" reconciliation, of human beings with God, over the horizontal reconciliation between persons that flows from it. It is worth noting, too, that although the initial discussion focuses on reconciliation between God and humanity in general, the document subsequently makes clear that sin is always personal and that the call for conversion is addressed fundamentally to individuals.[13] The progression of the document is from recognition of sin to longing for reconciliation, confession of fault to a merciful father, and reconciliation with God and others.

The basic structure of the document and its theological points of emphasis seem to be drawn more from the sacrament of reconciliation, in particular the form of individual private confession, than from engagement with the scriptural texts cited.[14] This emphasis on individual confession is also evident in the document's account of the Church's ministry of reconciliation. Although it states that the ministry of reconciliation is exercised by the whole Church, with the partial exception of the section on dialogue, the practical guidance given in the third section is focused on the activity of clergy. The document states that laypeople and clergy alike are entrusted with the message of reconciliation, but cate-chesis is discussed as being the task of pastors.[15] The lengthy section on the sacrament of reconciliation seems to be written principally for priests, with material on the character and formation of confessors and multiple references to "all of us priests"; the section as a whole also has a more technical and less pastoral tone than the rest of the document.[16] In *Reconciliatio et paenitentia*, the Church's ministry of reconciliation is largely conceived and discussed in sacerdotal terms.

What is the difficulty here? The tendency to think of the Church's ministry of reconciliation chiefly in terms of the role of its ordained ministers overlooks the more informal ministry of reconciliation as it is practiced by laypeople and Church organizations involved in grassroots peacebuilding, and the document misses the opportunity to develop a theology that speaks to their experience and supports them in their chal-lenges. The document's expansive understanding of the Church's mission of reconciliation is not matched by a similarly expansive understanding of the ways in which all the Church's members participate in that mis-sion. I argue later that closer attention to the relevant New Testament texts offers a much more expansive understanding of reconciliation as a ministry of the whole Church and that Catholic social teaching needs to develop a richer sense of what that means for laypeople.

Memory and Reconciliation (1999)

The second document to consider, *Memory and Reconciliation*, is not a magisterial document but is nevertheless instructive for our purposes here. It was commissioned by the then-president of the International Theological Commission, Cardinal Joseph Ratzinger, to deal with questions arising from John Paul II's calls in *Tertio millennio adveni-ente* for the "purification of memory" by confessing the past wrongs of the Church and his requests for forgiveness from various groups for the wrongs committed by Catholics in previous generations.[17] The focus of the document is thus strongly intraecclesial, and it does not discuss the Church's involvement in political truth and reconciliation processes.

Again, *Memory and Reconciliation* is interesting at least as much for what it does *not* say as for what it does say. In spite of the presence of "reconciliation" in the title, the document contains neither a definition of reconciliation nor any interaction whatsoever with the Pauline passages in which reconciliation is mentioned.[18] Instead, the concept is used loosely, and without specific theological content, to mean the end of enmity or antagonism between two parties based on confession of fault and forgiveness and a renewed relationship of friendship. More prominent in the document is the concept of the "purification of memory," which is explained as "eliminating from the personal and collective conscience all forms of resentment or violence left by the inheritance of the past, on the basis of a new and rigorous historical-theological judgement, which becomes the foundation for a renewed moral way of acting."[19]

Discussion of this purification process proceeds by way of a cautious analogy between the Church as a whole and an individual penitent—cautious because, as the document states, although the Church is a single subject, she is not a subject who sins.[20] We see here again an emphasis on the individual nature of sin, which is social only ever by analogy.[21] The document therefore clarifies that John Paul II's confession of faults on behalf of the Church is not a confession of subjective sinfulness, which can only apply to individuals, but a free association with the objective sin of Church members in preceding generations.[22] In other words, confessing the fault of the Church's members in the past does not mean that the Church as a whole or any of its present members are technically guilty of or responsible for these historical sins: it is an expression of solidarity, a way of acknowledging those sinful members as truly *belonging* to the Church rather than disowning them. All the same, the document stresses the need for careful discernment as to the subjective guilt of members in the past. Only "when there is moral certainty that what was done in contradiction to the Gospel in the name of the Church by certain of her sons and daughters could have been understood as such and avoided, can it have significance for the Church of today to make amends for the faults of the past."[23]

The document also reinforces a theological point not always clear in John Paul II's requests for forgiveness, namely, that such requests are addressed to God. God is the source of pardon; it is to God that the Church-penitent confesses her sin and from God that she asks forgiveness. The document expresses hope that this "purification of memory" will lead to renewed relationships with various groups and reciprocal acts of reconciliation from others where these are appropriate. However, this "horizontal" reconciliation seems to be envisaged largely as a hoped-for but by no means guaranteed fruit of "vertical" reconciliation: the primary focus is on the relationship between the Church-penitent, understood analogically as an individual, and God. The language of "purification of memory" is individual and introspective: this is about the Church purifying her own memory, and, in spite of some references to dialogue, there is no sense that those outside the Church might play a role in helping her recognize her past and present faults.[24]

Both *Reconciliatio et paenitentia* and *Memory and Reconciliation* demonstrate the ways in which recent Church teaching and reflection on reconciliation is shaped primarily by a sacramental and specifically confessional imaginary. This provides a natural bridge to the sacramental practice of reconciliation, and it also offers a potential bridge to the emphasis on open confession of wrongdoing that has characterized political truth and reconciliation processes, though neither document develops this link. In other respects, however, this sacramental focus leaves the Church's theology and practice of reconciliation with some significant limitations. When reconciliation is thought of first in "vertical" and individual terms as the individual's reconciliation with God, which then may or may not produce reconciliation on the "horizontal" and social level, it results in an essentially additive understanding of social reconciliation, as though a reconciled society is lots of individually reconciled people added together and relating together.[25] It is not clear that this makes good sociological sense, as we saw in chapter 5, and it is also not clear that this "additive" view of social reconciliation captures Paul's understanding of the relationship between God's initiative and our response. The individual confession paradigm, as noted above, also reorders the priorities in Paul's theology of reconciliation, which we will encounter in more detail in the next section.

Africae munus (2007)

Benedict XVI's *Africae munus* takes a significant step forward. This apostolic exhortation following the Second African Synod takes reconciliation, justice, and peace as its main themes. The Church in Africa is called to be salt and light, a witness and effective sign of reconciliation between human beings and God and between human beings them-selves.[26] As in *Reconciliatio et paenitentia*, there is a call to be reconciled to God and then to become ministers of reconciliation among people. Reconciliation is described early on as "not limited to God's plan to draw estranged and sinful humanity to himself in Christ through the forgiveness of sins and out of love. It is also the restoration of relation-ships through the settlement of differences and the removal of obstacles to their relationships in their experience of God's love."[27] The document cites the same Pauline texts as *Reconciliatio et paenitentia*, but there is more evidence that the theology of these texts shapes the conception of reconciliation in the document. While the document talks about the sacrament of reconciliation, for example, there is also a clear sense of the wider reconciling activity of the Church, along the lines of Ephe-sians: a call for the Church to exist as a reconciled body, transcending ethnic divisions, and thus to act as a witness of reconciliation to wider African society.[28]

Reconciliatio et paenitentia states that God initiates reconciliation, but this initiative of reconciliation is largely equated with the reconcil-ing presence and ministry of the Church, understood as God's objective work of reconciliation and the continuing offer of forgiveness.[29] In prac-tice, the document tends to treat repentance—approaching the reconcili-ation offered through the Church's ministry—as the "first move."[30] In *Africae munus*, the acknowledgment that reconciliation is God's initiative is better integrated: God's "discounting the sins of humanity" enables human beings to move past their differences and to grant and receive for-giveness.[31] The document talks about the power of the Spirit "to trans-form the hearts of victims and their persecutors" and about "granting and receiving forgiveness," allowing communities and families to find harmony.[32] This reflects closer dependence on scripture: Schreiter argues that Paul's understanding of reconciliation as God's initiative means that reconciliation begins with the victim in exactly this way.[33]

Africae munus also links the theme of reconciliation more closely to Catholic social teaching on peace. This is partly because the document clearly emerges from, and is addressed to, the particular and concrete situation of Africa; *Reconciliatio et paenitentia*, while more theologically systematic, is much more abstract. This means that the political is much more in view in *Africae munus*, in particular the relationship between the

Church and politics. The tensions between the spiritual and the political on the ground begin to emerge in the document itself.

Early on, the document claims that "reconciliation is a pre-political concept and a pre-political reality," thus establishing the Church's right to contribute to the conversation about reconciliation in Africa.[34] This statement is immediately followed by references to reconciliation being created "in people's hearts" and to striving for an "inner purification" and "inner development."[35] Later, the document states that "Christ does not propose a revolution of a social or political kind, but a revolution of love," even as it states that the Beatitudes "provide a new horizon of justice . . . through which we can become just and can build a better world."[36] As Katongole notes, the document as a whole is characterized by a distinction between the spiritual and political realms.[37] Even as the document calls for Christians to be "salt and light," transforming African culture from within, it repeatedly emphasizes that the Church's role is not political but spiritual.[38] The *instrumentum laboris* sheds light on the reason for this clear distinction between the political and the spiritual, commenting on the inappropriate involvement of bishops and priests in politics on a local and national level, which causes divisions in the Church, and the way that political figures can "use religion and religious institutions for their own purpose, while ignoring, among other things, the mission and function of religion and religious institutions in society."[39]

Interestingly, in *Africae munus* this caution about the distinction between the spiritual and political realms translates, to an extent, into a distinction between the clergy and the laity. Thus the document insists that bishops and priests do not "yield to the temptation of becoming political leaders or social agents" but exhorts laypeople to become involved courageously in political life.[40] The *instrumentum laboris* refers to the role of Church leaders in national reconciliation processes and in denouncing human rights abuses or electoral irregularities, but there is no mention of such borderline political activity in *Africae munus*, where references to transforming society and involvement in the political sphere apply to the laity only.[41]

The result is a tension between the document's vision of reconciliation, which includes a clear social and transformational dimension, and its caution about the Church's involvement in social and political life. As Katongole puts it, Benedict XVI "tries to walk a tightrope between a vision of reconciliation in its holistic and revolutionary dimension and a spiritual vision of reconciliation, based on the realization that the political realm lies outside the Church's competence."[42] Interviewed after the closing Mass of the synod, Benedict XVI spoke openly about this tension.

> The temptation could have been in politicizing the theme, to talk less about pastors and more about politicians, thus with a competence that is not ours. The other danger was—to avoid this temptation—pulling oneself into a purely spiritual world, in an abstract and beautiful world, but not a realistic one.[43]

This tension between the spiritual and political dimensions of reconciliation, Katongole argues, is never fully resolved, and in the end the document "pulls back from a dynamic vision of reconciliation as the basis of a new society in Africa."[44]

So while the concept of reconciliation holds much promise for Catholic social teaching, it is evident that some work is needed to realize its potential, especially for Catholic peacebuilding. In magisterial teaching as it stands, the tight connection between the concept of reconciliation and its sacramental form has limited the Church's imagination about what reconciliation is, who "does" it, and how. While the links between the theology of reconciliation and sacramental theology and ecclesiology are well developed, the links with Catholic social teaching are not as strong as they could be. *Africae munus* takes an important step forward, but it struggles with the tension between the spiritual and the political—a tension it tries to resolve, without much success, by appealing to the distinction between laity and clergy.

Part of the difficulty here is the fact that the concept of reconciliation is a relative latecomer to Catholic social teaching, and there is a lack of clarity in *Africae munus* about just what kind of a concept it is. In Catholic social teaching more widely, concepts like solidarity are more clearly deployed as natural law concepts: solidarity names a human duty that all people, regardless of their faith, can understand and a virtue for which all must strive. Communion, the corresponding theological concept, transposes solidarity into a theological and ecclesial key: Christians live communion because they are invited into the life of the Trinity. Reconciliation is described in *Africae munus* as a "pre-political concept and a pre-political reality," but the document draws on gospel texts rather than on natural law resources to expound its meaning. At the same time, political and international bodies have been using, and continue to use, the concept of reconciliation without any such theological meaning, and in this sense it is a sort of de facto natural law concept. *Africae munus* also reflects this reality, stating that reconciliation "is a task incumbent on government authorities and traditional chiefs, but also on ordinary citizens."[45]

It is possible, of course, for reconciliation to be used as both a natural law–type concept, applying to all people, and, in a deeper and richer theological sense, in relation to the Christian community, but the relationship between the two registers is not addressed, and key questions remain only half answered. Is reconciliation, following John Webster, a "shared task" that Christians simply engage in with more enthusiasm than others, or with a different motivation, or does the theological account of reconciliation mean that Christians contribute something distinctive?[46] *Reconciliatio et paenitentia* identifies the distinctively Christian practice of reconciliation in sacramental terms, and *Africae munus*, broadening the picture somewhat, suggests that Christians do indeed practice reconciliation in a distinctive way, shaped by God's word and by the sacraments and directed toward ecclesial communion and the realization of the kingdom at the end of time.[47] But what this particularly Christian practice of reconciliation looks like when pursued in the secular and political sphere—which the document assigns to laypeople—is less clear.[48]

Where to go from here? If the Catholic theology of reconciliation is currently somewhat boxed in by its sacramental form, then returning to scripture, and to the theology of reconciliation as it emerges in the letters of Paul and his school, may provide greater spaciousness. From the exploration of scripture in the next section, we can then explore how these might shape a vision of a distinctively Christian understanding of reconciliation and unpack how this relates to a Catholic theology and practice of active nonviolence.

RECONCILIATION IN PAUL

Reconciliation is one of the most important ways in which Paul talks about what God is doing in Christ, alongside other, perhaps more familiar tropes like redemption and sacrifice. The word usually translated as "reconciliation" (*katallasso* (verb); *katalage* (noun)) appears most often in the Pauline and Deutero-Pauline corpus, appearing in Romans, 2 Corinthians, Ephesians, and Colossians.[49] The root of the word means a change or exchange, and it is used to refer to situations in which the hostility between states, parties, or individuals is overcome and substituted for a relationship of peace, or acceptance into favor.[50] The concept of reconciliation is therefore social in origin, but Paul and his school use the word chiefly to refer to the relationship between God and creation. In Paul's hands, the concept of reconciliation describes a change from a situation of enmity and estrangement to one of peace and favor.[51] Paul argues that this exchange happens at God's initiative and that it occurs through the decisive events of the death and resurrection of Christ. In Paul's thought, the divine-human reconciliation thus achieved is cosmic and eschatological in scope, and it also has the present and concrete effect of breaking down division and enmity on the human level. Exploring these features in greater depth will help us gain a sense of the overall shape of Paul's theology of reconciliation.

Paul's statement, "While we were enemies, we were reconciled to God through the death of his son" (Rom 5:10), comes at the culmination of a long argument in the preceding chapters (Rom 1–5) in which he establishes why God's reconciling action was necessary. He begins by explaining that the relationship between God and human beings has become one of enmity. Enmity on the human side has consisted in willful disobedience to God (Rom 1:21, 1:28, 3:23), and Paul emphasizes that this is the case both for recipients of the law and for Gentiles (Rom 2:12). Being a recipient of God's law is no advantage or cause for boasting unless that law is kept, for only those who keep the law are righteous in God's sight (Rom 2:13). As it is, Paul insists, "There is no one who is righteous, not even one" (Rom 3:10), and "All have sinned and fallen short of the glory of God" (Rom 3:23). All human beings therefore stand in a relationship of enmity to and estrangement from God and are also absolutely unable to justify themselves, because they are held in the power of sin (Rom 3:9). On God's side the enmity consists in God's righteousness, which includes his judgment on human disobedience: the death to which all are subject because of sin (Rom 5:12). God's wrath is mentioned on a number of occasions (Rom 1:18, 3:5, 5:9), but the emphasis for Paul falls on the incompatibility of human sin and disobedience with God's rule rather than on God's being offended and bearing a disposition of anger toward human beings. This is consistent with Paul's emphasis that God is the author, rather than the recipient, of reconciliation.[52]

This brings us to a key point in Paul's theology of reconciliation, which I want to foreground in what follows: reconciliation is God's initiative. I have already noted the point of the cumulative argument of the first four chapters of the letter to the Romans, namely, that no one, neither Jew nor Gentile, is able to justify themselves in God's sight. Abraham was justified not by works but solely by his faith in God's gracious acting on his behalf, which was reckoned to him as righteousness (Rom 4:3, 22). The apex of the argument then comes in chapter 5, in which Paul states that *while we were still weak*, Christ died for us, the *ungodly* (Rom 5:6). The point is repeated more emphatically each time: "God proved his love for us in that *while we were still sinners*, Christ died for us" (Rom 5:8); and "*while we were enemies*, we were reconciled to God through the death of his son" (Rom 5:10). In the face of our absolute inability to justify ourselves, our faith in God's gracious and unilateral action on our behalf (Rom 4:5) is reckoned to us as righteousness (Rom 4:24). The whole argument of Romans 1–5 builds up to this confession of God as the sole agent of reconciliation and the death and resurrection of Christ as the event by which it occurs.

What does it mean for Paul to say that reconciliation occurs through the death and resurrection of Christ? Sometimes Paul connects the theme of reconciliation with the theme of sacrifice: Jesus is put forward "as a sacrifice of atonement by his blood" (Rom 3:25), and we are justified "by his blood" (Rom 5:9). Often, this language has been understood as implying a tight link between the concept of reconciliation and the concept of sacrifice, namely, that reconciliation is possible because the sacrificial death of Christ assuages God's wrath against the disobedience of sinners. Such a reading, however, risks oversystematizing the different modes in which Paul talks about the saving significance of the death and resurrection of Christ. The concept of reconciliation is social in origin, as I have already shown, and while I have also noted that Paul adopts the term to refer to the relationship between God and human beings, there is no need on this account to collapse the social metaphor of reconciliation into the cultic metaphor of sacrifice.[53] Perhaps more importantly, such a move also has the disadvantage of placing too exclusive an emphasis on the death of Christ as the precise locus in which reconciliation occurs, when for Paul, Christ's resurrection is a point of equal emphasis: he states that we are justified by Jesus's blood (Rom 5:9) but also that Jesus is raised "for our justification" (Rom 4:25). Christ's being laid in the grave and his being raised from it are both movements belonging to the one reconciling action of God; likewise, our being reconciled to God consists both in being united with Jesus in his death (Rom 6:3–5), and sharing in his resurrection (Rom 6:5). Our being reconciled does not just consist in our identifying with Jesus in his death, understood as the event in which the Father exhausts his wrath against humanity; our being reconciled also consists in an ongoing identification with the risen life of Jesus: "So you also must consider yourselves dead to sin and alive to God in Christ Jesus" (Rom 6:11). We are baptized into the death of Christ, so that, "just as Christ was raised from the dead by the glory of the Father, so we too might walk in newness of life" (Rom 6:4). Paul associates this walking in newness of life with the life of the Spirit (Rom 6:6; 8:2–17).

It is worth drawing out two points here. First, as Christoph Schwöbel puts it, reconciliation language in Paul "refers both to an event in the past and to an enduring relationship in the present, which is claimed to be eschatologically ultimate."[54] Reconciliation is therefore not a discrete, onetime event in the life of a believer but an ongoing relationship with the living Christ made possible by the work of the Spirit through which the love of God is poured into our hearts (Rom 5:5). Thus, Paul's appeal to the Corinthians to "be reconciled to God" (2 Cor 5:20) is consistent with his pleas that they live righteous lives: being reconciled signifies a way of life. Second, in this context of this overarching theological movement from death to resurrection, Paul's repeated references to blood and death have the effect not just of recalling sacrifice imagery but also of drawing attention to the *concreteness* of the events to which he is referring, and to the concrete change that these events must therefore effect in us. The author of Colossians, adopting what appears to be an early Christological hymn, seems to insert a reference to the "blood of the cross" and links the reconciliation of those "once estranged and hostile in mind, doing evil deeds" with the "fleshly body" of Christ (Col 1:21–2).[55]

This emphasis on the fleshly body of Christ brings me to the last point of emphasis in Paul's theology of reconciliation: the link between the reconciliation between God and human beings and reconciliation between human beings. On both a practical and a theological level, Paul was preoccupied by the relationship between Jewish and Gentile Christians and by the relationship between the Law (and the chosen people) and what God was doing in Christ. Understanding how Paul approaches Jewish-Gentile relations in particular is therefore key to understanding what he is saying about reconciliation between human beings more generally. Put simply, when Paul refers to the Law negatively, he is using it as *symbolic of division.* The Law divides the chosen people from those outside the covenant, both on a symbolic level and on a practical level. James Dunn argues that Paul's preoccupation with the "works of the Law," particularly in Romans and Galatians, should be understood in a social and historical context in which certain "works," in particular food laws, circumcision, and observance of special days and feasts, had become the key markers of distinctively Jewish identity and therefore of belonging to the covenant.[56] When Paul attacks boasting in the Law (Rom 2:23) or in "works," he is not attacking the Law per se, or external actions, but what Dunn calls "covenantal nomism"—the idea that God's grace extends only to those who wear the "badge" of the covenant, narrowly understood as the observance of certain practices.[57] What Paul is arguing against is an ethnonationalist mentality that would restrict the grace of God to the nation of Israel, when the covenant offered to Abraham included the promise that *all* the nations would be blessed through him. As Dunn puts it, Paul is attacking not activism but nationalism.[58] Paul therefore holds up Abraham's *faith in God* rather than works, the Law or membership of the chosen people, as what counted as justifying him. What justifies us, Paul says, is faith in the God who raises Jesus from death (Rom 4:24–25). So where Law and works are symbolic of division, sin and grace are levelers: nobody is righteous in the sight of God (Rom 3:23), and anyone can be justified through faith in Christ.

In Ephesians, Paul pursues a similar argument, using bodies as a way of expressing the meaning of the reconciliation achieved in Christ's death and resurrection. Before Christ, bodies were symbolic of distance and division: the literally uncircumcised Gentiles were distant from God, "strangers to the covenants of promise, having no hope and without God in the world," and they are also "aliens from the commonwealth of Israel" (Eph 1:12). He then goes on to claim that "in his flesh" Christ has "made both groups into one and broken down the dividing wall, that is, the hostility between us" (Eph 1:14). Jesus's death on the cross "puts to death the hostility" (Eph 1:16) and makes possible "one new humanity in place of the two" (Eph 1:15). Again, note that what dies is not "Israel" or "the Law" but *division and hostility itself:* hostile division between two groups is overcome in Jesus's single body. In Galatians, in which Paul returns to the themes of Romans explored above—and in which bodies are also very much in view—this overcoming of hostility is widened still further: "There is no longer Jew or Greek, there is no longer slave or free, there is no longer male and female; for all of you are one in Christ Jesus" (Gal 3:28).

Two things should be emphasized here. First, Paul's theology of reconciliation has very clear implications for the Church, in which it must be concretely obvious that, for those in Christ, hostility is dead and divisions are overcome. This is more than obvious from both Paul's letters and the Acts of the Apostles, in which we see repeated wrangling about the relationships between Jewish and Gentile Christians. To Paul's mind, where there are divisions within the Christian communities as a result of ethnonational identities taking precedence over unity in Christ, the gospel has simply not been understood. Second, although the Church's embodiment of unity in Christ is indispensable and nonnegotiable, it is only part of the picture. It needs setting in both eschatological and cosmic perspectives. The concept of reconciliation also includes eschatological hope. Paul expresses its significance in the future tense: "justified by the blood of Christ, we *will* be saved from the wrath of God" (Rom 5:9), and "having been reconciled, we *will* be saved by his life" (Rom 5:10). This hope for the fullness of salvation includes the hope of being united with Christ in a resurrection like his (Rom 6:5). Importantly, it also includes hope for the renewal of the whole of creation, which has been "groaning in labor pains until now" (Rom 8:19–25).[59] Dunn reinforces the same point in connection with the Christ hymn in Colossians, which states that in Christ "God was pleased to reconcile to himself all things" (Col 1:20): here *ta panta,* "all things," implies a reconciliation that is not restricted to human creation alone but cosmic in its scope and implications.[60]

I argued earlier that Church teaching on reconciliation is shaped by a sacramental imaginary and by a specifically confessional imaginary. Like any lens, it has its uses: it focuses the broad theme of reconciliation into a narrow and practical point, namely, how it takes shape in the sacramental ministry of the Church. But, like any lens, it also narrows the theology of reconciliation as we encounter it in Paul and in some cases significantly reshapes his priorities. In the next section, I want to broaden the focus of the Church's theology of reconciliation, starting from the key points of Paul's theology as I have just outlined it. I draw out three areas— reconciliation as God's initiative, as cosmic and eschatological in scope, and as overcoming human boundaries—and unpack their significance for a Catholic theology and practice of active nonviolence.

GOD'S INITIATIVE

Paul insists that reconciliation is God's initiative, extended to us while we are helpless in our sins and utterly unable to justify ourselves. Reconciliation means God not counting our sins against us and instead holding out to us the free gift of justification in Jesus. In light of this gift of reconciliation, we are called to live reconciled lives; in light of this free gift, utterly unearned, we are called to let go of the old human boundaries that divided those deserving of grace from those undeserving of grace.

Reconciliatio et paenitentia states, "This initiative on God's part is made concrete and manifest in the redemptive act of Christ, which radiates through the world by means of the ministry of the Church."[61] Early on, John Paul II identifies the Church's gaze on the world with the gaze "anxious, yet full of hope" of the pastor: the Church is identified with the father who stands waiting for the prodigal son, and, practically speaking, the document chiefly has in view fathers—priests—and their ministry of reconciliation through preaching, catechesis, and the sacraments. In *Reconciliatio et paenitentia*, the Church is a minister of reconciliation in that she stands ready, making available the offer of God's reconciliation through the sacraments: God's initiative is identified with the Church's continual offer of mercy. If we were to choose an image to represent this understanding of the Church's ministry of reconciliation, it might be a water tank—an objective structure, standing ready to offer grace to those who approach it. God's initiative is identified with the ministry of the Church, and the Church is a sort of container and conduit of reconciliation.

If "container" is the best image to explain how Church teaching understands the relationship between God's initiative of reconciliation and the Church's ministry, then the best image to capture its understanding of the relationship between God's initiative and our response is perhaps "cellular." *Memory and Reconciliation* distinguishes between vertical and individual reconciliation with God and horizontal reconciliation with others. Vertical reconciliation enables horizontal reconciliation, and many vertically reconciled individuals add up to a horizontally reconciled community, society, and world. That document conceives vertical reconciliation in individual and introspective terms, and it may or may not effect reconciliation on a horizontal level. Imaginatively, we are in the confessional here: examining our conscience, confessing fault to God, being vertically reconciled, and then going out to be reconciled horizontally with those whom we have wronged. Thus we might envision the relationship between individual and social change as cellular: as each individual cell is transformed, so eventually is the whole organism.

These images have their uses, but they need to be broadened and complemented by others that perhaps better capture the dynamic of reconciliation as Paul understands it. Here, I want to draw on the image of breathing. We usually think of breathing as something we do actively: we draw air in through the mouth and nose, and the chest expands. Physiologically, in fact, it happens the other way around: the intercostal muscles expand the rib cage, the diaphragm draws downward, and the resulting negative pressure draws air in through the mouth and nose. This image is closer to the relationship between God's initiative and our response as Paul understands it. It is our being expanded by the discovery of grace that draws others into the space of reconciliation. The first move—reconciling us while we are still in sin—is all God's, and recognition of grace received, not recognition of sin, is our human starting point. Breathing, which seems like our activity, is in fact passive and simply *will* happen if we do not hinder it by holding our breath or blocking our airway. In the same way, it is the nature of grace to flow because it is the nature of God to give, and reconciliation—the grace and forgiveness of God—can and will flow to others if we do not hinder it.[62] This image gives us two principles: first, our action in response to God's initiative is perhaps best characterized in terms of corresponding or, better still, not getting in the way; and second, it is the nature of reconciliation to flow, and reconciliation has to flow through us. Just as we cannot oxygenate our bloodstream if we hold our breath or obstruct the flow of air to our lungs, we cannot be ministers of reconciliation if we are not part of the flow of God's reconciling grace, which must transform us—both personally and ecclesially—in order to reach others. This gives us two leads to pursue, one about the ministry of reconciliation and one about reconciliation and nonviolence.

The Ministry of Reconciliation: "Not Hindering"

The metaphor of breathing, I have suggested, gives us a helpful image of the relationship between God's initiative and our response: our being expanded by grace draws others into the space of reconciliation. The initiative is God's, whose freely given grace will flow through us to others if we do not hinder it. In the narratives of Acts, the incorporation of Gentile Christians into the early Church—one of the concrete issues Paul is wrestling with in some of the texts explored earlier—is framed in just these terms, as "not hindering God."[63] In the account of Peter's vision in the house of Simon the Tanner (Acts 10), God makes the first move, telling Peter, "What God has made clean, you must not call profane" (10:15). As Peter is recounting this to Cornelius, the Holy Spirit comes upon all his listeners in what is clearly presented as a second, Gentile, Pentecost. Once again, the emphasis falls on God's initiative in giving the Holy Spirit before these Gentiles have even received the baptism of water (10:44). As the Holy Spirit has ignored the boundary, Peter follows suit: "Can anyone withhold the water for baptizing these people, who have received the Holy Spirit just as we have?" (10:47). When Peter arrives in Jerusalem he tells the brethren, "If then God gave them the same gift that he gave us when we believed in the Lord Jesus Christ, who was I that I could hinder God?" (11:17). "Not hindering God" is perhaps the best way of characterizing human action in response to God's initiative of reconciliation. God has not made a distinction, and therefore the Holy Spirit tells Peter (11:12) and the Christian community (15:9) not to make any distinction. God leads, and human beings follow by getting out of the way, or "not hindering," the flow of God's grace. This is the equivalent of Paul's "not counting" of sins in 2 Corinthians 5:19, where he states that God's reconciliation takes the form of "not counting" our sins against us—a ministry of reconciliation that is then handed on to us. Our being reconciled with God and with one another takes the form of a responsive letting-go, an open-handedness with mercy received.

I develop this understanding of the ministry of reconciliation below, but it is worth noting that there are implications for the "who" of ministry here. In Acts 11, the Spirit even overflows the distinction between those present at the original Pentecost event, and those Gentiles who are given the same Spirit later on: the same Spirit is given to both (11:17; see also 15:8). If we look at these passages expecting to find in them some understanding of the apostles' distinctive role in the ministry of reconciliation, we have to admit that the emphasis falls on the apostles' *response* to God's initiative of reconciliation rather more than their mediation or dispensing of it. Peter's role in admitting Cornelius and his family to baptism is framed, in minimalist terms, as "not hindering": the apostles are basically playing catch-up and describe their own activity and decision making in these terms. While these are certainly not the only passages to which we might look for an understanding of the role of the ordained in reconciliation, there is little here to support the idea that the Church's ministry of reconciliation is concentrated in the ordained priesthood, though we can certainly recognize that it appears in a distinctive way there.[64] Rather, the whole thrust of these passages is toward overcoming any sense of an "inner circle" and an "outer circle" within the Christian community with regard to who receives, manifests, and ministers the reconciliation that God has achieved in Christ. The ministry of reconciliation, understood as not hindering, belongs to the whole Church.

Reconciliation and Active Nonviolence

One of the things the image of breathing and flow highlights is the intrinsic relationship between means and end in God's work of reconciliation. The end is the reconciliation of all creation in Christ (Col 1:20–21; Eph 1:10), and the means is reconciliation (2 Cor 5:18–20), which includes the overcoming of the boundary between human beings and God created by our sin (Rom 5:10) and the overcoming of human boundaries to God's reconciling work, which now in Christ is extended to all people (Rom 5:15; Eph 1:14; Gal 3:28). God's overcoming sin and division happens by sin and division being overcome in us; the new creation includes our concrete transformation and renewal. And as *Reconciliatio et paenitentia* puts it, the Church does not just *have* the means of reconciliation, but she *is* a means of reconciliation, a means to the end that is the reconciliation of all things in Christ. I want to argue that this intrinsic connection between means and ends in the theology of reconciliation means that the Church's practice of reconciliation is necessarily one of active nonviolence.

This may seem like stating the obvious—violent reconciliation, after all, sounds like an oxymoron—but in what follows I want to show how it is rooted in Paul's theology of reconciliation, which deepens both what I mean by "nonviolent" and what I mean by "active." Here, let me unpack just one implication: the Church's practice of reconciliation involves the spiritual and practical challenge of "loving first." At the heart of Paul's argument in Romans is the claim that God acts unilaterally to reconcile us through the death of his son while we were still weak (Rom 5:6), while we were still sinners (5:8), and while we were enemies (5:10). The first move is not our repentance but God's "not counting" our sin against us and acting to reconcile us to himself. Our response is to "be reconciled" to God, to live renewed lives, and to be ministers of reconciliation. This ministry of reconciliation, I have argued, means not hindering the flow of grace to others. The ministry of reconciliation also means, like God, being willing to love first.

One of the legacies of violent conflict is deeply divided communities, something especially apparent in contemporary intrastate conflicts. In situations like post-genocide Rwanda, survivors have had to live in close proximity to those known or suspected to have participated in the killings or in close proximity to their families. In Uganda, former child soldiers with the Lord's Resistance Army are often rejected by the villages from which they were abducted; in Colombia, too, efforts to reintegrate demobilized guerrillas in local communities often meet with significant difficulties, as those who have suffered from violence reject those they see as perpetrators. In Guatemala, the army recruited and frequently compelled members of indigenous communities to participate in the repression and massacre of their own people.[65] Long after the direct violence has subsided, communities like these are often enduringly divided by a lack of justice, by mutual recriminations, by suspicion, or by a silence that refuses any discussion of what occurred and who was responsible.[66] No reconciliation can occur until the truth of what happened has been established and there has been a confession of culpability.

In such situations, the Church has sometimes been an important witness to truth, on both a local and a national level. In Guatemala, for instance, local pastors were sometimes able to resist the silence surrounding massacres and disappearances by compiling the names of the dead.[67] During the repression in El Salvador, Óscar Romero read out the names of the disappeared each week on a radio program that was broadcast nationally. But in addition to calling for the truth, Paul's theology of reconciliation suggests that the Church's practice of reconciliation must involve a willingness to love first. Schreiter argues:

> An important corollary flows from this insight that God takes the initiative, that reconciliation is something that we discover rather than achieve. This insight reverses a moment in the process of reconciliation that we usually expect. We expect that evildoers should repent and so seek forgiveness, that those who have wreaked terror and oppression on a society should see the wrongness of their ways and engage in repentance and reparation. However, in the Christian understanding of reconciliation, it works the other way around. We discover and experience God's forgiveness of our trespasses, and this prompts us to repentance. In the reconciliation process, then, because the victim has been brought by God's reconciling grace to forgive the tormentor, the tormentor is prompted to repent of evildoing and to engage in rebuilding his or her own humanity.[68]

This is profoundly challenging, but it is a clear implication of Paul's theology of reconciliation. There is not space here to explore all the issues raised, but let me make two points.

First, on a practical level, loving first and pursuing justice often proceed in difficult tension with one another, but to say that Christians must be willing to love first is not to say that the demands of justice should be abandoned, still less that Christians should uncritically support blanket amnesties where these are proposed in exchange for truth or to encourage a community to "move past" violence.[69] For the grace of forgiveness to appear as such, there must be some recognition of its being undeserved, and therefore some recognition of sin, even if this does not come first as a confession of guilt. As a practice of active nonviolence, loving first can still hold evildoers fast to what they have become, even as it releases them by "not counting" it.[70] A small vignette, recorded by Bernard Noel Rutikanga, serves to illuminate this point. Father George, a Tutsi and a Roman Catholic priest, escaped the genocide in Rwanda and, some time later, was engaged in pastoral work in prisons. There, a prisoner to whom he had given some secondhand clothing insisted on speaking with him.

> "Father, I would like to tell you something which has been heavy on my heart since you started working with us. It pains me to see you working for our comfort while some of my colleagues here and I killed your mother, taking everything from her house, including the clothes on her body." The prisoner started to cry, and Fr George became like someone who has been struck by lightning.[71]

Father George's practical loving first, in the context of justice, enabled the man to confess his guilt, to seek forgiveness, and eventually to be reconciled with the man whose mother he had killed. In this connection, the second point is that reconciliation is a journey, eschatologically long, and forgiveness is a process—one with which we may not be finished during our lifetime. Though pursuing Paul's vision of reconciliation may mean calling Christians to love first, it also means recognizing that this love must flow: it cannot be forced, nor, ultimately, can it be legislated. The grace of reconciliation works on fragile human nature, and the transformation it works must happen at a human pace or not at all.

Loving first, understood as part of a Christian practice of reconciliation, can also take more institutional forms. Especially in contexts of conflict where communities are divided along religious lines, offering services like healthcare and education to all without discrimination is a concrete way of loving first and can be an effective way of peacebuilding. Especially in contexts where state provision is weak or absent, such services can be important ways of proclaiming, defending, and upholding human dignity. They can also be expressions of the dynamic of gratuity we see at work in the theology of reconciliation: practical love extended to others across boundaries of alienation, mistrust, or enmity, which can transcend and even overcome those boundaries over time. It is important not to be romantic about this: great risk and personal cost may be involved. And, for example, schools that educate Christian and Hindu children side by side or clinics that treat the local majority Muslim population as much as the Christian minority do not necessarily build relationships across boundaries or encourage reconciliation.[72] But equally, it is important not to instrumentalize the peacebuilding potential of such institutions or treat them as mere sideshows in the Church's life. In his 2017 Message for the World Day of Peace, Pope Francis quotes Benedict XVI's insistence that nonviolence "is realistic because it takes into account that in the world there is *too much* violence, *too much* injustice, and therefore that this situation cannot be overcome except by countering it with *more* love, with *more* goodness. This '*more*' comes from God."[73] He went on to stress that "for Christians, nonviolence is not merely tactical behaviour but a person's way of being, the attitude of one who is *so convinced of God's love and power* that he or she is not afraid to tackle evil with the weapons of love and truth alone."[74] Institutional ways in which the Church offers "more love" and "more goodness" are part of her ministry of reconciliation, and they can be part of a realistic and effective practice of peacebuilding through active nonviolence.

COSMIC SCOPE

I have argued that for Paul there is an intrinsic relationship between our being reconciled and our reconciling, which I described using the image of breathing and flow: being reconciled is how we reconcile. This obtains on an individual as well as a communal level: for Paul, the church manifests and ministers the reconciling grace of God by its existence as a reconciled community, which includes both living a new life in the Spirit and transcending existing human boundaries of race, nation, sex, and social status (Gal 3:28). The church exists as a concrete sign of the new creation that God has inaugurated in Christ (2 Cor 5:17–20).[75] But at the same time, God's work of reconciling and renewing is not identical with the Church or confined to it. God's work of reconciliation involves the concrete transformation of us as individuals and as communities, but its ultimate horizon is cosmic and eschatological.

It is characteristic of Catholic theology to take a both-and approach, emphasizing both the free gift of grace and the necessity of our concrete transformation. Salvation is not just something given to the creature from without but also something grown into and merited, grace that becomes bone of our bone and flesh of our flesh. Our becoming a new creation is *real*, and transformation must begin now, even as it extends beyond the bounds of our earthly life. In the context of a Catholic theology of reconciliation, this means that we have to hold together both the cosmic scope of reconciliation and its human scale. On the one hand, we have to say that God's plan for the fullness of time is the uniting of all things in Christ (Eph 1:10), the reconciliation of all things (Col 1:20), and that this will involve real and profound transformation. On the other hand, we have to account for the way in which the cosmic scope of God's activity takes place in an eschatological time frame and at a human scale and pace. We need to hold together the limitless demand that we be reconciled to God and to one another in the concrete circumstances of our lives, and the reality of our incapacity and frailty. Our best progress, as well as our failure, needs healing and completing in Christ. This is not just a practical point, but a theological one: our nature, frailty, and limitations are comprehended in God's "plan for the fullness of time," and the cosmic scope and human scale of reconciliation are not in tension with one another.

As might be expected, the Catholic theology of reconciliation as it stands deals with this "gap" using a framework drawn from sacramental theology. The Church is a sacrament of reconciliation and called to be a living sign of what she proclaims. The distance, as it were, between her reconciling ministry and her being reconciled is discussed in terms of the distance between the objective truthfulness of the Church's proclamation and the effectiveness of the Church's sacramental ministry and her appearance as a "concrete living witness" to reconciliation.[76] This is even clearer in *Memory and Reconciliation*, which discusses the distance between the Church's objective holiness, grounded in Christ, and her subjective holiness as she appears to the world.[77] But here I want to move away from the sacramental logic of reality and sign, substance and accident, and talk about the gap in terms of "now" and "not yet."

I quoted earlier Schwöbel's description of reconciliation in Paul as simultaneously an event in the past, an enduring relationship in the present, and an eschatologically ultimate future. Reconciliation is something God has decisively done in Christ, something God is doing—particularly but not exclusively in the Church—and something that God will bring to completion in the eschatological future. This allows us to talk about genuine growth and progress in reconciliation: even now the Spirit of God is concretely at work in human communities, and the renewed relationships that emerge, even falteringly, are truly part of God's renewal of all things. The connection is direct, but it is also mystical: the kingdom of God does not progress like the installation of new software but rather in a mysterious, hidden way, like a seed growing secretly. So while we can speak of and work for the growth and progress of reconciliation, and believe in the certainty of its eventual triumph, we need to remain somewhat agnostic about how that progress happens and what it looks like. The reconciliation of all things in Christ is not just a known we are working toward but have not yet achieved but also an unknown breaking in whose appearance we must attentively discern.

What does this mean for a Catholic practice of active nonviolence? I want to draw out two points: timing and discernment and effective eschatological imagination. Below I discuss each in turn.

Timing and Discernment

Drawing from a range of case studies of Christian peacebuilding, Cejka and Bamat offer a typology of nonviolent peacebuilding activities spanning the conflict cycle, from ongoing or preventive initiatives (prayer services, demonstrations for peace) through various activities carried out during violent conflict (warning, sheltering, accompanying), longer-term initiatives (mediation, relationship building), and postviolence initiatives (memorializing, pursuing justice). Commenting on this typology, Cejka and Bamat state:

> Faith communities must be able to read the signs of the times. They must have a reasonably good analysis of social conditions and the ways in which power is exercised within and upon a given context. They must also have a sense of *timing*. They should know when they can take preventative action, when mediation may be fruitful, and when it is time to witness to past atrocities or focus on rebuilding broken relationships.[78]

Time and intensity, they note, "tend to frame and structure the realm of the possible."[79] Above, I argued that God's initiative of reconciliation is cosmic in scope and that the call to be reconciled to God and to one another demands our complete transformation, but the scale here is human: this call comes to us "in the realm of the possible." Sometimes it will be time for acting, risking, demanding more of ourselves and others; sometimes it will be time for grieving, withdrawing, regrouping. The key questions are, "What does God's work of reconciliation ask of us now?" and "At this moment, with its particular opportunities and limitations, where and how can we work for transformation that will be deep and real?" Depth and reality of transformation take time and cannot be forced, and they are the only way to sustainable peace.

Against a view of nonviolence as a fatalistic or passive attitude toward conflict, I have emphasized that active nonviolence is both realistic and effective. It is realistic in a theological sense in that it is "God's work in God's way," and therefore corresponds to the ultimate end of creation and its deepest reality, and realistic also in the practical sense of being "in the realm of the possible," even though it is often difficult and costly. It can also be an effective response to violent conflict and an effective approach to sustainable peacebuilding. From a Catholic perspective, the effectiveness of active nonviolence is also a matter of faith. Sometimes its effectiveness will be evident and measurable on a human time scale, but often the picture will be mixed: conflict ebbs and flows and changes shape, and even what seems like solid progress can be undone in an instant conflagration. In such contexts, the eschatological framework just explored helps Catholic peacebuilders keep in view a belief in the mystical effectiveness of nonviolent action. The "more love," "more goodness," of which Benedict XVI writes may not appear to have the upper hand, but our belief in its final triumph allows us to act consistently in the faith that this "more" is what ultimately endures, while "all the footgear of battle, every cloak rolled in blood will be burnt as fuel for the fire" (Is 9:5).

Effective Eschatological Imagination

Exploring the theology of reconciliation as a resource for a Catholic practice of active nonviolence is not about getting the right theory lined up behind our practice but about cultivating a moral imagination that can initiate, structure, and support faithful action. Lederach argues that the ability to transcend violence while still living in it "is forged by the capacity to generate, mobilize, and build the moral imagination," and he goes on to list four disciplines or capacities he regards as essential, the first of which is "the capacity to imagine ourselves in a web of relationships that includes our enemies."[80] If we believe that the ultimate horizon of reconciliation is cosmic and eschatological, then this places us in a web of reconciled relationships that includes all that exists; proximately and concretely, it places me in a web of relationships that includes my enemies. This is more than a matter of recognizing our de facto interdependence with those with whom we are in conflict: it is a profession of faith that my peace is bound up with their peace, my flourishing with their flourishing.

This helps us with one of the questions noted earlier, where I drew attention to the fact that in *Africae munus* it is not clear what kind of a concept reconciliation is. Over time, concepts like solidarity have become part of a somewhat clearer theological framework: the basic fact is human interdependence, and the corresponding virtue is solidarity, which is transposed into a theological key as communion and has its end in our participation in the life of the Trinity. Reconciliation is used much more loosely, to describe both a general human duty and a specifically Christian task. Though the "bilingualism" of the concept of reconciliation—its use in the register of both natural law and gospel—is not necessarily a problem, and can be an advantage, Paul's theology of reconciliation can help us introduce some helpful distinctions here. His conviction about the cosmic scope of reconciliation—*ta panta*, "all things"—indicates that the basic fact of natural law that we have in view is the fact of *our common humanity in a common home*. The ultimate end of reconciliation is not just human communion with the Trinity, but a new creation (2 Cor 5:17–19). Both *Reconciliatio et paenitentia* and, more recently and fully, *Laudato sí* recognize that reconciliation also involves nonhuman creation.[81] The virtue that corresponds to this fact is perhaps best described in terms of fraternity and mutuality. More than friendship, fraternity involves a recognition of common origin, of the fact of relationship and of the fact of shared space—a common home. Where fraternity and mutuality have been damaged, there is a duty of reconciliation, meaning here the end of enmity and the restoration of relationships of mutual respect and the recognition of interdependence. Transposed into a theological key, the call to reconciliation includes not only restoring fraternity and mutuality on the level of creation but also reconciliation with God and inclusion in the Father's "household" (Eph 1:19). Its ultimate horizon is the new creation and the unity in Christ of all things in heaven and on earth.

Thomas Aquinas, in his commentary on 1 Timothy, refers to the Church's peace as intermediate between the peace of the world and the final peace of the kingdom.[82] The author of Colossians, similarly, places the Church midway between the two poles of common humanity and common home and the reconciliation of all things in Christ. All things are created in Christ and for Christ, and all things "hold together" in him; he is the "first born" of the dead—the firstborn of the new creation—and "the head of the body, the church"; and all things will be finally reconciled to God in him (Col 1:15–20). The question is *how* the Church lives between these two poles, and here I want to suggest that reconciliation adds something to the concept of communion and helps specify it further. In *Reconciliatio et paenitentia* the two overlap considerably, such that the call to reconciliation is effectively a call to repent and return to the communion of the Church.[83] The cosmic and eschatological horizon of reconciliation encourages us to stretch this further. The ministry of reconciliation the Church is called to exercise is not ultimately turned inward, directed to the upbuilding of the Church as a kind of oasis or island of reconciliation. Rather, the Church is called to live proleptically out of the final reconciliation of *all* things, and its ministry of reconciliation means acting as a catalyst of reconciliation beyond the bounds of ecclesial communion.

OVERCOMING HUMAN BOUNDARIES

This brings us to the final point in Paul's theology of reconciliation that I want to explore: his belief that God's work of reconciliation in Christ involves overcoming human boundaries. Earlier, I described the ministry of reconciliation in terms of not hindering, and here I want to make the connection between the ministry of reconciliation so understood and the very existence of the Church. The particular letting-go and not-hindering that constitutes the Church at its roots has to do with the overcoming of established human boundaries, whereby one group is chosen and favored and has access to God and another is "excluded," "alienated," "without hope and without God" (Eph 2:12). Paul is not attacking covenant, nor is he attacking the particular works he names—circumcision, food laws, and so on—as practices of fidelity to the Law or the covenant, both of which he understands as blessings for the world. What he is attacking are human practices, even and perhaps especially religiously mandated ones, that are weaponized to create an identity over against and superior to another, with which God is identified, and to which grace is believed to be restricted. In Paul's ministry, the boundary in question is that between the covenant people, the Jews, and the Gentiles: God's grace, Paul argues, has overflowed this boundary, and we must not hinder God by demanding that Gentiles keep the Law. But note here that what is overcome in Jesus is not just a particular boundary (Jew-Gentile) and a particular set of requirements (the Law), but the *whole idea of God's grace being restricted to a particular group simply by virtue of its being a particular group* (Gal 3:27–29). What is overcome in Jesus is any such boundary to the grace of God, which will flow as far as we will let it. This "letting go" of the covenant boundary is what it means for the Jewish people to become a blessing to the nations: they are indeed chosen, but their being chosen does not preclude others from also being called.[84]

In Dunn's terms, what Paul denies is not activism but nationalism—not individual or social practices per se but the use of those practices to create and reinforce identity-by-division and to exclude from the saving action of God those designated as "outside."[85] As Paul understands it, the whole shape of God's saving action is overcoming boundaries of enmity, between sinners and God and between Jew and Gentile. Reconciliation, then, is what creates the Church; or, to put it another way, the Church's whole being is founded on the overcoming of boundaries—and not just the boundary between Jew and Gentile, but the overcoming of any humanly bounded grace. The Church comes into being not as a new "super-group" to which grace is then restricted but *in* the action of overcoming. Now nothing is counted (2 Cor 5:19) except Abraham's faith, which is what counted as justifying him (Rom 4:3). For the purposes of this chapter, this is where I want to place the emphasis: what is important is not just that the Church comes into being as a new social body in which existing social differences are transcended, but *how* this comes about. The mere fact of transcending differences to unite around a single new cause is not enough, because it can trade in the same kind of religious identity politics: Catholic and Orthodox communities, for example, historically in conflict, can unite around the demonization and exclusion of Muslim immigrants. If some human differences are transcended but a hard boundary to grace remains, then this is not true reconciliation. A genuine response to God's reconciling initiative does not ask, "How far does it extend?," but recognizes that it is intrinsically limitless.[86]

Resisting Division

I have argued that the Church's founding grace has to do with the overcoming of boundaries that create a people "alienated," "estranged," "without hope and without God," and the overcoming of the kind of identity politics—whether religious or secular—that create such divisions. Part of the Church's ministry of reconciliation, then, is to resist division by existing as a body that transcends existing ethnic, national, political, and ideological divisions. What does this mean for Catholic nonviolence as, in Pope Francis's phrase, a "style of politics for peace"?

Africae munus already has this possibility in view: in the Eucharist, Catholics are called to recognize a fraternity "stronger than that of human families, than that of our tribes."[87] But overall, as we have seen, the document shies away from a robust account of the Church's role in reconciliation in the social and political spheres, preferring to speak of reconciliation as being created "in people's hearts" and involving "inner purification" and "inner development."[88] The confessional imaginary is in evidence here, but the principal reason for this preference for "inner" language is a concern not to overreach the Church's sphere of competence, as well as concrete concerns about the inappropriate political involvement of priests and bishops. Yet the risk of this retreat to "inner" language is that the spiritual realm becomes implicitly understood as inner, individualized, and private, while the political realm is outer, social, and public. This is clearly not what Benedict XVI intends: he is aware of the tension and wants "to demonstrate a concrete but spiritual world."[89]

Katongole's *Journey of Reconciliation* takes up the challenge, setting out to demonstrate what a concrete but spiritual practice of reconciliation looks like and to explore its significance for politics in Africa. His work draws on William Cavanaugh, whose *Torture and Eucharist* demonstrated how torture was used during the Pinochet regime in Chile to atomize the body politic, isolating people and dividing them against one another.[90] In the Chilean context, the Church, particularly the practice of the Eucharist, became a concrete way of reconfiguring the social body as a site of resistance to torture and repression.[91] Katongole's work takes this insight and connects it with the theology of reconciliation in Paul, exploring how reconciliation creates the Church as a new body that transcends ethnic difference. This emphasis on the creation of a new people is partly about resisting the ways in which modern African politics, drawing on the legacy of colonialism, continues to amplify, manipulate, and weaponize tribal and ethnic identities.[92] It is also part of a deeper argument about resisting the kind of nature/grace distinction that keeps Christian identity safely in the "spiritual" realm, floating above supposedly "natural" identities that are assumed to be basic, and thus left uncritiqued and untransformed by the gospel. Katongole argues that Christian, ecclesial identity should be seen as primary; following Cavanaugh, he also argues for a redefinition of what we mean by "political."

> If politics is defined not as the achievement of state power but more broadly as the ordering of bodies in space and time, then we should be able to see how—as in Chile, Poland, the Philippines and other places—the church can enact Eucharistic bodies in space and time that stand as a counter-politics to violence and injustice, while avoiding both Church-state entanglement, and the secularization and irrelevance of the Church in the West.[93]

Viewed this way, "the decisive question is what kind of politics the story of God's love shapes."[94] Katongole's book offers numerous examples of instances where the Christian narrative has shaped communities able to withstand politicized tribal divisions, from Maggy Barankitse's Maison Shalom in Burundi to the students of Buta seminary, who died together rather than separate themselves into Tutsi and Hutu.[95]

It is clear that Katongole sees this kind of resistance to division not as a communion turned in on itself but as part of the Church's ministry of reconciliation—as something *for* others—and here I simply want to amplify and extend Katongole's point. As we have explored Paul's understanding of reconciliation, it has as much to do with the *overcoming* of politics, understood in a certain sense, as its redefinition. By this, I mean that Paul's understanding of God's reconciling action in Christ, and its overflowing of human boundaries, calls radically into question any state making (or any social-body making) that depends on one group's self-definition over against excluded others.[96] What is overcome in Christ is any alignment between the grace of God and identity-by-division; what emerges is not a new social body on the old human plane of exclusion or competition but a whole new creation. Katongole's understanding of politics as "the ordering of bodies in space and time" goes some way toward dissolving the tension in *Africae munus* between the spiritual and political, which limits the document's account of reconciliation as a concrete, social practice. Christian reconciliation, he argues, does not compete on the level of state power, but it does result in the creation of a new and concrete social body that transcends, resists, and critiques existing political, ethnic, or tribal divisions. But we need to keep in view, too, that even this "ordering of bodies in space and time" happens in a new way. Katongole argues that Christians in the first centuries understood their new, Christian identity as basic, in the sense that it replaced or displaced existing racial identities, and he quotes Michael Budde to this effect: "Early Christians saw themselves, and were seen by others, as more than just a new 'religious' group, more than a new idea unleashed in the ancient world, and more than a voluntary club like other social groupings of association. . . . Early Christians were more often seen as part of a new ethnic group, even a new race of people, in the Roman World."[97]

But what we are looking at here is not a "new race" or "new ethnic group" constituted in the old way: Paul's account of reconciliation, as we have seen, would disallow any idea of a new chosen people along the same exclusive and boundaried lines of the old. Rather, the reconciling grace that creates this new social body also overruns its boundaries, both concretely, now, and eschatologically, as everything in heaven and on earth will be brought together under Christ as head (Eph 1:9). Just as the reconciling grace of God stretches and reshapes human structures and ways of relating, so our descriptions of God's action in terms of "people" and "body" employ human language and concepts but also stretch and reshape them in light of new purposes.

The theology of reconciliation that I have explored shows that the Church is called to exist as a sign of unity, resisting division in and through her own communion. It also highlights the need for the Church to remain vigilant and discerning, refusing to allow Christian, Catholic, and ecclesial identity to become part of the discourse of identity-by-division. For the Church to trade in the logic of identity-by-division is for her to become catastrophically separated from her founding identity and the source of her life. The poet Denise Levertov, addressing the phrase "the arts of war," says that "the arts draw their life from the soul's well, and warfare / dries up the soul and draws its power / from a dark and burning wasteland." The poem goes on:

> When Leonardo
> set his genius to devising
> machines of destruction he was not acting in the service of art,
> he was suspending
> the life of art
> over an abyss,
> as if one were to hold
> a living child out of an airplane window
> at thirty thousand feet.[98]

For the Church to trade in the rhetoric of identity-by-division, or to become implicated in politics of this kind, is for her to suspend her life over an abyss in just this way. To give just one example: in March 2019, the Roman Catholic Diocese of Gurk-Klagenfurt in Austria refused permission for the annual Bleiburg Mass to be celebrated. The Mass commemorates the killing of Croat soldiers and civilians allied to the Nazi-sympathizing Croatian wartime government by Yugoslav partisans. In recent years, it has become a gathering point for far right activists and Ustaše supporters. A letter from the diocese read: "The Mass in the field near Bleiburg has become part of a manifestation that is politically instrumentalised and is part of a political-nationalistic ritual that serves a selective experience and interpretation of history."[99] The Croatian bishops refuted the charge, but my point here is that the Church must remain alert and discerning in just this way about the weaponizing of Christian and ecclesial identity. The temptation here may be strongest precisely where Christian identity and existence are threatened by non-Christian others. In such contexts the Church's ministry of reconciliation, lived as active nonviolence, means not just transcending division within herself, but resisting being co-opted, willingly or unwillingly, as an agent of division.

Surprising Solidarities

Finally, I want to argue that the ministry of reconciliation opens the Church to the possibility of surprising solidarities.

As the Algerian civil war escalated in 1995–96, the Cistercian monks of Tibhirine were faced with a decision: whether to return to France, and to safety, or to remain in Algeria among the Muslim community alongside whom they had been living, praying, and ministering. The decision, dramatized in the 2010 Xavier Beauvois film, *Of Gods and Men*, was to remain, in the knowledge that to do so was to expose themselves to the risk of death. The final testament of Dom Christian de Chergé makes clear that, though the monks were aware of the risks of staying, they were not seeking martyrdom or glorifying self-sacrifice.

> I have lived long enough to know that I am an accomplice
>   in the evil
> which seems to prevail so terribly in the world,
> even in the evil which might blindly strike me down.
> I should like, when the time comes, to have a moment of spiritual
>   clarity
> which would allow me to beg forgiveness of God
> and of my fellow human beings,
> and at the same time forgive with all my heart the one who would
>   strike me down.
> I could not desire such a death.
> It seems to me important to state this.
> I do not see, in fact, how I could rejoice
> if the people I love were indiscriminately accused of my murder.
> It would be too high a price to pay

for what will perhaps be called, the "grace of martyrdom"
to owe it to an Algerian, whoever he might be,
especially if he says he is acting in fidelity to what he believes
    to be Islam.[100]

There is a helpful corrective here to a kind of understanding of non-violence as a grim determination to go under the wheel of fate. More could be said here, but I want to draw out two different points.

First, the monks' decision to remain in Algeria was a refusal to be divided: not a refusal to be divided among themselves as a Christian community but a refusal to be divided from those "children of Islam," as de Chergé calls them, whom they loved and served. The examples Katongole gives in *The Journey of Reconciliation* are drawn from a context in which politicized tribal divisions are a major challenge. In that context, emphasizing that the communion of the Church transcends and resists ethnic and political divisions makes sense. Both *Africae munus* and Katongole's work draw on sacramental language and practices to make the point: the water of baptism is thicker than the blood of trib-alism, and communion in the Body and Blood of the Lord creates a "bond of fraternity . . . stronger than that of human families, than that of our tribes."[101] But in the decision of the Cistercians of Tibhirine, we see a refusal to be divided that extends beyond the bounds of Christian communion. At the same time, this refusal to be divided clearly arises from specifically Christian moral imagination: it is more than a deci-sion to stand in generic human solidarity with other suffering violence. De Chergé's testament gives us a window into the kind of radical moral imagination of reconciliation explored above. His eschatological vision allows him to see himself in a web of relationships that includes even his killer.

Obviously, my death will appear to confirm those who hastily judged me naïve or idealistic: "Let him tell us now what he thinks of his ideals!" But these persons should know that finally my most avid curiosity will be set free. This is what I shall be able to do, God willing: immerse my gaze in that of the Father to contemplate with him His children of Islam just as He sees them, all shining with the glory of Christ, the fruit of His Passion, filled with the Gift of the

Spirit whose secret joy will always be to establish communion and restore the likeness, playing with the differences. . . . And also you, my last-minute friend, who will not have known what you were doing: Yes, I want this THANK YOU and this GOODBYE to be a "GOD-BLESS" for you, too, because in God's face I see yours. May we meet again as happy thieves in Paradise, if it please God, the Father of us both. Amen! Inshallah![102]

In the monks' decision to stay we also see the kind of "overcoming" of politics I explored earlier: their refusal to be divided from the people was a refusal of the religious-nationalist narrative that demanded such division as the price of peace and security.

Part of the Church's ministry of reconciliation is her refusal to be divided. This means that the Church must resist the politics of division in and through her own communion and refuse to trade in—indeed actively resist—the violent rhetoric of identity-by-division. What the theology of reconciliation also shows us, I want to argue, is that the Church's resistance to division does not just apply within her own communion. To live with the eschatological vision of the unification of all things in Christ means to be open to surprising, boundary-crossing solidarities that are effective signs of that final reconciliation.

The theology of reconciliation presents the Church with the opportunity to speak to the heart of human longing and to the heart of political processes of truth-telling and reconciliation that continue to unfold in countries striving to move away from recent violence and build sustainable peace. I have argued that the Church's theology of reconciliation needs significant work if it is to speak directly and compellingly to such situations. A richer theology of peacebuilding, better connected to the Church's social teaching on peace, has the potential to support Catholic peacebuilders and to encourage ordinary Catholics to consider themselves ministers of reconciliation in their own contexts. In this chapter, I have focused on broadening the Church's theology of reconciliation, by returning to the theology of reconciliation as we find it in Paul. There we find a rich and challenging account of reconciliation, which can resource the theology and practice of active nonviolence. Discovering reconciliation as God's initiative encourages Catholics to develop practices of "loving first" as forms of effective peacebuilding. Exploring the cosmic and eschatological scope of reconciliation in Paul encourages forms of active nonviolent peacebuilding that are discerning and that build up and draw on the moral imagination as a source of resilience and hope. Connecting with Paul's own journey of understanding, as he realizes and then preaches God's overcoming of boundaries in Christ, encourages the Church to resist division, not just within her own communion, but as a ministry of reconciliation exercised in a divided world.

SEVEN

Desire for Peace

The purpose of this final chapter is to explore in greater depth one of the key themes of Catholic social teaching on peace: the idea that all people desire peace. For Augustine, as shown in the first chapter, the idea of desiring peace is a capacious one, encompassing robber barons and dead bodies as well as those who long for peace in eternal life. As the tradition develops, the sense of what it means that all people desire peace develops too, until we reach John XXIII and the post-*Pacem* tradition, where the claim that all people desire peace comes to mean something more like a universally shared, positive, conscious, and rational desire for a just peace. The first part of this chapter places these two understandings of desire for peace side by side and, looking particularly at the post-*Pacem* tradition, asks what might have been lost in this adoption of an unequivocally positive account of desiring peace.

In the second part, the chapter draws together some of the critical questions that I have already touched on: whether the vision of the essential unity and harmony of humanity that underpins Catholic social teaching undercuts its ability to address situations of conflict; whether, to balance this optimistic vision of human goodwill and capability, we need more resources that enable us to address the realities of struggle, tragedy, and ambiguity that inevitably beset the seeking of peace amid a fallen creation; whether, alongside the natural law tradition that sees the pursuit of peace as running with the grain of our nature, we need a deeper sense of just how utterly we need to be transformed, both personally and socially, and how long and slow and hard-fought that transformation is *in via*. This final chapter asks two questions: If all people desire peace, then how does that *desire* manifest itself within fallen creation on its way back to God? And if all people desire peace, how does that *peace* manifest itself within fallen creation on its way back to God? The chapter goes on to address these questions in Christological perspective, because Christ is the way of fallen creation back to God and because the account of peace that all people desire must, in the end, be Christological in shape, "for he is our peace" (Eph 2:14). For the same reason, the resurrection narratives stand at the heart of the constructive work in this chapter, because the peace that all people seek, however confusedly, is the gift of the risen Jesus.

The work of this chapter is a conclusion, insofar as it draws together many of the themes we have encountered so far and makes some more wide-ranging constructive suggestions about the development of the Catholic theology of peace. It is not conclusive, however: the theological key is reflective, creative, and experimental, and more questions will be raised and more ideas touched on than can be satisfactorily pursued within the bounds of the chapter. Part of my purpose is, in this way, to sketch out some of the tasks that lie ahead for this growing edge of Catholic social teaching.

DESIRING PEACE

Central to Augustine's argument in Book XIX of *The City of God against the Pagans* is the idea that all people desire peace: "Whoever joins me in an examination, however cursory, of human affairs and our common human nature will acknowledge that, just as there is no one who does not wish to be joyful, so there is no one who does not wish to have peace."[1] Peace, he continues, is the ultimate aim of warfare, by means of which people exchange an existing state of peace for one more to their liking. As the book progresses, it becomes clear that Augustine's conception of both "peace" and "desire" is not quite what we might expect: not only does it include those with malicious intent, like robbers, who wage wars to impose the terms of their own peace, but also dead bodies, which can scarcely be said to desire in any straightforward sense at all. Peace here means something like "a state of rest in the right order" (*tranquillitas ordinis*), and desire means the inbuilt and natural weight of created things toward such a state of rest—something rather more like the law of gravity than the desire for an ice cream.[2] It is in this sense that a person strung up by their feet desires peace.

> For example, if someone were to hang upside-down, this position of the body and disposition of the limbs would certainly be a perverted one. For what nature places above would be beneath, and what nature intends to be beneath would be above. This perversity disturbs the peace of the flesh, and therefore causes distress. Nonetheless, the spirit is at peace with its body and strives to secure its health: it is precisely for that reason that there is pain. And even if the spirit is driven out of the body by the latter's distresses, still, as long as the disposition of the body's members remains intact, what is left is not without a kind of peace: which is why there is still something to hang there. And if the earthly body presses down towards the ground, and strains against the bond by which it is suspended, it tends towards the position of its own peace, and by the voice of its own weight, so to speak, entreats a place where it may rest.[3]

Several points are worth drawing out here regarding the relationship of order to disorder, and true peace to unjust peace. First, Augustine uses the example of the upside-down man to describe *dis*order in terms of the perversion of true order. All disorder is predatory on some prior order: even that which is perverse, he says, "must of necessity be in, or derived from, or associated with, and to that extent be at peace with, some part of the order of things among which it has its being or of which it consists. Otherwise, it would not exist at all."[4] Total disorder is not possible: all disorder includes some measure of order.[5] Second, in the upside-down man example, desire for peace takes the form of pain: pain is the language, as it were, by which what is disordered expresses its desire for order.[6] Third, there is in the upside-down man a kind of peace simply by virtue of his ongoing bodily integrity, even when dead. Augustine holds that there can be more order and less order, more peace and less peace, "kinds of peace" even amid manifest disorder and suffering. But Augustine is also quite clear that, in another sense, "the peace of the unjust is not worthy to be called peace at all." All that is not true order is *dis*order, and therefore all that is not true peace is, in some sense, in conflict.

What is true of the upside-down man is true of the political order. In one sense, Augustine acknowledges that there are kinds of peace and that even the peace of the earthly city can be made use of and is "not to be despised."[7] But all social and political order that is not fundamentally ordered in obedience to God is really a kind of *dis*order. Viewed in one direction, insofar as it inevitably contains some elements of order, such disorder is on the way to being true order. But equally, and certainly in Augustine's view in *City of God*, such disorder is understood not as an approximation of true order but as a corruption of it, and just to the extent that it is corrupt, it has no lasting significance eschatologically.[8] Like the upside-down man, disorder of this kind is a sign of decay, not a sign of growth. It is important to note, too, what Augustine labels as the root sin of this kind of disorder: pride. Pride refuses to acknowledge God: it "hates a fellowship of equality under God, and wishes to impose its own dominion upon its equals, in place of God's rule."[9] Just like the robber barons, we exchange the true peace of God for an unjust peace, an alternative order more to our liking. Only worship of God and obedience to the eternal law can result in true order, true justice, and true peace.

I will return to some elements of Augustine's vision later, but now I want to look at the account of desiring peace in the post-*Pacem* tradition, in order to demonstrate the contrast between Augustine's account and the twentieth-century tradition. *Pacem in terris* itself echoes Augustine almost verbatim: "For who is there who does not feel the craving to be rid of the threat of war, and to see peace preserved and made daily more secure?"[10] But where desire for peace for Augustine is something automatic and instinctive, something that can manifest itself as pain or grief, for John XXIII desire for peace is a rational response to a good manifestly obvious as such. We have already noted the encyclical's strong, neo-scholastic natural law framework and its confidence about the human capacity to perceive and follow the order inherent in creation. John XXIII's account of desire for peace takes on this hopeful hue: it is "common sense" that true and lasting peace cannot be secured by parity of arms but only by mutual trust. Relationships between states must be regulated "in accordance with the principles of right reason: the principles, that is, of justice, truth and vigorous and sincere coopera- tion."[11] Desire has come to mean the force of right reason and goodwill, and peace, too, has taken on a more positive coloring.[12] Where peace for Augustine could include robber barons and dead bodies, peace for John XXIII has come to mean a positive order "founded on truth, built up on justice, nurtured and animated by charity, and brought into effect under the auspices of freedom."[13] This much more straightforwardly positive account of peace is partly the result of increased engagement with scrip- ture: in the post-*Pacem* tradition, the concept of peace becomes more ex- plicitly scriptural in content, and more explicitly Christological. In the post-*Pacem* tradition, as we have already seen, there is also a sense of progress that is arguably alien to Augustine. *Pacem in terris* claims that there exists an objective moral order with God as its author, but John XXIII understands earthly peace more in terms of progress toward the peace of the kingdom of God rather than as an Augustinian falling away from divine order.[14]

The post-*Pacem* tradition has not replicated John XXIII's levels of confidence about human goodwill and rationality, but it nevertheless takes forward his basically positive account of what it means to desire peace. *Gaudium et spes* defines peace as "the fruit of the order built into human society by its divine Founder, an order to be given practical ex- pression by men ever thirsting for more perfect justice," and there is a clear sense that this positive understanding of peace is what people desire.[15] The document sees continuity between human aspirations and the call of the gospel; again, the image is one of growing toward divine order rather than falling away. Nevertheless, *Gaudium et spes* has a much clearer sense of the ambivalence of the human person, torn between good and evil, and the way in which this ambivalence is reflected on the social and political level: there is reference to the "hard struggle against the powers of darkness" and the "cross which the flesh and the world puts on the shoulders of all who dedicate themselves to peace and justice."[16] John Paul II's encyclicals and messages for the World Day of Peace continue very much in this line—keenly aware of the power of sin and ideology but with the same basically positive account of what it means to say that all people desire peace. His 1987 message, for example, quotes Paul VI's definition of peace as "something that is built up day after day in pursuit of an order intended by God, which implies a more perfect form of justice among people" and then continues in the next sentence with the phrase, "this harmonious order for which all peoples long."[17] We saw earlier that John Paul II's experience of communism made him alert to the power and dangers of ideology and the ways in which this could play out in the politics of blocs, but what is interesting is the way that such political systems are regarded as antipeace or peace denying rather than, as Augustine might describe them, perverse or defective forms of peace: the concept of peace itself remains unequivocally positive.

What I have aimed to illustrate here is the contrast between the sense of Augustine's claim that "all people desire peace" and the sense of the same claim in post–*Pacem in terris* Catholic social teaching. The question now is whether in this development, alongside the significant positive gains, something useful has been lost, and here I want to draw on the analysis of earlier chapters to suggest that the answer to this question should be yes.

WHAT IS MISSING

In the first two chapters, I characterized the development of Catholic social teaching on peace across the two millennia surveyed in terms of a shift from discontinuity to continuity across a whole series of relationships, including earthly and heavenly, imperfect and perfect, temporal and eternal, present and future. Where Augustine emphasizes the discontinuity between the temporal peace of the earthly city and the perfect peace of eternal life with God, the tradition as it develops through Aquinas and into the twentieth century shifts toward a sense of continuity or growth between the imperfect peace of the present and the fullness of peace in the kingdom. In surveying the twentieth century, I also noted the impact of the shift in the prevailing understanding of the relationship between nature and grace, from a more extrinsic to a more intrinsic relationship. There I raised the question of whether contemporary Catholic social teaching's sense of progress or smooth ascent between earthly peace and the peace of the kingdom was perhaps too smooth, a little too confident in the idea that peace, in Paul VI's words, "marches on and is establishing itself in the world with a certain invincibility."[18] I suggested that Catholic social teaching on peace might need to develop theological resources better able to hold the realities of setback and tragedy that also often mark the task of peacebuilding.

The same concerns emerged in the chapter on pastoral accompaniment, where I drew attention to the need for theological resources that would support the experience of those accompanying communities through violent conflict, resources that took account of the costliness of remaining in such situations and the difficulties of discernment. One of the aims of the constructive work undertaken in that chapter was to draw attention to the need for deeper theological balancing work. From its earliest beginnings Catholic social teaching has insisted that harmony, not conflict, is the essential truth of human society, and it is arguable that this insistence has led it to underestimate the force of sin in social and political life and overlook the reality of hostility in human relationships with one another and with God.[19] The constructive work in that chapter offered a way of thinking about the work of peacebuilding against this backdrop, describing God's work of consolation as a kind of unrelenting fidelity in the face of human indifference and hostility.

In the chapter on solidarity, I looked at the tendency of Catholic social teaching to focus on the macro level of structural change and the micro level of personal conversion and overlook the realities of peacebuilding "in the middle" and "in between." I noted, again, the need for theological resources that would take account of the experience of people in situations where they must discern a course of action that, far from being self-evident to all reasonable people of goodwill, is deeply ambiguous and fraught with risk. The constructive work in this chapter drew attention to the importance of Christological themes and incorporated resources from the *Spiritual Exercises*. The aim here was to encourage Catholic social teaching to look steadily at the world's darkness and the force of sin and to ask what it means to participate in Christ's "making redemption" in a world that, in Todd Whitmore's expression, is not merely imbalanced or out of order, but threatening.[20]

In the chapter on social sin, I explored some of the ways in which the Church's tendency to use the language of personal sin and personal conversion fails to engage with the complex social character of structural and social injustice. Transforming such contexts, I argued, is not just a case of individuals recognizing and doing the right thing: transformation will require a gradual bringing-to-light of injustices embedded at the level of perceptions of reality, bodily responses, and even built environments. Drawing on Rahner's account of concupiscence as our inability to be "all-of-a-piece" despite even our best intentions, I suggested that both personal and social transformation needed to be seen in eschatological perspective. Like the whole life of grace, growing toward peace means entering into a process of complete transformation, the magnitude of which exceeds both our capabilities and our understanding and with which most of us only partly correspond during our lifetime.

In the chapter on reconciliation and Catholic nonviolence, I argued that the Church's teaching on reconciliation, currently shaped by sacramental theology, needs further work to connect it more effectively with Church teaching on peace. Drawing on Paul's theology of reconciliation, I suggested that the Catholic practice of reconciliation involves the overcoming of human boundaries, including both practices of resistance—refusing to be divided—and forging surprising solidarities beyond the Church's bounds.

In drawing attention to the realities of risk and ambiguity, tragedy and setback, costliness, conflict, resistance and struggle, and the sheer magnitude of the call to transformation, I have not just been drawing attention to counterfactuals on the level of concrete experience. My argument has been that these experiences highlight the need for what Nicholas Lash calls "corrective pressure" on the tradition as it stands.[21] Without denying the central claims of that tradition about the essential unity of humanity and without weakening our vocation to cooperate with God in the work of the kingdom, Catholic social teaching needs a stronger sense of the reality and pervasiveness of conflict, a stronger sense of the power of sin and the way it weakens our vision and our wills, and a stronger sense of ways in which God's work of redemption appears in such a context not just like the steady, quiet growth of dough rising but also as struggle in and with a broken creation. It needs a more textured account of the peace for which we long, and the ways in which we long for it, a more textured account of the shape our desire takes, touched by sin as it is, and the ways in which it needs to be transformed as well as pursued. Catholic social teaching on peace needs an account not just of how we must grow toward peace but also of how we must *change*.

DESIRING RESURRECTION

An account of how we must change is the work of the present chapter, and it is at this point that I want to turn to the theme of resurrection. My constructive work thus far has focused on the cross as a way of talking about God's redemptive action in a broken creation, but a theology of peace must also include the resurrection, as the sign and first fruits of the renewal of that creation. Some of the images Jesus uses to speak about the coming of the kingdom, the image of the seed growing secretly (Mk 4:26–29) and the leaven in the dough (Lk 13:21), are images of a transformation that happens quietly and mysteriously; they are also images of a transformation *from within*. A long tradition reads these parables as Jesus speaking about himself, as he does more directly in John's gospel (Jn 12:23–24): Jesus himself is the seed sown into creation, dying into creation, in order to raise it from within. If the cross has something to tell us about the kind of struggle, the kind of dying involved in our redemption, then resurrection has something to tell us about the shape of our transformation. That transformation is something sown in us at the deepest possible level—the level of our bodies, personal identities, and social relationships—and that rises in and through the renewal of these things.[22] If the resurrection of Christ has something to tell us about the "how" of the transformation to which we are called, it also has something to tell us about the end of that transformation, and about the kind of peace that we desire. Peace is the greeting and gift of the risen Jesus to his disciples (Jn 20:19, 26), and so to say that we desire peace is to say that we desire, in however clouded or complex a way, something that is ultimately given by Christ and something that he gives from the far side of death.

Rowan Williams's *The Truce of God* begins with a discussion of popular depictions of violence on television and film. The kind of violence we imagine and depict has something to tell us, Williams argues, about what we fear and about our response to it. Through a range of themes—alien attacks, psychopaths, animals, natural, or supernatural forces—popular culture depicts violence as something that just happens, something overwhelming that overtakes us from without. The implication "is that violence is never something ordinary human beings *decide to do*" and that we can therefore defend ourselves "without many qualms about how we do so, because we are not dealing with agents like ourselves, whose motives and methods would need scrutiny."[23] Our popular narratives tell us that violence is something that does not belong to the moral world of responsibility and everyday choices.[24]

Williams's instinct is a good one: the stories we tell ourselves have much to tell us about ourselves, about our desires, our fears, and the kinds of reality we instinctively inhabit. So what stories do we tell ourselves about resurrection? Recent studies in Britain suggest that even though formal religious beliefs are in decline, belief in life after death remains common: more people believe in some kind of life beyond death than believe in God.[25] On some level, perhaps even alongside our skeptical rationalism, we deeply *want* to believe that death is not the end. The abiding popularity at funerals of the quotation from a Henry Scott Holland sermon, beginning, "Death is nothing at all, I have only slipped away to the next room," is a window into this kind of widespread desire for resurrection, understood as a continued life, without pain or suffering, resumed after the brief interruption of death. This kind of death, which is really "nothing at all," and this kind of resurrection, which gives our loved ones back to us unchanged, is easy to desire. But this is not the only cultural current: the abiding and renewed popularity of comics, films, and television series about vampires and zombies suggests that we are also terrified of what comes back from the dead, or what cannot be killed, whether "undead" humans, viruses, or prehistoric creatures. The heroes and heroines of such stories are engaged in an epic struggle to return the universe to its proper order, by killing or returning to the dead those creatures that belong there but refuse to stay put.

These cultural patterns suggest two things. The first is a deep ambivalence about resurrection, as well as a profound fascination with it: on one level, we long for resurrection; on another, we are terrified of it.[26] The second is that our cultural familiarity is often with something that is to one side of resurrection, or a kind of pseudo-resurrection: either a death that is "nothing at all" and a life that resumes basically unchanged or a kind of resurrected life that is really a resuscitation. We find it much harder to imagine the absolute discontinuity of a real, final death, and a resurrection that is not a reversal of that death but, as MacKinnon puts it, the beginning of a "strange and elusive sequel."[27] This is the kind of resurrection with which we have to deal in the Gospels, which are just as insistent about the reality of the death of Jesus as they are about the reality and strangeness of his resurrected presence.[28]

The gospel accounts of the resurrection of Jesus reflect the deep human ambivalence about resurrection that I have been discussing. Mark uses four different Greek words to describe the fear of the women who find the empty tomb, and his account ends with the women running away, "and they said nothing to anyone, for they were afraid" (Mk 16:6, 8). The other gospel accounts are less stark, but they show nevertheless that encounters with the risen Jesus are characterized by terror as well as joy, doubt as well as belief, and hesitation as well as touching and embrace. In Matthew's gospel, the women run from the tomb with "fear and great joy" (Mt 28:8), and Jesus's first words as he comes to meet them are, "Greetings! Do not be afraid."[29] In Luke's gospel, as the two unnamed disciples are relating their encounter with Jesus on the road to Emmaus, Jesus appears among the group: they are "startled and terrified, and thought that they were seeing a ghost" (Lk 24:37). It is worth noting, too, that the appearances of the risen Jesus and his demonstrations of his realness (the invitation to touch in Lk 24:39 and Jn 20:27, the eating of grilled fish in Lk 24:42–43) do not altogether remove this ambivalence. Luke tells us that the disciples were still "disbelieving and wondering," and the final verses of Matthew's gospel say that "when they saw him, they worshipped him; but some doubted" (Mt 28:17). In these narratives desire and fear, known and unknown, circle around each other.

My contention in this chapter is that this ambivalence about resurrection, so evident in the gospel narratives of encounters with the risen Jesus, is also the fundamental human attitude toward peace, the peace that, ultimately, is the gift of the risen Christ and inseparable from him. All people long for peace, I will argue, but not in straightforward or unequivocal ways: like resurrection, we desire it and we fear it in equal measure. Lederach records John Brewer, a peacebuilder from Northern Ireland, naming exactly this ambivalence.

In our context of thirty plus years of troubles, violence, fear, and division are known. Peace is the mystery! People are frightened of peace. It is simultaneously exciting and fearful. This is mystery. Peace asks a lot of you. Peace asks you to share memory. It asks you to share space, territory, specific concrete places. It asks you to share a future. And all this you are asked to do with and in the presence of your enemy. Peace is mystery. It is walking into the unknown.[30]

We cannot help desiring peace, but that desire does not necessarily take salutary shape in a broken creation in which both our desires and the ways in which we pursue them are distorted by sin. Our desire for peace is often, in Sebastian Moore's phrase, "a desire with fear in the saddle," and like our desire for survival and immortality, it can take shape as naked self-preservation and selfishness, empire building, and domination.[31] We need some account of the ambivalence of our desire for peace, some sense of what shape that desire takes in human relationships and why, and some account of how it might be transformed toward a purer peace, more purely desired.

PIECEMEAL PEACE

When it was evening on that day, the first day of the week,
and the doors of the house where the disciples were
were locked for fear of the Jews,
Jesus came and stood among them and said,
"Peace be with you."

(Jn 20:19)

Invincibility, immortality, the continuance of life scarcely broken by a death that is nothing at all—all these are easy to desire, but genuine resurrection is a rather more frightening prospect. A desire for real resurrection is a desire to share in the life of Christ, and this means sharing in his death.[32] Between us and the new, indestructible life in Christ for which we long lies a real death in which all is absolutely surrendered into the hands of the Father. But where the death of Jesus is a simple returning to the Father, ours, as well as a going to the Father, is a dying to self, a laying-to-rest of our deep resistance to God. From where we are *in via*, the prospect of resurrection is both a source of hope and a source of fear: we desire it, but we are divided against ourselves.

In Augustine's account, to be human is to desire peace but also to be divided against oneself in just this way. He traces this division back to the Fall and the original human rebellion against divine authority.

> He who, in his pride, had pleased himself, was now, by God's justice, handed over to himself. This was not done, however, in such a way that man was now placed entirely under his own control. Rather, he was divided against himself, and now, instead of enjoying the freedom for which he so longed, he lived in harsh and miserable bondage to the devil: a bondage to which he consented when he sinned.[33]

After the Fall, human beings are divided, both on an individual level and among themselves. On an individual level, we exchange an original integrity and peace for a disordered and divided nature; on a social level, we exchange an original freedom and equality for slavery to sin and to one another.[34] This first sin of pride, of putting ourselves in the place of God, is then compounded by our refusal to see our sin and ask pardon for it and by our determination to blame one another.[35] Like blaming, covering ourselves is a response to the fragmentation caused by the Fall. Shamefully, painfully aware of the inner warfare caused by sin, we seek ways of covering our disobedience and hiding our loss of integrity.[36]

We cannot help seeking peace, but the fragmentation of our nature caused by sin inevitably distorts both the peace we pursue and the way we pursue it. We saw earlier that for Augustine all human order—in the sense of "order" created by human will in defiance of God—is, in a sense, disorder, a corruption of the true divine order. Like a little child who has broken something priceless and beautiful, all our attempts to put it back together cannot undo the original breakage, and try as we might to put the pieces back into their proper order, all our childish order is still disorder. The same is true of human peace: all our peace is in some way fragmented or divided because, I want to argue, our attempts to secure it so often *proceed* by way of fragmentation and division. On an individual level, we secure our peace of mind by suppressing or projecting what threatens it, whether our sense of failure or rejection, our fears, our knowledge of our own wrongdoing, or our memories of pain. Faced with our inner chaos, we try to create order by imposing our own division of good from bad, light from dark, acceptable from unacceptable. Our attempts to secure peace on an inner level involve a good deal of "covering and blaming," through which we seek, in complex and unconscious ways, to conceal this inner warfare and chaos both from ourselves and from others. On a personal level, true peace, understood as the resolution of this fragmentation and division by which we have created a kind of order for ourselves, can appear dreadfully threatening. Though we may long for this true peace and pursue it in all kinds of inchoate and unconscious ways, the return of what we have tried to shut out or kill off can appear to our conscious selves as a frightening return to primal chaos. We long for resurrection, but, at the same time, we lock the door out of fear. It is only over time and with considerable courage that we can admit—in the sense of "let in"—the still-living presence of what we thought was dead, and allow the work of a new creation to begin in us.

What is true of the desire for and pursuit of peace on an inner, psychological level is also frequently true on the interpersonal level. In a world already broken by sin, securing peace on the level of interpersonal relationships can also mean division: preserving our peace by guarding against the demands and chaos of others, shutting out or withdrawing from those with whom it is too difficult to engage, and deploying death-as-solution when relationships are broken past any hope of resolution.

Peace-as-division is evident, too, on a social level, where we see the human tendency to secure the peace and unity of the group or nation by excluding what threatens it: the poor, the religiously or ethnically other, the criminal, the violent, even the mentally ill. Our attempts to create order in this way involve a process of division and othering, in which what threatens the unity and peace of the whole is identified, separated out, and either contained or expelled. The public and political conversation about asylum seekers and refugees in the United Kingdom is a good example: asylum seekers are routinely represented in both popular and political discourse as a threat to the peace, prosperity, and unity of British society. Mainstream media use language about the United Kingdom being "swamped" or "invaded" and highlight stories that associate people seeking asylum with terror attacks and criminality. The political system, in a different way, employs dehumanizing language and practices that both enact and reinforce the belief that maintaining the peace and well-being of British society means deterring, detaining, and deporting asylum seekers. This is just one example of the way in which piecemeal peace proceeds by way of division and exclusion, but there are countless others.

These distorted ways of pursuing peace on a social level also involve a kind of covering and blaming of which we are hardly, if at all, aware. In projecting our sense of threat outward, and making it a feature of the objectively dangerous other, we "cover" our fear and the fragmentation that underlies it by blaming the other: "She tempted me so I ate" becomes "They are dangerous so we reject them." I explored in the chapter on social sin how this kind of othering and exclusion, covering and blaming, settles out like a sediment, ceasing to appear to us as an attitude, feeling, or choice and becoming instead a solid fact about the world that must be negotiated. Thus sinful disorder takes concrete shape in our built environment, in our political systems, in ideological oppositions, and international trade relationships.[37] As Williams puts it:

> We are all of us, in some measure, shut off from each other: our own individual options for violence fade into the background of endemic violence. We are born into a world where there is *already* a history of oppression and victimization: our moral and spiritual growth does not occur in a vacuum. And so, before we can be conscious of it, the system of oppressor-victim relations absorbs us.[38]

We cannot say, "All people desire peace," without taking account of the ways in which that desire is conceived and pursued in a climate of sinful division that envelops us from our birth and that shapes and misshapes our moral and spiritual horizons. In a broken creation, the desire for peace—a "desire with fear in the saddle"—frequently works itself out in perverse forms of order that proceed by division.

In a disordered creation, all our order is disorder; in a divided creation, our seeking of piecemeal peace proceeds by way of division. But it is important to note here, also following Augustine, that though all order that is not aligned with God's is in some sense *dis*order, it is not disordered in the same way or to the same extent. Likewise, although in a fragmented creation we secure peace by means of division, not all division is the same.[39] Division can take the form of racism or nationalism, but it can also take the form of justice, defense of the innocent, necessary self-protection, or the pursuit of the common good.[40] But all such efforts, even when intended in good faith to contribute to the building of a more just or peaceful world, are the result of the distortion and fracturing of God's original unity and inevitably replicate elements of it, even as they strive to repair it. It is important to be absolutely clear that not all such division is *sinful*—it may be necessary, deeply regretted, much wept over—but I want to argue that all such division is the *fruit* of sin, in the sense that it emerges from and remains within the constraints of broken creation.[41] "Securing peace" in this sense is a contradiction in terms, like "compelling love" or "seizing authority": because it proceeds by division, it damages what is sought in the very act of grasping it.[42] That is, in reaching for peace, we are reaching for wholeness, unity, and rest, but in proceeding by division, we cannot help compromising the wholeness that we seek.

This acknowledgment that our attempts to secure earthly peace can only proceed by way of division in no way lessens the imperative to seek peace. It is simply to acknowledge that, in a broken creation, all our attempts to secure such peace inevitably bear the marks of the brokenness that is our climate.[43] In *City of God* XIX, Augustine gives the example of a judge who feels compelled to take his seat: though unavoidable ignorance means he may end up torturing or killing the innocent, "judgement is also unavoidable because human society compels it."[44] In a broken creation we are compelled to grapple with the forces of sin and try to wrest them toward justice, and we are to some extent compelled to proceed by way of division, whether more or less just. Pain, as well as longing, is one of the shapes that the desire for peace takes in a disordered creation. Sometimes seeking peace by division is necessary, but even when it appears unavoidable, the act of shutting out, cutting off, or "death-as-solution" is often also experienced as tragedy, as a fruit of the irreparable brokenness of things. Like the upside-down man, something about the pain of the situation, even when it cannot be otherwise, speaks to us of disorder. The desire for peace in such situations may be present as a conscious longing for reconciliation, but it may be buried even deeper still, present to us only as a pain that things must be so—or so we feel. This is the pain of conscience, the kind of pain we heard in the voice of the Colombian guerrilla quoted earlier: "Father, it is not me. . . . I want it over, but I can't."[45] Buried deeper yet, and paradoxically, the desire for peace may take shape as a sense of the *necessity* of our hard hearts in such a world and a determination not to relent. That such a hard-hearted determination is necessary speaks to us, though distantly, of the strain of disorder and division.

This pain, I want to argue, speaks to us in two directions. In one sense, it is the voice of *loss*: loss of innocence, loss of unity, loss of the possibility of relationships without competing and incompatible needs, and all of this like the memory of a beautiful country we have never seen. This is the voice of original peace and the harmony for which our nature longs. But here I want to suggest a distinction that offers a gentle corrective to one of the problematic tendencies noted earlier in Catholic social teaching. In the face of accounts of society that would make a state of conflict the ultimate or permanent truth about humanity, Catholic social teaching has always insisted on peace as the original condition and vocation of humanity. But this insistence on harmony as the original and deepest truth of human nature, and the insistence that efforts to achieve peace therefore run with the grain of our nature, has resulted in a tendency to underestimate the force of sin in human relationships and the degree of struggle involved in working toward a more just and peaceful social order. There is in modern Catholic social teaching a certain—and absolutely proper—idealism about the possibility of peaceful, just international relations and the reconciliation of peoples with God and with one another. But, as Williams observes, there can be no "return to primordial harmonics, purely innocent difference": to be in history is to be inevitably "shaped by privation, living at the expense of each other."[46] There is no going backward. And so I want to argue that the pain I have described speaks to us not just from the past, as the voice of loss of a peace that now can never be; ultimately, it is not a tragic voice but a hopeful one, and it speaks to us, however faintly we hear it, about the possibility of a different kind of peace altogether.

The peace that is the gift of the risen Jesus is not piecemeal peace as the world gives. It is a peace that arrives with the presence of the one who was cut off and killed, and killed precisely as a means of securing peace: "It is better that one man should die for the people." But in this context, the presence of Jesus, alive, is not the *undoing* of this act of cutting off and killing: the cutting off, the death, was final. Jesus's presence in the locked room, then, is a starting again, a new creation. It is the presence of absolute gratuity, and he gives freely there what we long for but cannot ask from the victim of our attempts to grasp it: peace. And because there can be no undoing, no going backward, that peace must necessarily take the shape of *forgiveness*, reconciliation, and the growth toward healing of the wholeness we have so damaged.

TRUE PEACE

I want at this point to return to the distinction between what Augustine calls the peace of the earthly city and the peace of the city of God. I do not want to use the terms "earthly peace" and "heavenly peace," because these come with associations that I want to resist, namely, that heavenly peace is something that happens after earthly peace and somewhere else. I also resist using Augustine's terms, because the earthly city and the city of God are too easily wrongly understood as "world" and "church"—a point to which I return later. Above, I have used the terms "piecemeal peace" and "true peace," and these terms will serve. By "piecemeal peace," I mean the kind of humanly secured peace I have just been discussing, the peace that, in sinful or less sinful, distorted and less distorted ways, we pursue from within the brokenness of creation. It is a peace that, in Anna Rowlands's nice phrase, "fails towards" and *can* only ever fail toward God's order of creation.[47] By "true peace" or "the peace of God," I mean something different: not a heavenly peace of "elsewhere" or "someday," but the peace of our last end *as it comes to meet us within broken creation.* This is the peace of the risen Christ, which is not defined or contained by the locked doors by which we secure our piecemeal peace. It is not disembodied or ghostly but real and touchable, and I want to argue that it can, in an imperfect way, be received and lived by us concretely *in via.* This peace is not something constructed by us but something received; it does not proceed by division but by receiving the other—the other whom we have cast out as the victim and price of our smaller peace.

I have already touched on the ambivalence of the human desire for peace and the ways in which we fear as well as long for it. Sebastian

Moore's *The Crucified Is No Stranger* draws on Jungian tropes to explore human ambivalence in the face of God's call to wholeness. We deeply desire wholeness and freedom, but we also dread it: there is a force in us that resists the power "that calls man into being[,] . . . to identity, to personhood, to himself," and that constantly undermines that call to wholeness.[48] The mystery of evil, Moore argues, "is the inability of the death-wish to be simply a death-wish: its necessity to justify itself by removing the very *grounds* for requiring of us a more intensely personal life."[49] Our personal refusal to enter into life becomes hostility toward the God who calls us toward it. Jesus is God's invitation into fullness of life, an invitation that we reject and crucify rather than accept. "But my crucifying," Moore claims,

> is my way of entry, for it represents my non-personhood forced into its characteristic action, which is the destruction of wholeness. So there I am, out in the open at last. But once out in the open, I lose the fight to keep what I *thought* was myself but was really my anonymity. Forced to hear myself saying, "I hate that which makes for life," I expose myself to sorrow, and sorrow, if I give it free rein, bears me into the heart of the crucified where I discover myself. . . . We crucify Jesus rather than be him, and thus, through the healing power of sorrow, we become him.[50]

In the crucifixion, our covering and blaming tactics are stripped away, exposing our hostility to God, and to ourselves fully alive in God. This hostility takes shape as the "destruction of wholeness," our preference for the security of our own self-willed fragmentation rather than a wholeness that lies beyond our power.[51]

Moore's work focuses on the symbol of the cross as the moment and locus at which God reveals and begins to heal this refusal of wholeness, but I want to return to the theme of the resurrection and make a connection with the theology of consolation that I sketched out in the third chapter, where I described the resurrection as God's concrete refusal of human self-destructiveness. In Jesus crucified, we see that the desire for peace, the true peace of God, is something we resist, a hope that we strive to bury as we try to content ourselves with the divided and piecemeal peace of our own construction. The risen Jesus is God's refusal of our division of things, our willingness to settle for death-as-solution because it is "better to have one person die for the people" (Jn 18:14). In Jesus risen, we meet a God more faithful to us than we are to ourselves, who presents us with the possibility of a real, risen life beyond the death that we inflict on ourselves and on each other. What the resurrection shows us is that though there is no going backward to the original peace before the Fall, there is a possibility of going *for-ward* to a life on the other side of violence and death. We fear this unknown life, and what the journey toward it will demand of us, but we also deeply desire it.

This is a central theme of Williams's *Resurrection*, which draws together some of the themes that I have already discussed: the resurrection as the sign of God's unrelenting fidelity to us and Sebastian Moore's instinct that the moment of our transformation is one of simultaneous recognition and admission. For Moore, that moment takes place at the cross, when I realize that this victim on the cross is both my victim and my *self.* But the moment of recognition that locates at the cross I want to locate at the resurrection, when Jesus enters the room in spite of the locked door. Jesus appears there as what we dread: the return from the dead of what we have shut out. He appears there not just as the one we crucify in dramatic ways, but the one from whom we cut ourselves off in all kinds of ordinary, understandable, and perhaps unavoidable ways: the one betrayed, the one abandoned, the one we could not love enough, the one we sacrificed because of our need for safety or out of fear, the one who it was better to sacrifice for a greater good or to save "the people." Jesus also appears there as our *unknown* victim, the one we were unaware of cutting off, or who never existed for us, but who now confronts us: "Lord, when did we see you . . . ?" (Mt 25:44). Jesus appears there, too, as the reconciliation for which we perhaps deeply long but from which we have cut ourselves off, or from which we are separated by the "death" of impossibility. And he appears there, in the locked room, not as reproach or condemnation or vengeance but as forgiveness, as healing, and as restoration: he comes with the greeting, "Peace be with you."[52]

This needs some unpacking. In the Acts of the Apostles, the disciples preach in the streets of Jerusalem that "God has made him both Lord and Messiah, this Jesus whom you crucified" (Acts 2:36). In this proclamation, Williams says, the exaltation of the condemned Jesus is presented by the disciples not as threat but as promise and hope. The condemning court, the murderous "city," is indeed judged as resisting the saving will of God; but that does not mean that the will of God ceases to be saving. The rulers and the people are in rebellion; yet they act "in ignorance" (Acts 3:17, Luke 23:34), and God still waits to be graciously present in times of "refreshing" (Acts 3:19). And grace is released when the judges turn to their victim and recognize him as their hope and their saviour.[53]

What the apostles announce is not a reversal, in which the one judged returns, vindicated by God, to judge and condemn his judges; rather, what they announce is the risen Jesus as the insistent mercy of God, who consistently refuses to condemn, threaten, or reject. The point here is one I mentioned at the beginning of the chapter: the transformation happens from within, in that "the divine judgement on the world is *not* delivered from a supernatural plane, but is enacted within the relations of human beings to each other."[54] As James Alison puts it, "The resurrection is forgiveness: not a decree of forgiveness, but the presence of gratuity as a person."[55] The presence of the risen Jesus in the locked room simply *is* God's overcoming of our self-inflicted alienation from God, self, and others.

Williams goes on to argue that this event is not a one-off but part of a pattern. The disciples' proclamation of the resurrection is an announcement that God is with the victim, and not just this victim, Jesus, but every victim, and purely because they *are* a victim. Looking backward, Jesus's death and resurrection reveal God's perennial identification with the victim throughout salvation history.[56] Looking forward, Jesus's death and resurrection reveal the pattern of God's salvation, which is also concretely enacted and received within the relations of human beings to one another.

> When we make victims, when we embark on condemnation, exclusion, violence, the diminution or oppression of anyone, when we set ourselves up as judges, we are exposed to judgement (as Jesus himself asserts in Matt. 7:1–2), and we turn away from salvation. To hear the good news of salvation, to be converted, is to turn back to the condemned and rejected, acknowledging that there is hope nowhere else.[57]

Again, the point here is not simply the reversal or inversion of our relationships of oppression and exclusion.[58] This, Williams argues, would be a distortion of true reconciliation and restoration: the inversion of the oppressor-victim relationship is not the point, for the "judge-victim relationship must itself be transformed."[59] The point of the resurrection, and the presence of the victim not as threat but as forgiveness, is that it makes possible new kinds of relationship.[60] As Williams puts it, "When God receives and approves the condemned Jesus and returns him to his judges through the preaching of the Church, he transcends the world of oppressor-oppressed relations to create a new humanity, capable of other kinds of relation—between human beings, and between humanity and the Father."[61]

Piecemeal peace, the peace gained by division, othering, and exclusion, can only be transcended by overcoming division itself. This means *admission*, in the double sense of genuine letting-in of the other from whom we have cut ourselves off and allowing their presence to bring home to us the truth of our guilt and the truth of the brokenness in which we have played our part. The risk, of course, is considerable, because forgiveness cannot be demanded or guaranteed. We can open ourselves to encounter and ask for forgiveness, but the initiative and the power of reconciliation lies with the victim. It is only through their gracious act of forgiveness that the relationship of oppressor and victim can be transcended and a new kind of relationship made possible. This is what I meant earlier by saying that true peace cannot be grasped or secured, only received; this is also what Williams means by claiming that "grace is released *only* in confrontation with the victim" and that the victim "alone can be the source of renewal and transformation."[62]

This moment of admission and encounter with the victim is constantly endangered by our fearful urge to secure peace by division. Faced with the presence of the victim by whose exclusion we have purchased our peace, and thus confronted with our guilt, the urge may be to exalt them and exclude ourselves from grace: they become all light, and we become all darkness. Aware that in this moment of admission we are "at the mercy" of our victim, unsure that we will receive the forgiveness we seek, we exclude ourselves from it, and in doing so we perpetuate the untruth that peace can be gained only by division. Victim and oppressor cannot exist in the same space, so, acknowledging our guilt, we absent ourselves, and the locked door remains. Alternatively, we may be unable to resist the desire to divide the multivalent brokenness in which we are all enmeshed into "good" and "bad," pure victim and irredeemable oppressor. Earlier, I suggested that there were some cases in which peace-by-division was necessary. Take, for example, situations of religious tension in which fear of attacks mean that Christian communities rely on compounds around churches, with armed guards at their gates. In such a case, to describe militants as victims as well as oppressors and Christians as oppressors as well as victims seems nonsensical or even morally offensive, and the temptation is to deny any such mutuality, indeed to deny the need for reconciliation altogether. Again, the logic of division prevails, and the locked door remains: victim and oppressor cannot exist in the same space. In such profoundly difficult situations, to resist a black-and-white division between innocent and guilty is not to say that all hurts are equal; nor is it to excuse violence and abuse, or make its victims culpable for the piecemeal peace they have secured by cutting themselves free of their abusers. It is rather to cling to the truth that in a creation damaged by sin, all are wounded, all are sinful, and all are in need of reconciliation, and thus to hold open a space of encounter. This is what Christian de Chergé expressed: a recognition of his own complicity in the world's brokenness that enabled him to see even his murderer as a "last minute friend" and hold open the possibility of reconciliation, even if only eschatologically as "happy thieves in paradise."[63]

It is worth emphasizing at this juncture the eschatological character of true peace: it can indeed come to meet us within fallen creation, and concretely so, but sometimes it is simply beyond our strength. True peace, as I have already stated, is something we receive, not something we grasp: forgiveness cannot be forced, and attempts to do so just result in division going underground rather than being overcome. In many cases, the true peace of reconciliation is approached iteratively, and the encounters in which we give or receive forgiveness must happen over and over again. In other cases, true peace can barely be approached at all, and the desire for true peace is lived simply as the conscious experience of division *as* division, rather than as necessary or desired, and as the hope that even those divisions that seem most insurmountable by our own powers will, in the end, be healed. But it is important to state, too, that this vision of eschatological possibility should galvanize us rather than leave us passively waiting for the reconciliation of all things in Christ: reconciliation is indeed God's initiative, as explained in the previous chapter, but we are also called to let it flow through us.

TO BE A NEW CREATION

So far I have argued that if we talk about all people desiring peace, we need to account for the ways in which sin distorts the peace we pursue and the way in which we pursue it. In the first part of the chapter, I drew on the resurrection narratives to explore human ambivalence in the face of peace and to draw a contrast between piecemeal peace—the peace of division, secured by cutting ourselves off from one another and from aspects from ourselves—and the true peace of the risen Christ, which returns us to one another and to ourselves. These are different not just in degree but also in kind: piecemeal peace originates within a creation broken by sin, and cannot help reflecting and carrying forward some of that brokenness, whereas the peace of the risen Christ makes possible new kinds of relationships and thus enables a kind of peace and unity not secured by division. I have argued that although the fullness of true peace is an eschatological reality, it also comes to meet us in history as a concrete possibility.

We need now to take a closer look at how these two kinds of peace exist side by side *in via*. The task of exploring a politics of true peace belongs to another, future project, and here I want to make only a few brief comments about the relationship between true peace and the Church.[64] It is not possible to address fully every ecclesiological implication of the argument I have made thus far, but it is important to set out a few key principles.

The first principle is that the possibility of true peace in history is not separable from the Church. The final chapters of the Gospels tell the stories of the disciples' renewed relationship with the risen Jesus, in encounters in which the wounds of denial (Jn 21:15–17), abandonment (Jn 21:1–13), and doubt (Jn 20:24–29) are healed.[65] With this healing comes a new mission to all people, "beginning in Jerusalem" (Lk 24:47). There then unfolds, in Acts and the letters of Paul, the larger story of the new kinds of relationships made possible by the resurrection, relationships of forgiveness and "letting-in" that overcome human divisions of class, sex, nation, and religion.[66] What we see is the emergence of a new community "in Christ," a community that emerges through and is defined by the overcoming of established boundaries between Jew and Gentile, slave and free, wealthy and poor, and male and female. This community is real: Acts and the letters of Paul furnish ample evidence of a growing community that holds within it all these different classes of people. It is also far from being a perfect embodiment of true peace, and there is also clear evidence of the tensions and questions that arise in that new unity.[67] As I showed in the previous chapter, Acts and the letters of Paul also demonstrate that overcoming division is a key part of the Church's understanding of what God was doing in Christ, and therefore of its self-understanding. This appears perhaps most clearly in Paul's announcement of the new creation in 2 Corinthians.

> So if anyone is in Christ, there is a new creation: everything old has passed away; see, everything has become new! All this is from God, who reconciled us to himself through Christ, and has given us the ministry of reconciliation; that is, in Christ God was reconciling the world to himself, not counting their trespasses against them, and entrusting the message of reconciliation to us. (2 Cor 5:17–19)

The initiative is with God: "all this is from God," who by "not counting their trespasses against them" makes the first move in reconciling a creation unable to help itself. The message of reconciliation is then handed on to us, as ambassadors and inhabitants of the new creation. In this new creation, the old divisions have passed away. In Ephesians, Paul speaks about the way in which the death of Christ breaks down "the dividing wall, that is the hostility" between Jews and Gentiles, "that he might create in himself one new humanity in place of the two, thus making peace, and might reconcile both groups to God in one body through the cross" (Eph 3:14–16). In Galatians, Paul claims that there is no longer Jew or Greek, slave or free, male or female, "for all of you are one in Christ Jesus" (Gal 3:28). This process of reunification of all things under Christ begins in the body of the Church, but it has a cosmic and eschatological scope (Col 1:15–20).

These passages help us answer more fully the question I asked at the beginning of the chapter: If all people desire peace, then how does that peace manifest itself within broken creation on its way back to God? I have already sketched out part of the answer: true peace manifests itself in the emergence of new relationships which are free from the division, covering, and blaming by which we try to secure our peace in a broken creation. This peace is not something grasped or secured by us but something received; it is the fruit of God's initiative of reconciliation. Further, this true peace is really present within broken creation: the Church is the body that the peace of the risen Christ creates, and in this sense it literally embodies true peace. It is therefore an indispensable part of the Church's identity and mission to be an agent of true peace and the overcoming of division.

But if the first principle is that the Church and the presence of true peace in history are not separable, the second principle is that they are not identical. My discussion of piecemeal peace and true peace has focused on the personal and interpersonal level, partly because if we recognize the complexity of the relationship between the two on a personal level and the magnitude and depth of the transformation required of us, we will be more inclined to resist too swift or easy a transfer to the general or political level. It is just not possible to identify "Church" with "true peace" and "world" with "piecemeal peace," for at least two good reasons. First, as an ecclesial body, as on an individual level, we live between piecemeal peace and true peace. It hardly needs saying that the Church falls well short of living true peace; what is perhaps less obvious, and worth pointing out, is the fact that the Church is a Church of sinners and thus sometimes needs to pursue peace-by-division even within her own bounds.[68] Second, the way that the resurrection overcomes human divisions also means that true peace can be found outside the Church. We have already seen how, in the book of Acts, the initiative of God and the action of the Spirit constantly run ahead of the apostles' understanding, so those who are not yet included in the "we" of the Church are already gathered in by the action of God. The gift of the Spirit of the risen Jesus is poured out even upon those who have not yet received baptism (Acts 10:44–48), and we can therefore expect to find those outside the Church who, in different ways, embody true peace.

These two principles are important because they enable us to uphold and insist on the Church's vocation to embody and pursue true peace within history without making overconfident claims about the Church's achievement or distinctiveness in this regard on a social level. Some recent Catholic theological reflection in this area has emphasized the need for the Church to exist as a distinctive social body, characterized by its ability to overcome the problematic ethnic, political, and social divisions of the surrounding culture.[69] Some of these theologians are writing from situations of violent conflict or oppression, where the Church's ability to rise above such "natural" categories, and resist the violent uses to which they are put, is very important.[70] Yet I remain somewhat chary of theological schemes that place a premium on the Church's social distinctiveness or argue that the Church is (or ought to be) a "whole new world" on a social level, for two reasons. The first is empirical: as Kathryn Tanner points out, Christian identity is simply not a "whole cloth" cultural alternative.[71] Christianity takes ordinary practices of the surrounding culture, adapts, and reorients them, but in doing so it does not create a whole new Christian world, in the sense of a comprehensive, sufficient, and distinctive web of cultural practices.

The second reason is theological. The Church is indeed a sign of the new creation in Christ, but its newness does not consist in being a new social group on the same plane and in the same way as other social groups, as though after Pentecost we simply have the usual babel of social groups plus one new supergroup, the Church. The significance of the Pentecost event is not that people speak a single new language but that they newly understand one another: division is overcome when differences are transcended, not displaced. There is a danger, as we saw in the previous chapter, that theological overinvestment in the social distinctiveness of the Church leads to continuing trade in the currency of identity-by-division. But it is humility, balance, and care that are needed here, not the rejection of any and all claims that the Church should model a different way of living. I do want to describe the Church as a new unity, but it is important to specify the kind of new unity that it has: the Church's peace, in Williams's words, "is a healed history, not a 'total harmony' whose constructed (and thus scarred) character doesn't show."[72] At its best, our identity as Church includes, mends, and transcends our other identities rather than displacing them, and it is significant that the Church in some way shows signs of the ongoing struggle and "scars" of its new unity. To take an example, if a garment is mended "invisibly," then there is nothing to show that its original perfection was ever damaged or that it was restored; a visible mend in a garment shows the fact of damage *and* that it has been mended. The fact that the Church exists as a "visible mend" is what makes it a sign of hope and a sign of God's intention to reconcile the whole of creation. It is also—or also should be—what makes the Church an *effective* sign of that reconciliation and an agent of eschatological mending.

Mary McClintock Fulkerson's *Places of Redemption*, a study of a racially and ably diverse congregation in the southern United States, provides an excellent example of what I mean here. Against the background of a racially divided nation and a racially divided Church, well-meaning liberal claims "not to see" differences of color or disability are problematic, because they fit into wider patterns of obliviousness or "will-to-disregard" that perpetuate injustice by refusing to name or confront it.[73] Congregants at Good Samaritan often claimed "not to see color" or "not to see difference, only Christians," but defining Christian identity as a kind of "amiable tolerance," Fulkerson argues, can perpetuate a "denial of the inherited residuals of racism and projection of premature reconciliation by those most fearful of losing power."[74] She argues that "generically inclusive behaviours are not simply kindly Christian displays of love for humanity; rather they reproduce daily racism and able-ism."[75] In the context of such willful obliviousness, Fulkerson argues that what Good Samaritan became was "a place to appear."[76] In other words, what made the church a potentially transformative and healing place for those who attended it was not its existence as a whole new world in which race and ability were invisible but its existence as a visible mend, and one in which the work of mending was still ongoing. Like the scars of the risen Jesus, the visible mend of the Church's diversity shows in a very concrete way the path that God's saving work has taken and the reality of the struggle with the powers of evil. The Church's scarred unity should not just speak to us of a natural and original harmony, but also of the costliness of the ongoing struggle with sin and the magnitude of our call to transformation in Christ.

The work of mending is still ongoing, and that, perhaps, is at the root of my resistance to accounts of the Church's peace that place heavy emphasis on the necessity of its existence as a distinctive social option. As discussed in the chapter on social sin, the evil against which we struggle is not just a feature of our social environments, but also of ourselves: our bodily habituations, our patterns of thought, even our understandings of reality. Our worldly identities and Christian identities are intermixed at just this level, inseparable as leaven and flour. And the transformation to which we are called, that shift from piecemeal peace to true peace, reaches into the deepest parts of who we are. We must be changed, but, as *Pacem in terris* puts it, "it is the law of nature that all things must be of gradual growth."[77] If we claim too quickly that the Church—unlike the world—is "reconciled and reconciling," then we may miss the ways in which the line between piecemeal peace and true peace runs through the Church as a body. Such a move may result in conflict within the Church being denied or suppressed, prematurely reconciled or projected outward as a feature of "the world"—the irony of a piecemeal peace purchased by shutting out the Church's own conflict and sin. The Church's ability to be reconciled and reconciling, to be a manifestation and agent of true peace, depends on her resisting this kind of division and having the humility and strength to remain in the difficult space of encounter with her own sin, conflict, and darkness. Her ability to embody true peace depends on her ability to return to this space of encounter, in which she receives the forgiveness of the risen Christ, over and over again. It is a law of grace, as well as nature, that new life must be of gradual growth.

PURSUING PEACE

I have explored in this chapter one of the central and abiding claims of Catholic social teaching on peace—that all people desire peace. Taking a closer look at how the understandings of both "desire" and "peace" have shifted from Augustine to the present, I suggested that we need to attend to two questions. If all people desire peace, then how does that *desire* manifest itself within broken creation on its way back to God? And if all people desire peace, then how does that *peace* manifest itself within broken creation on its way back to God? Drawing on the resurrection narratives, I first explored the ambivalence of human desire for peace, arguing that it is always present but complex, deeply buried, and in need of transformation. I then went on to explore the ways in which we pursue peace in distorted as well as salutary ways, revisiting and fleshing out a distinction between the piecemeal peace secured by division and the true peace that is the gift of the risen Christ. I argued that this distinction between piecemeal peace and true peace is a helpful one, because it gives us the beginnings of a language in which to express the relationship between these two kinds of peace as being one of radical change and transformation, as well as growth. And rather than posit a distinction between a kind of peace available now and another available in a distant eschatological future, or a kind of peace available on earth and another kind available in heaven, it gives us a way of talking about how these two different kinds of peace can and do exist side by side in broken creation on its way back to God. The Church is where true peace is most fully revealed, not because we live it perfectly, or even because we live it well, but because it is revealed there with the face and name of Jesus, whose gift it is. It is the Church's task to proclaim the hope, embody the possibility, and hasten the advent of that true peace in the world.

NOTES

Introduction

1. See BBC News, "Pope Francis Kisses Feet of Rival South Sudan Leaders." See also Jason Horowitz, "Pope Francis, in Plea for South Sudan Peace, Stuns Leaders by Kissing Their Shoes."

2. ICIN, "New Hope Trauma Centre of Iraq."

3. John L. Allen Jr., "Trauma Forms the Invisible Ruins ISIS Left Behind on the Nineveh Plains."

4. Throughout the book, I generally refer to the Catholic Church rather than to the Roman Catholic Church. This signifies all churches in communion with Rome, so in addition to the Roman Catholic Church (the Latin Church specifically), it includes the twenty-three Eastern Rite Churches, of which the Chaldean Catholic Church is one example.

5. BBC News, "Pope Francis Warns on 'Piecemeal World War III.'" See also the collected references in *National Catholic Reporter*, "World at War Is a Common View for Francis."

6. O'Brien, "Stories of Solidarity," 401.

7. "Peacemaking is not an optional commitment. It is a requirement of our faith. We are called to be peacemakers, not by some movement of the moment, but by our Lord Jesus. The content and context of our peacemaking is set not by some political agenda or ideological program, but by the teaching of his Church." See USCCB, *The Challenge of Peace*, Summary II.C. See also Paul VI, *Evangelii nuntiandi*, §29.

8. See Hehir, "Catholicism and Democracy," 25.

9. See, e.g., Todd Whitmore's reflections on how the precarious nature of life in seriously poverty-stricken countries challenges the distinction in Catholic just war reasoning between direct and indirect threats to life. Whitmore, "Peacebuilding and Its Challenging Partners," 155–89.

10. Sobrino, *Witnesses to the Kingdom*, 75.

11. Lisa Cahill's *Love Your Enemies* is a fine example of a book that seeks to engage with the Church's tradition of teaching on peace as a whole, and Kenneth Himes has also undertaken valuable mapping work in his "Peacebuilding and Catholic Social Teaching" and "Papal Thinking about Peace."

12. Appleby, "Peacebuilding and Catholicism," 5.

13. As far as I am aware, the term is first used in Benedict XVI, *Caritas in veritate*, §72.

14. Cahill, "Peacebuilding: A Practical Strategy," 47.

15. The USCCB document, *The Challenge of Peace*, portrays pacifist and just war approaches as complementary in this way in §121. See also Miller, *Interpretations of Conflict*, 17–18.

16. Kenneth Himes disagrees with this tactic on the grounds that "sharing a presumption against violence is not enough to establish complementarity when one side considers the presumption absolute and the other does not." See Himes, "Pacifism and the Just War Tradition," 341.

17. Its most well-known advocate and practitioner is the Mennonite peacebuilder and sociologist John Paul Lederach. See Lederach, *Building Peace*.

18. The language of destructive patterns of relating I borrow from Liechty and Clegg, *Moving Beyond Sectarianism*, 103.

19. Lederach and Appleby, "Strategic Peacebuilding," 34.

20. Drew Christiansen describes peace in Catholic social teaching as a "convoy concept," including many separate but related requirements. See Christiansen, "Catholic Peacemaking, 1991–2005," 22.

21. For more on this theme, see Hawksley, "Drawings for Projection."

22. Lederach and Appleby, "Strategic Peacebuilding," 28.

23. For the assertion that reconciliation cannot be less profound than the division itself, see John Paul II, *Reconciliatio et paenitentia*, §3.

24. The amount of Christianity still coursing through the bloodstream of most Western democracies means that quasi-theological beliefs about them can often to be found mixed up in even the most secular approaches to conflict.

25. The traffic is two-way: Séverine Autesserre's work indicates that international peacebuilding interveners may also have something to learn from peacebuilding as conceived and practiced by Catholic agencies, whose emphasis on long-term accompaniment and supporting local partners makes them comparatively effective and allows them to avoid some of the pitfalls of agencies involved in short-term peacebuilding interventions. See Autesserre, *Peaceland*, 85–86, 103–5.

26. Francis, "Nonviolence, a Style of Politics for Peace," §6, §1.

Chapter 1

1. For an overview, see Harnack, *Militia Christi*. James T. Johnson argues for a fairly continuous tradition of Christians serving in the Roman army. Johnson, *The Quest for Peace*, 15–17.

2. At the same time, Tertullian's claim in his *Apology*, "We sail with you, we fight with you, and till the ground with you," is one of the earliest pieces of evidence that Christians fought in the imperial army. See Tertullian, *Apologia* ch. 42.

3. Origen, *Contra Celsum* VIII.73–75.

4. Musto, *Catholic Peacemakers*, 95–96.

5. In an interesting critical comment on early Christian pacifism, Lytta Basset points out that both Tertullian and Lactantius emphasize divine vengeance and suggests that unable to act on their anger against their persecutors, they transferred it to God to enact in their stead. See Basset, *Holy Anger*, 31.

6. As Hunter points out, the prohibition on clerics taking arms and on the ordination of former soldiers suggests ongoing Christian unease regarding the ethics of military service and bloodshed. See Hunter, "A Decade of Research on Early Christians and Military Service," 89.

7. Cf. James T. Johnson's claim that these early fathers were writing in expectation of Jesus's imminent return, and therefore urging a general withdrawal from public life and an "interim ethic." See Johnson, *The Quest for Peace*, 13.

8. Cahill, *Love Your Enemies*, 41.

9 Origen, *Contra Celsum* VIII.73. See also Tertullian, *Apologia* ch. 30: "Looking up to heaven, the Christians . . . are ever making intercession for all the Emperors. We pray for them long life, a secure rule, a safe home, brave armies, a faithful senate, an honest people, a quiet world—and everything for which a man and a Caesar can pray."

10. It is worth noting that this question does not go away: it is still being discussed in debates on the ethics of war in seventeenth-century Salamanca, expressed in terms of the relationship between the natural law (equated with the Old Testament) and the gospel.

11. Augustine, *Contra Faustum* XXII.70.

12. Miller treats Augustine's thought on the ethics of war and killing in the context of a larger discussion on the presumption against harm. What distinguishes Augustine from the tradition that precedes him is the way he circumscribes the "duty of nonmaleficence . . . by distinguishing between realms of morality in three ways: self/other, interior/exterior acts, and

private/public authority. Augustine restricts the force of nonmaleficence by confining it to the first term in each of these pairs." See Miller, *Interpretations of Conflict*, 20–21.

13. Langan, "The Elements of St. Augustine's Just War Theory," 20. In *City of God* Augustine will emphasize still more strongly the tragic character of coercive violence.

14. In *On Free Choice of the Will*, Augustine reserves killing to those with proper judicial or military authority and argues that those lacking this authority may not kill, even in self-defense. See Augustine, *On Free Choice of the Will* I.4–6. See also Augustine, *Letter to Publicola*, §5. Cahill points out that this restriction of killing to those with proper authority may also concern the motivation that justifies the act, e.g., its use as punishment. See Cahill, *Love Your Enemies*, 69.

15. It is "when force is required to inflict the punishment, that, in obedience to God or some lawful authority, good men undertake wars, when they find themselves in such a position as regards the conduct of human affairs, that right conduct requires them to act, or to make others act in this way." Augustine, *Contra Faustum* XXII.70.

16. Augustine, *Contra Faustum* XXII.75.

17. Augustine, *Contra Faustum* XXII.78.

18. Augustine, *Contra Faustum* XXII.71.

19. This is evident in his discussion of self-defense in *On the Free Choice of the Will* I.5, where he states that people should not kill in defense of those things (life, liberty, chastity) that can be lost. See Langan, "The Elements of St. Augustine's Just War Theory," 27; Miller, *Interpretations of Conflict*, 19–20.

20. Augustine, *Contra Faustum* XXII.74.

21. Augustine, *Contra Faustum* XXII.75.

22. Augustine, *Letter to Boniface*, §6.

23. Augustine, *Contra Faustum* XXII.79.

24. Augustine, *City of God* XIX.13.

25. Augustine, *City of God* XIX.12.

26. Varro calculates 288 possible sects in all, based on multiplying possible principles of differentiation, but then reduces all the possible differences between the schools to three fundamental ones: whether the "primary objects of nature" are sought for the sake of virtue, whether virtue is sought for the sake of the primary objects of nature, or whether each is sought for its own sake. Augustine disagrees with each of Varro's options, on the grounds that they concern only happiness in the here and now. See Augustine, *City of God* XIX.2.

27. Augustine, *City of God* XIX.4.

28. Augustine, *City of God* XIX.13.

29. By contrast, the end of the wicked of the earthly city is "everlasting misery" in a state of continual war: "The force of pain is in such conflict with the body's nature that neither can yield to the other. . . . [P]ain continues always, in order to torment, while nature remains in order to feel the pain." Augustine, *City of God* XIX.28. Ordinarily, either pain would be victorious in this struggle, and the person's suffering would end in death, or nature would be victorious, and the person's suffering would end in healing.

30. Augustine, *City of God* XIX.17, 27.

31. Augustine, *City of God* XIX.20.

32. Augustine writes, "The peace which is our [Christians'] peculiar possession, however, is ours even now, with God by faith; and we shall enjoy it eternally with him by sight. But the peace we have here, whether shared with other men or peculiar to ourselves, is only a solace for our wretchedness rather than the joy of blessedness." Augustine, *City of God* XIX.27.

33. Te Selle, *Living in Two Cities*, 123.

34. Augustine, *City of God* XIX.11, 28.

35. Augustine, *City of God* XIX.14. I find persuasive Oliver O'Donovan's view that Augustine does not have a concept of the secular in the way we understand it: a sphere shared by Christians and non-Christians in which the same goods are used to different ends. For Augustine, things are only properly used when directed to their right end; directed to their wrong end, they are simply *ab*used. See O'Donovan, "Augustine's *City of God XIX* and Western Political Thought." For an alternative view, see Markus, *Saeculum*.

36. Augustine, *City of God* XIX.14–15.

37. Augustine, *City of God* XIX.27.

38. Augustine, *City of God* XIX.17.

39. Augustine, *City of God* XIX.26, 17.

40. O' Donovan, "Augustine's *City of God XIX* and Western Political Thought," 144–47. Contrast this with the 1971 Synod of Bishops document *Justitia in mundo*, which states, "Action on behalf of justice and participation in the transformation of the world fully appear to us as a constitutive dimension of the preaching of the Gospel, or, in other words, of the Church's mission for the redemption of the human race and its liberation from every oppressive situation." Synod of Bishops, *Justitia in mundo*, §6. Quoted in Himes, "Commentary on *Justitia in mundo*," 352.

41. Augustine, *City of God* XIX.16. Lisa Cahill argues that Augustine's view of the ideal Christian emperor in *City of God* "hints at larger transformative possibilities." See Cahill, *Blessed Are the Peacemakers*, 134.

42. O'Donovan, "Augustine's *City of God XIX* and Western Political Thought," 146. Brown notes, in a similar vein, that "the Christian ruler differs

from the pagan, not in the amount of power he wields, nor in the state which he maintains: he differs only in his awareness of where this power stands in God's order, to what it is related, what ends it may serve." See Brown, "Saint Augustine and Political Society," 23.

43. "Therefore, for as long as this Heavenly City is a pilgrim on earth, she summons citizens of all nations and every tongue, and brings together a society of pilgrims in which no attention is paid to any differences in the customs, laws and institutions by which earthly peace is achieved or maintained. She does not rescind or destroy these things, however. For whatever differences there are among the various nations, these all tend towards the same end of earthly peace. Thus, she preserves and follows them, provided only that they do not impede the religion by which we are taught that the one and supreme God is to be worshipped." Augustine, *City of God* XIX.17.

44. Augustine, *City of God* XIX.14.

45. Johnson, *Ideology, Reason, and the Limitation of War*, 47–48.

46. Instead, the authority to wage war belonged to "princes without superior." In theory, this was an attempt to limit the constant conflict between warring nobles in Europe, in practice, it translated into "might makes right." As Johnson puts it, "if a prince could make war and get away with it, he had authority to do so." See Johnson, *Just War Tradition*, 170.

47. Pieper, *The Silence of St. Thomas*, 60; original emphasis.

48. Aquinas's theory of human knowledge gives a very positive account of the ability of human beings to grasp the truth of created things. John Jenkins's account of Aquinas's theory of human knowledge is helpful here: Jenkins, *Knowledge and Faith in Thomas Aquinas*, 102–8. See also Aquinas, *Summa Theologica* I.8.5–6.

49. Aquinas, *Summa Theologica* I–II.1.8 s.c., referring to Augustine.

50. Aquinas, *Summa Theologica* I–II.62.1 co.

51. Aquinas, *Summa Theologica* I–II.1.8 co.

52. Aquinas, *Summa Theologica* I–II.5.5 co.

53. Aquinas, *De Regno*, §107.

54. Aquinas, *De Regno*, §§108–10.

55. Aquinas, *Summa Theologica* II–II.29.1 co. Concord is defined as the unity of desire between individuals. It does not necessarily entail the unity of desire of individuals within themselves.

56. Aquinas, *Summa Theologica* II–II.29.2.

57. For natural law, see *Summa Theologica* II–I.94.2; for human law, see II–I.95.2. Human law participates in eternal law only so far as it is derived from natural law, and in the following question Aquinas states, "The natural law is a participation in us of the eternal law: while human law falls short of the eternal law" (II–I.96.2 ad 3).

58. Aquinas, *Summa Theologica* II–I.93.3. Aquinas states that "virtue is natural to man inchoatively. This is so in respect of the specific nature, in so far as in man's reason are to be found instilled by nature certain naturally known principles of both knowledge and action, which are the nurseries of intellectual and moral virtues, and in so far as there is in the will a natural appetite for good in accordance with reason" (*Summa Theologica* I–II.63.1 co).

59. Aquinas, *Summa Theologica* I–II.98.1 co.

60. Aquinas, *Summa Theologica* II–II.29.3 ad 3.

61. Aquinas, *Summa Theologica* II–II.29.3 ad 4.

62. Compare Aquinas's statement on happiness: he argues that true and perfect happiness cannot be had in this life (*Summa Theologica* I–II.5.3 responsio), but he adds, "Men esteem that there is some kind of happiness to be had in this life, on account of a certain likeness to true Happiness. And thus they do not fail altogether in their estimate" (I–II.5.3 ad 3).

63. Aquinas, *Summa Theologica* II–II.40. This is a major argument of Reichberg, *Thomas Aquinas on War and Peace.*

64. Aquinas, *Summa Theologica* II–II.40.1 co.

65. See Aquinas, *Summa Theologica* I.96.4: "Man is naturally a social being, and so in the state of innocence he would have led a social life. Now a social life cannot exist among a number of people unless under the presidency of one to look after the common good; for many, as such, seek many things, whereas one attends only to one." Cf. Augustine, *City of God* XIX.15: "He [God] did not intend that his rational creatures, made in his own image, should have lordship over any but irrational creatures: not man over man, but man over the beasts. Hence the first just men were established as shepherds of flocks, rather than as kings of men. This was done so that in this way God might indicate what the order of nature requires, and what the desert of sinners demands." Augustine does regard the exercise of authority as natural within the family, however.

66. Aquinas, *De Regno*, §117.

67. Aquinas, *De Regno*, §118.

68. Gregory Reichberg notes that Aquinas, in his commentary on 1 Timothy, refers to the peace of the Church as mediate between the peace of the world and true peace. See Reichberg, *Thomas Aquinas on War and Peace*, 3.

Chapter 2

1. Aquinas, *Summa Theologica* II–II.40.1 co.

2. Johnson, *Ideology, Reason, and the Limitation of War*, 55.

3. Johnson, *Ideology, Reason, and the Limitation of War*, 47–48.

4. Johnson argues that it is English Puritans who came up with the idea of holy war. See Johnson, *Ideology, Reason and the Limitation of War*, 81–105. It

is in this period that "the role of religion in justifying war has become what we would call ideological" (169).

5. In the two centuries following the European "wars of religion," Cavanaugh points out, we see not the birth of modern liberalism but the rise of absolutist governments with confessional states. See Cavanaugh, *The Myth of Religious Violence*, 132.

6. Cavanaugh, *The Myth of Religious Violence*, 142–51.

7. Johnson notes that even in the later medieval period, "in real political terms no pope, even after Huguccio's recasting of right authority to include the papacy, was able to command the arms of the secular princes of Christendom except when the princes perceived it to be in their interest to be so commanded." See Johnson, *Just War Tradition*, 160.

8. Cavanaugh, *The Myth of Religious Violence*, 162.

9. Cavanaugh, *The Myth of Religious Violence*, 161.

10. Cahill, *Love Your Enemies*, 83.

11. Vitoria, *De Indis* II.1, II. Summary.

12. Vitoria, *De Indis* II.3.

13. Suárez, *De Bello et De Indis*, §6, cited in Johnson, *Ideology, Reason and the Limitation of War*, 168.

14. Christiansen, "Commentary on *Pacem in Terris*," 224.

15. Charles Curran argues that "even the post–Vatican II [social teaching] documents tend to use the Scriptures in proof-text fashion. . . . The documents do not consider the Scriptures in and for their own sake; they use the Scriptures to give support to moral teachings." See Curran, *Catholic Social Teaching*, 45.

16. "The created intellect cannot see the essence of God, unless God by his grace unites himself to the created intellect, as an object made intelligible to it." Aquinas, *Summa Theologica* I.12.4 co.

17. See Turner, *Thomas Aquinas*, 170. Human beings cannot know of nature's insufficiency to its own ends independently of grace: if we naturally knew what we lacked, then what we lack must be natural and therefore available to us.

18. Johnson, *Ideology, Reason, and the Limitation of War*, 169.

19. Rosenthal, "The Problem of the *Desiderium Naturale*," 338.

20. Suárez, *De Legibus* II.6.

21. Komonchak, "Theology and Culture at Mid-Century," 582.

22. De Lubac, *The Mystery of the Supernatural*, 61.

23. Shadle, *The Origins of War*, 36–48.

24. Leo XIII states that it must not "be supposed that the solicitude of the Church is so preoccupied with the spiritual concerns of her children

as to neglect their temporal and earthly interests." See Leo XIII, *Rerum novarum*, §28.

25. See Leo XIII, *Rerum novarum*, §§5–11. He concludes, "The common opinion of mankind, little affected by the few dissentients who have contended for the opposite view, has found in the careful study of nature, and in the laws of nature, the foundations for the division of property, and the practice of all ages has consecrated the principle of private ownership, as being pre-eminently in conformity with human nature, and as conducing in the most unmistakable manner to the peace and tranquillity of human existence." Leo XIII, *Rerum novarum*, §11.

26. Leo XIII, *Rerum novarum*, §17.

27. Leo XIII, *Rerum novarum*, §19.

28. Leo XIII, *Rerum novarum*, §19.

29. Leo XIII, *Rerum novarum*, §25.

30. Leo XIII, *Rerum novarum*, §§18–21.

31. Benedict XV repeats his plea to stop the fighting in *Allorché fummo chiamati*, published eight months later, in July 1915.

32. Benedict XV, *Ad beatissimi*, §§5, 7. Benedict XV also cites the love of money (§7) as among the causes of the war.

33. Benedict XV, *Ad beatissimi*, §17.

34. Benedict XV, *Ad beatissimi*, §17.

35. Benedict XV, *Ad beatissimi*, §18.

36. His encyclical *Pacem Dei munus pulcherrimum* (1920) speaks explicitly about these efforts in §2.

37. Benedict XV, *Ad beatissimi*, §30.

38. As Ashley Beck points out, this recent history of Vatican isolationism was one of the reasons Benedict XV's attempts at diplomatic resolution of the war were ignored or rebuffed. See Beck, "How Catholic Teaching about War Has Changed," 130–46. During the papacy of Benedict XV's predecessor-but-one, Pius IX, King Victor Emmanuel III had claimed the city of Rome as his capital, entering the city after a short siege on 20 September 1870 and leaving the pope "a prisoner in the Vatican." The political wrangling between the Italian government and the Holy See that followed would not be resolved until the conclusion of the Lateran Accords in 1929.

39. Pius XI, *Ubi arcano*, §§11–13.

40. Pius XI, *Ubi arcano*, §16.

41. Pius XI, *Ubi arcano*, §27.

42. Pius XI, *Ubi arcano*, §§10–11.

43. "We have already seen ... that the principal cause of the confusion, restlessness, and dangers which are so prominent a characteristic of false peace

is the weakening of the binding force of law and lack of respect for authority, effects which logically follow upon denial of the truth that authority comes from God, the Creator and Universal Law-giver." Pius XI, *Ubi arcano*, §39; see also §§28, 47.

44. Pius XI, *Ubi arcano*, §48. The same emphasis is present in Pius XII's *Summi pontificatus* (1939), which attributes war and other social ills to "the denial and rejection of a universal norm of morality as well for individual and social life as for international relations; We mean the disregard, so common nowadays, and the forgetfulness of the natural law itself, which has its foundation in God, Almighty Creator and Father of all, supreme and absolute Law-giver, all-wise and just Judge of human actions." *Summi pontificatus*, §28.

45. Pius XI, *Ubi arcano*, §48. I discuss later how this separation between Church and society is in Henri de Lubac's sights twenty years later, as he criticizes the extrinsicist relationship between nature and grace.

46. For peace and justice, see Pius XI, *Ubi arcano*, §34: "Peace does not consist merely in a hard inflexible justice. It must be made acceptable and easy by being compounded almost equally of charity and a sincere desire for reconciliation."

47. Pius XI, *Ubi arcano*, §41.

48. Pius XI, *Ubi arcano*, §44.

49. Pius XI states, "Recently the representatives and rulers of practically every nation, motivated by a common and instinctive desire for union and peace, have turned to this Apostolic See in order to bind themselves closer to us. . . . [I]t is becoming increasingly evident on all sides, and especially from actual experience, what great possibilities for peace and happiness, even here below, such a union with Us possesses for human society." Pius XI, *Ubi arcano*, §64.

50. "No merely human institution of today can be as successful in devising a set of international laws which will be in harmony with world conditions as the Middle Ages were in the possession of that true League of Nations, Christianity." Pius XI, *Ubi arcano*, §45.

51. Pius XI, *Ubi arcano*, §59.

52. Pius XI, *Ubi arcano*, §11. Pius XI's comments on education are largely directed against education that is "not only secular and non-religious but openly atheistical and anti-religious" (§29). Education about God and God's law is what is necessary to promote peace. A similar point is made in Pius XII's *Summi pontificatus*, which criticizes "the much vaunted civilization of society, which has made ever more rapid progress, withdrawing man, the family and the State from the beneficent and regenerating effects of the idea of God and the teaching of the Church" (§30).

53. Pius XI, *Ubi arcano*, §49.

54. John XXIII, *Pacem in terris*, §1.

55. As Curran puts it, Jesus Christ and grace do not really enter the picture. See Curran, *Catholic Social Teaching*, 28.

56. Christiansen, "Commentary on *Pacem in Terris*," 223–24.

57. On the development of the concept of dignity in Catholic social teaching from Pius XI's *Mit brennender sorge* and *Divini redemptoris* to John XXIII's *Pacem in terris*, see Rowlands, *Catholic Social Teaching*.

58. John XXIII's support for human rights also distinguishes him from his immediate predecessors. Christiansen has a helpful excursus on the history of rights talk in Catholic teaching in his "Commentary on *Pacem in Terris*," 217–43.

59. Christiansen, "Commentary on *Pacem in Terris*," 224.

60. See John XXIII, *Pacem in terris*, §93: "There may be, and sometimes is, a clash of interests among States, each striving for its own development. When differences of this sort arise, they must be settled in a truly human way, not by armed force nor deceit or trickery. There must be a mutual assessment of the arguments and feelings on both sides, a mature and objective investigation of the situation, and an equitable reconciliation of opposing views."

61. Shadle, in *The Origins of War*, notes the influence of Jacques Maritain (142) and points out that the structure of *Pacem in terris* reflects the structure of Kant's *Perpetual Peace*, which distinguishes the *ius civitas*, the *ius gentium*, and the *ius cosmopoliticum* (160 n. 43). Whether or not there are more direct links to the liberal tradition, I think it is fair to say that *Pacem in terris* reflects what Hollenbach calls "the modern self-confidence that human beings, if sufficiently enlightened, could finally bring the conditions of their social existence under the control of human reason, thus placing social life at the service of a more humane existence." Hollenbach, "Social Ethics," 6.

62. Quoted in Weigel, *Tranquillitas Ordinis*, 89. It is worth noting that the conviction that human beings can overcome war also has roots in the Catholic tradition, in the work of humanists like Vives and Erasmus.

63. E.g., John XXIII, *Pacem in terris*, §38, §54.

64. See Benedict XVI, *Caritas in veritate*, §67. Cahill comments, "This vision of just governance for the common good, even when paired with Benedict's conception of 'objective truth,' has much in common with the post–World War II ideal of 'liberal internationalism.' There is reason to suspect that both visions fly in the face of the real roles, capacities and limits of the United Nations; and of emerging, much more complicated, forms of global authority and control in 'the globalization era.'" See Cahill, "*Caritas in Veritate*," 306.

65. John XXIII, *Pacem in terris*, §157.

66. In an essay on the disappearance of the sense of the sacred, de Lubac wrote of "a sort of unconscious conspiracy between the movement which led to secularism and a certain theology, and while the supernatural was exiled and proscribed, we began to think that the supernatural was thus placed beyond the reach of nature, in the one place where it must reign." Henri de Lubac, quoted in translation in Komonchak, "Theology and Culture at Mid-Century," 584.

67. See, e.g., Weigel, *Tranquillitas Ordinis*, 90; Tillich, *Theology of Peace*, 176–77.

68. Weigel, *Tranquillitas Ordinis*, 90. The judgment is perhaps a little harsh: the encyclical was certainly heeded by the Catholic peace movements and bolstered grassroots Catholic support for human rights. John XXIII's faith in goodwill and the power of mutual trust to overcome enmity was not mere make-believe: he had managed to forge a relationship of trust with Khrushchev that enabled him to play a role in averting nuclear catastrophe during the Cuban Missile Crisis the previous fall. See Christiansen, "Commentary on *Pacem in Terris*," 217–43.

69. Tillich, *Theology of Peace*, 177–78.

70. Tillich, *Theology of Peace*, 179.

71. Tillich, *Theology of Peace*, 181.

72. Thomas Merton offers an interesting theological defense of John XXIII's optimism as essentially Thomist and mystical. See Merton, *Redeeming the Time*, 179–87.

73. Christiansen argues that "as a social ethic it [*Pacem in terris*] was incomplete. As a result of its optimism, it failed to recognize the tensions inherent in divided societies between rights advocacy and peace-making, and appeared to discount the hostility and conflict that the quest for human rights would provoke. John's vision of peace as a world community upholding human rights captured the end-state of a process that in lived experience would be fraught with conflict." Christiansen, "Commentary on *Pacem in Terris*," 233.

74. See Yzermans, *American Participation in the Second Vatican Council*, 215; see also Alberigo and Komonchak, *History of Vatican II*, vol. 4, 322.

75. De Lubac, *Surnaturel*.

76. De Lubac, *The Mystery of the Supernatural*, 167. De Lubac's insistence that human beings have a natural desire to see God emerges in part from his engagement with patristic thinking on the *imago Dei*: see 136.

77. While agreeing broadly with de Lubac's anti-extrinsicism, Rahner felt that *la nouvelle théologie* endangered the gratuity of grace by making nature unthinkable without it. He therefore held on to the necessity of the concept of nature as a *Restbegriff*, a remainder concept. See Rahner, "Concerning the Relationship between Nature and Grace," 315.

78. Pius XII, *Humani generis*, §26.

79. De Lubac's interpretation of Thomas remains controversial. For a critical appraisal, see Feingold, *Natural Desire*. For a helpful overview of the debate as it relates to issues of politics, see Bushlack, "The Return of Neo-Scholasticism?"

80. See Komonchak, "Theology and Culture at Mid-Century," 582.

81. O'Malley, *What Happened at Vatican II*, 46–49. These characteristics are less pronounced in more social encyclicals. We have seen persuasion and appeal in *Ad beatissimi* and *Ubi arcano*, for example, though both these encyclicals as well as *Summi pontificatus* contain strong denunciations of error.

82. Cardinal Ottaviani argued that "councils speak in a style that is orderly, lucid, concise and not in the style of a sermon or pastoral letter of some bishop or other, nor even in the style of an encyclical of the supreme pontiff." See O'Malley, *What Happened at Vatican II*, 142.

83. The practical objections came especially from bishops whose countries of origin did not reflect the rapid progress of the West. Tchidimbo of Guinea said, "The schema has been conceived for Europe and perhaps for America, but not sufficiently for the Third World." See Alberigo and Komonchak, *History of Vatican II*, vol. 4, 290.

84. "Nature and 'supernature' were paired off in such a way that the second came to seem to jealous reason as nothing but a vain shadow, a sham adornment. To the degree that the one became a complete system, the other, correlatively, became, to the eyes of the thinker, something superfluous." De Lubac, *Surnaturel*, 173–75. In his memoirs on his writings, de Lubac wrote, "If too often today the general life of humanity is withdrawing from Christianity, it is perhaps because too often Christianity has been uprooted from the inner vital organs of man." See De Lubac, *Mémoire sur l'occasion de mes écrits* (Namur: Culture et vérité, 1989), 189, quoted in translation in Komonchak, "Theology and Culture at Mid-Century," 582.

85. One bishop, Del Rosario of the Philippines, criticized the "squirrel cage mentality," which had human beings scurrying around the cage of this life getting nowhere and only hoping they ran well enough to be liberated by God to go to heaven. See Alberigo and Komonchak, *History of Vatican II*, vol. 4, 296.

86. The work of the Jesuit Teilhard de Chardin, recently censured by the Holy Office, received both warm mention and implicit criticism; see Alberigo and Komonchak, *History of Vatican II*, vol. 4, 285–26; O'Malley, *What Happened at Vatican II*, 289. The bishop of Mainz, Hermann Volk, "wanted the chapter [III] to stress fidelity to the gospel, not just 'generous cooperation in correctly building an earthly city.'" See Alberigo and Komonchak, *History of Vatican II*, vol. 4, 299.

87. Ratzinger, "Commentary on Part I, Chapter I," 123–24.

88. Ratzinger, "Commentary on Part I, Chapter I," 119–20.

89. Ratzinger, in particular, remained unhappy with the eventual form of part 1 of the constitution. In a commentary published in 1966, he argued that the Ariccia text left the proper subject of Christian theology—Christ and his work—on ice while it started out with a general anthropology. His criticism was that the subject of Christ was never properly retrieved from the "deep freeze" where it had been left. See Ratzinger, *Die Letzte Sitzungsperiode Des Konzils*, 34. In subsequent years, Rahner also voiced his disquiet: "Although I took no part in the elaboration of *Gaudium et spes* at the Council, I would not deny that its undertone is too euphoric in its evaluation of humanity and the human condition. What it says may be true, but it produces the overall impression that it is enough to observe its norms, and everything will more or less turn out well. It does not insist enough on the fact that all human endeavours, with all their sagacity and goodwill, often end up in blind alleys; that in questions of morality, when we really face the whole of reality, we get lost in obscurities which no moral formula can wholly remove. In short, as Scripture says, the world is in a bad way and it will stay that way, even if, as we are obliged to do, we fight against evil to the death." See Rahner, "Christian Pessimism," 157. For a good overview of the development and controversy over Schema XIII, see Peterson, "Critical Voices."

90. O'Malley, *What Happened at Vatican II*, 267. Rowland takes a critical view in her *Culture and the Thomist Tradition*, 18.

91. These voices included those of the *periti* Rahner and Ratzinger, as well as Karol Wojtyła. See O'Malley, *What Happened at Vatican II*, 258.

92. Moeller, "History of the Constitution," vol. 5, 18.

93. On this point, see Hollenbach, "Commentary on *Gaudium et spes*," 270–71.

94. Vatican II, *Gaudium et spes*, §78.

95. Vatican II, *Gaudium et spes*, §78.

96. The reference is to Gerard Manley Hopkins's poem "Peace." See Hopkins, *God's Grandeur*, 28.

97. See Aquinas, *Summa Theologica* II–II.40.2.

98. Vatican II, *Gaudium et spes*, §78.

99. The affirmation of conscientious objection provoked some disagreement, particularly from among the American bishops, and §78 adds, "so long as this can be done without harm to the rights and duties of others or of the community." See Yzermans, *American Participation in the Second Vatican Council*, 215–19.

100. *Lumen gentium* had reshaped the relationship between the laity and the clergy by affirming the universal call to holiness: "It is obvious then to all

that all of Christ's faithful, no matter what their rank or station, have a vocation to the fullness of the Christian life and the perfection of charity, and that this sanctity results in the promotion of a more humane way of life even in society on earth." Vatican II, *Lumen gentium*, §40.

101. See Johnson, *Ideology, Reason, and the Limitation of War*, 64–80.

102. Himes has a perceptive critique of this tension in his "Pacifism and Just War in Roman Catholic Social Teaching," 329–44.

103. See, e.g., Musto, *The Catholic Peace Tradition*, 193: "The scriptural tradition replaced the un-Christian traditions of Roman law, natural law or Aristotelian logic. This change opened the door for a gradual discarding of the just-war tradition. Its evangelical outlook and concern for individual conscience also put Vatican II firmly behind the rediscovered tradition of biblical pacifism." The introduction to chapter 5 of *Gaudium et spes* includes four scriptural citations (two from Isaiah, one from the Sermon on the Mount, and one from Ephesians) but, as already noted, these chapter introductions were added at a later date for stylistic reasons. It is not clear that the approval of "renunciation of violence" proceeds from a consideration of these scriptural texts or others.

104. Vatican II, *Gaudium et spes*, §80.

105. John XXIII, *Pacem in terris*, §127.

106. In *Allorché fummo chiamati*, Benedict XV asks whether "the cost of the long drawn-out struggle is too great, too great," and adds, "Nor let it be said that the immense conflict cannot be settled without the violence of war."

107. Johnson argues that recent Catholic teaching on peace departs from the traditional just war doctrine in giving undue priority to three prudential *jus ad bellum* criteria: last resort, the expectation that the overall good achieved will outweigh the evil of war, and a reasonable hope of success. These are listed in the *Catechism* as "the traditional elements enumerated in what is called the 'just war' doctrine." See Johnson, "Just War, as It Was and Is." The reference is to *Catechism of the Catholic Church*, §2309.

108. Vatican II, *Gaudium et spes*, §78.

109. A point made by way of criticism in Johnson, "Just War, as It Was and Is."

110. After returning from the UN trip, Paul VI was welcomed back into St. Peter's to thunderous applause. See O'Malley, *What Happened at Vatican II*, 262–64. The few objections to the section on war came largely from those prelates whose countries of origin possessed nuclear weapons: the American bishops and, to a lesser extent, the English bishops. See Yzermans, *American Participation in the Second Vatican Council*, 215–21, 247–48.

111. Paul VI, *Populorum progressio*, §7.

112. *Rerum novarum* calls for the existing social order to be perfected in love, rather than structurally reformed: "It is impossible to reduce civil society to one dead level. . . . [A]ll striving against nature is in vain." Leo XIII, *Rerum novarum*, §17. *Ad beatissimi* and *Summi pontificatus* also emphasize the need for the restoration of respect for natural relationships of authority and obedience and personal conversion.

113. CELAM, "Peace," §§6–7.

114. In its opening paragraph the Medellín document mentions the "sinful situation" of Latin American societies, further developing in Catholic social teaching the concept of social sin.

115. CELAM, "Peace," §10. The document goes on to denounce "the unjust action of world powers that works against self-determination of weaker nations who must suffer the bloody consequences of war and invasion" (§32).

116. There are differing assessments of how successful *The Challenge of Peace* is, both in addressing the tensions in *Gaudium et spes* and in addressing the problems of nuclear war and the arms race. For an overview of some critical responses, see Cahill, *Love Your Enemies*, 209–11. George Weigel offers a particularly critical assessment of *The Challenge of Peace* in Weigel, *Tranquillitas Ordinis*, 257–85.

117. See USCCB, *The Challenge of Peace*, §17. The preceding paragraph states, "Catholic teaching on peace and war has had two purposes: to help Catholics form their consciences and to contribute to the public policy debate about the morality of war. These two purposes have led Catholic teaching to address two distinct but overlapping audiences. The first is the Catholic faithful, formed by the premises of the gospel and the principles of Catholic moral teaching. The second is the wider civil community, a more pluralistic audience, in which our brothers and sisters with whom we share the name Christian, Jews, Moslems, other religious communities, and all people of good will also make up our polity" (§17).

118. USCCB, *The Challenge of Peace*, §20.

119. The Reformed theologian John Webster argues, "The Church is not simply as it were a volunteer willing to spend itself in a task for which others are also suited, but in which they decline to involve themselves. The Church engages in actions which are given to it to do by its constitution as that gathering of humanity which confesses that in Christ, God has reconciled the world to himself." See Webster, "The Ethics of Reconciliation," 118.

120. See, e.g., *Gaudium et spes*, §77: "The Council wishes passionately to summon Christians to cooperate, under the help of Christ the author of peace, with all men in securing among themselves a peace based on justice and love and in setting up the instruments of peace"; see also §78: "all Christians are

urgently summoned to do in love what the truth requires, and to join with all true peacemakers in pleading for peace and bringing it about."

121. USCCB, *The Challenge of Peace*, §§21–22.

122. USCCB, *The Challenge of Peace*, §32.

123. USCCB, *The Challenge of Peace*, §§33–55.

124. USCCB, *The Challenge of Peace*, §51.

125. USCCB, *The Harvest of Justice*, sec. D.

126. The document states that "application of these [just war] principles requires the exercise of the virtue of prudence; people of good will may differ on specific conclusions." It goes on to acknowledge that "the increasing violence of our society, its growing insensitivity to the sacredness of life and the glorification of the technology of destruction in popular culture could inevitably impair our society's ability to apply just-war criteria honestly and effectively in time of crisis. In the absence of a commitment of respect for life and a culture of restraint, it will not be easy to apply the just-war tradition, not just as a set of ideas, but as a system of effective social constraints on the use of force." USCCB, *The Harvest of Justice*, Introd., B.2.

127. *The Harvest of Justice*, Introd., B.1.

128. John Paul II, *Centesimus annus*, §23; see also John Paul II, "Homily at Drogheda"; Benedict XVI, "Midday Angelus." The most significant shift toward nonviolence is found in Pope Francis's Message for the World Day of Peace, 2017, "Nonviolence, a Style of Politics for Peace." In 2016, the Pontifical Council for Justice and Peace and Pax Christi jointly organized the conference, "Nonviolence and Just Peace: Contributing to the Catholic Understanding of and Commitment to Nonviolence," in Rome, selections from which were published as Dennis, *Choosing Peace*.

129. John Paul II references the role of nonviolent action in the fall of the Eastern bloc in *Centesimus annus*, §23. Francis's "Nonviolence, a Style of Politics for Peace" references Gandhi, Khan Abdul Ghaffar Khan, Martin Luther King Jr., and Leymah Gbowee (§4).

130. Benedict XVI, "Midday Angelus." Emphasis in original.

131. Francis, "Nonviolence, a Style of Politics for Peace," §3.

132. John Donahue argues, "Whatever the intellectual power and depth of papal teaching, the encyclicals rarely touch the lives of everyday Catholics. If Catholic social teaching is to form people's consciences, inspire their imaginations, and shape their lives, it must weave biblical theology into its presentations." See Donahue, "The Bible and Catholic Social Teaching," 11. The same need for Catholic social teaching to incorporate scripture more integrally is echoed by Schneiders, "New Testament Reflections on Peace and Nuclear Arms," 91–105.

133. By "spiritualities," I mean "a disciplined way of living out the Gospel message that becomes a concrete embodiment of the Catholic imaginary." See Schreiter, "The Catholic Social Imaginary and Peacebuilding," 223.

134. See Webster, "The Theology of Reconciliation," 214.

135. USCCB, *The Challenge of Peace*, §20.

136. Williams is commenting on John Milbank's *Theology and Social Theory*. See Williams, "Saving Time," 321.

137. Lederach, *The Moral Imagination*, 54, 60–61.

Chapter 3

1. Gomes, "Forty 'Missionaries' Killed Worldwide in 2018."

2. Glatz, "Vatican: 13 Priests, 1 Religious Brother, 1 Nun and 8 Lay Workers Killed in 2017."

3. Mexico is the deadliest place to be a priest. It is estimated that thirty-two have died since 2006. See Associated Press, "Catholic Priest Murdered in Mexico."

4. Lay workers in the Catholic Church go by various titles and levels of official incorporation into the local and national ministerial structure. In this chapter I use "lay worker" to include catechists, leaders of base ecclesial communities, parish lay assistants, and so on.

5. Henao states, "The mandate of accompaniment is a community one, not destined to be carried out by a small or select group of people. It is the community that must accompany, moved by the Spirit who motivates them and makes itself present. The accompaniment can be personal, like that carried out by the Good Samaritan (Lk 10.30–36), but it can also be collective like the appearances of the Risen One, particularly the text about the Emmaus road (Lk 24.13–25)." Henao, "And They Shall Make War No More," 188–89.

6. *Pacem in terris* mentions the difficulties facing minority groups in states (§§94–96), and *Gaudium et spes* briefly refers to civil war and the violence of state repression (§§73–75).

7. *Africae munus*, Benedict XVI's apostolic exhortation after the second synod on Africa, has a clearer sense of the roles played by midlevel and grassroots actors; see §§100–146.

8. Lederach gives a good overview of peacebuilding roles fulfilled by the Church in Colombia in "The Long Journey Back to Humanity."

9. Henao prefers to speak of "autonomy" rather than "neutrality": "On this issue, the Colombian Episcopate points to autonomy as the governing principal [*sic*]: 'We reaffirm our independence and autonomy as Pastors to the People of God to announce the Gospel and denounce all that oppose His

Kingdom and His justice. We will not allow conflicting groups to force any of us—bishops, priests, men or women religious or pastoral workers—to align with any one group.' The church has chosen the option of autonomy, which does not mean the same as neutrality. We choose to support affected communities, the civilian population and, especially, the victims. It is an option that provides us an independent space to accomplish the task of promoting the search for peace and to negotiate from different angles. But, most of all, this autonomy creates a position of relationship to and accompaniment of initiatives that arise from the local level, from community proposals." See Henao, "Lessons Learned."

10. Whitmore, "Peacebuilding and Its Challenging Partners," 178.

11. Séverine Autesserre notes that the longitudinal presence of Catholic organizations and actors makes their peacebuilding interventions more sustainable and effective than similar initiatives designed and implemented by expatriate peacebuilders without strong local connections. See Autesserre, *Peaceland*, 103, 105.

12. Henao, "Lessons Learned," 9.

13. Henao, "And They Shall Make War No More," 185.

14. "The breakdown of solidarity in communities that were identified historically by common values and strong relationships can happen due to the pressure of physical or psychological threats, corrupting influences, or where there are disputes over development issues where one takes a different view from the rest of the community. Due to these multiple threats, the surest form of support is through a strategy of accompaniment and close association so as to foster dialogue and allow for the rebuilding of trust." Henao, "And They Shall Make War No More," 186.

15. Henao, "And They Shall Make War No More," 186.

16. Henao, "And They Shall Make War No More," 186.

17. Henao, "And They Shall Make War No More," 186.

18. Henao, "And They Shall Make War No More," 186.

19. Henao, "And They Shall Make War No More," 188.

20. Henao, "And They Shall Make War No More," 189.

21. Henao, "And They Shall Make War No More," 189.

22. Henao, "And They Shall Make War No More," 187–88. Henao adds that "this strong idea of a fraternal mysticism, in response to a 'throwaway culture' and in support of a 'culture of encounter', is precisely the key to pastoral accompaniment" (190).

23. Henao, "And They Shall Make War No More," 188.

24. Pastoral accompaniment "represents the pedagogical value of a conscious presence in the midst of conflict and the prophetic vision." See Henao, "Lessons Learned," 13.

25. John Paul II, *Reconciliatio et paenitentia*, §§8–9.

26. Stoebe, "Nḥm (Pi) to Comfort," 734–37.

27. See also, e.g., Ps 23:4 and 119:76, and Job's complaints about his useless comforters in Jb 16:2.

28. See, e.g., Is 21:1 and 51:12 and particularly Lamentations 2.

29. It is used thirty times in relation to God, compared to only seven usages in connection with human beings. See Stoebe, "Nḥm (Pi) to Comfort," 738.

30. Fabry, "Nḥm," 343, with quotation from J. Jeremias, "Die Reue Gottes," *Biblische Studien* 65 (1975).

31. As with God's regret at having made Saul king in 1 Sam 15:11, 35, which Fabry points out paves the way for his covenant of steadfast love with the House of David. See Fabry, "Nḥm," 343.

32. See also Amos 7:5–6: "Then I said, 'O Lord God, cease, I beg you! How can Jacob stand? He is so small!' The Lord relented concerning this; 'This also shall not be,' said the Lord God."

33. Stoebe, "Nḥm (Pi) to Comfort," 738.

34. Stoebe, "Nḥm (Pi) to Comfort," 736.

35. Of 119 occurences of the verb stem in the entire Hebrew Bible, Isaiah accounts for 19, 9 of which are in Deutero-Isaiah. See Stoebe, "Nḥm (Pi) to Comfort," 735.

36. See Childs, *Isaiah*, 296. The Babylonian context of Is 40–55 is widely accepted but not unchallenged; for a critique and alternative view, see Barstad, *The Babylonian Captivity*.

37. See Watts, *Word Biblical Commentary: Isaiah 34–66*, 78–79. See also Childs, *Isaiah*, 295–96.

38. There is some debate as to whether Is 40 should be understood as a revisiting or readjustment of the prophetic call narrative in Is 6. For Childs on the call narrative, see Childs, *Isaiah*, 295: "In a conscious dependency on chapter 6, chapter 40 does not offer a new independent call narrative, but rather provides a reapplication of Isaiah's call."

39. Childs, *Isaiah*, 296. Childs also argues that this announcement of "new things" provides an interpretive bridge between First and Second Isaiah.

40. On highway imagery and its possible link to the Babylonian context, see Westermann, *Isaiah 40–66*, 38–39.

41. Peter Stuhlmacher's summary provides a helpful point of departure for the wealth of scholarly writing and debate in this area. See Stuhlmacher, "Isaiah 53," 147–62.

42. Moltmann writes of the impact of his war experience on his theology at the beginning of *The Crucified God*: "Shattered and broken, the survivors of

my generation were then [1948–49] returning from camps and hospitals to the lecture room. A theology which did not speak of God in the sight of the one who was abandoned and crucified would have had nothing to say to us then" (1).

43. "The only way past protest atheism is through a theology of the cross which understands God as the suffering God in the suffering of Christ and which cries out with the godforsaken God, 'My God, why have you forsaken me?'" Moltmann, *The Crucified God*, 227.

44. "When God becomes man in Jesus of Nazareth, he not only enters into the finitude of man, but in his death on the cross also enters into the situation of man's godforsakenness. . . . He humbles himself and takes upon himself the eternal death of the godless and the godforsaken, so that all the godless and godforsaken can experience communion with him." Moltmann, *The Crucified God*, 276.

45. Moltmann, *The Crucified God*, 263.

46. Moltmann, *The Crucified God*, 278.

47. "These realities are not another kingdom separate from God, nor are they just similes and equivalents of his kingdom. They are synecdochically, to take up Luther's language, real presences of his coming omnipresence." Moltmann, *The Crucified God*, 337.

48. There are echoes of this theme in Paul's use of allusions to the Exodus story and "hardening of hearts" in Romans 9: "God's freedom to be merciful has, for Paul, another side: namely, God's freedom *not* to show mercy, but to turn human rebellion to his own purposes, as in the case of Pharaoh (Rom 9:17)." See Wagner, *Heralds of the Good News*, 53.

49. This is a key emphasis of Sebastian Moore in *The Crucified Is No Stranger*. "It cannot be too much insisted that man's evil is turned, in the deepest analysis, on himself. In it he hates *himself* as the free being he knows himself to be. He hates himself free. Which means, he hates himself free from evil. He hates himself free from sin. So, he hates himself as he sees himself in Jesus, the man free from sin" (24; original emphasis). For Moore, "what the crucified Jesus is forever bringing to an end is not simply the otherwise endless process of violence provoking violence, but what itself powers this process, the endless fear of man for himself, the endless flight of man from himself, the endless crucifixion of man by himself" (25).

50. James Alison writes, "The intelligence of the victim comes from a freedom in giving oneself to others, in not being moved by the violence of others, even when it perceives that this free self-giving is going to be lynched as a result. The free self-giving is not a seeking to be lynched, but is completely open-eyed about the probability of just this happening." See Alison, *Knowing Jesus*, 45.

51. Wagner draws attention to Paul's use of Isaianic texts throughout Romans to make exactly this point: "Both Paul and Isaiah are convinced that it is God's power alone that will ultimately overcome his people's apostasy. In the Isaianic vision, Israel's hope for salvation rests entirely on God's initiative and action. Seeing the helplessness of his people and motivated by his mercy rather than by Israel's deserts (Isa 59:16; 60:10), the Lord himself ventures forth to remove Israel's ungodliness and to restore their fortunes. Similarly, in Romans 11, Paul depicts the salvation of 'all Israel' as a divine act prompted by God's mercy and accomplished by God himself (Rom 11:26–27, 31–32)." See Wagner, *Heralds of the Good News*, 292.

52. On this point, see Alison, *Knowing Jesus*, 19–20, who criticizes the sleeping and rising or seed and plant images of Jesus's resurrection: "This is unhelpful because it suggests that the power behind the change was within the changed one, just as the butterfly is implicit in the caterpillar. Whereas the point of Jesus' resurrection was that there was no power at all within the dead Jesus. The power to raise him was purely from the Father, not a hidden resource in some remote corner of Jesus that hadn't been reached by death. The raising of Jesus was not, if you like, a logical continuation of the life and power that had been in Jesus before. Rather, the raising of Jesus was the gratuitous giving-back of the whole life and death that had ended on Good Friday—the whole of Jesus' humanity includes his human death."

53. Radcliffe, *Sing a New Song*, 27.

54. William Cavanaugh's *Torture and Eucharist* provides an in-depth study of how the celebration of the Eucharist during the Pinochet regime in Chile was a way of reconstituting the social body that was being dismembered and fragmented by torture and disappearances.

55. Emmanuel Katongole writes about the importance of lament in a Christian understanding of reconciliation. See Katongole, *The Journey of Reconciliation* 11, 40–44, 52–55. For an interesting example of intentional use of mourning rituals in a conflict situation, see Rios-Oyola and Acarón, "Peacebuilding and Dance in Afro-Colombian Funerary Ritual."

56. This is part of the argument of Judith Butler, *Frames of War*.

57. Stauffer, "An Interview with Judith Butler."

58. Butler states, "An increased attunement to that [grief] could only make us more humane." See Stauffer, "An Interview with Judith Butler."

59. I explore this further in chapter 6.

60. Benedict XVI talks about this vocation of the Church with reference to the ecological crisis in *Caritas in veritate*, §51: "The Church has a responsibility towards creation and she must assert this responsibility in the public sphere.... She must above all protect mankind from self-destruction."

61. 2 Cor 5:18: "All this is from God, who reconciled us to himself through Christ, and has given us the ministry of reconciliation; that is, in Christ God was reconciling the world to himself, not counting their trespasses against them, and entrusting the message of reconciliation to us."

62. Alison, *Knowing Jesus*, 45.

63. See Cahill, "A Theology for Peacebuilding," 303. For a critique of social trinitarianism along these lines, see Tanner, "Trinity," 319–32.

64. For "culture of life," see John Paul II, *Evangelium vitae*, §§78–101. The document is largely concerned with the culture of life in relation to the issues of abortion and euthanasia, but it does refer to violent conflict, and the theme of the culture of life could usefully be developed further in relation to the Church's teaching on peace.

65. Cejka and Bamat, *Artisans of Peace*, 260.

66. See Vanier, *Our Life Together*, 294–95, 304–6.

67. Neuhaus, "Fr. David Neuhaus S.J.: Witness Interview." At the time of this interview, Neuhaus was patriarchal vicar for Hebrew-speaking Catholics in the Latin Patriarchate of Jerusalem.

68. In Colombia, the Jesuit Centro de Investigación y Educación Popular has played an important role in documenting violence and recognizing victims, as well as contributing to the study and analysis of peace initiatives and social mobilization. Its director, Francisco de Roux S.J., has been involved in mediation of high-level peace talks between the Revolutionary Armed Forces of Colombia (FARC) and the Colombian government. See www.cinep.org.co.

Chapter 4

1. Interview with Fr. Darío Echeverri, quoted in Lederach, "The Long Journey Back to Humanity," 34–35.

2. The *Compendium of the Social Doctrine of the Church* lists four permanent principles of Catholic social teaching: the dignity of the human person, the common good, subsidiarity, and solidarity. See Pontifical Council for Justice and Peace, *Compendium*, §160.

3. Ronald Reagan's speech to Members of the British Parliament in 1982 provides a brief and clear articulation of this vision of liberal peacemaking. See Reagan, "Address to the British Parliament, House of Commons, London."

4. Benedict XVI's brief comments on peacebuilding in *Caritas in veritate* recognize this: "Even peace can run the risk of being considered a technical product, merely the outcome of agreements between governments or of initiatives aimed at ensuring effective economic aid" (§72).

5. UN Secretary General Boutros Boutros-Ghali's *An Agenda for Peace: Preventative Diplomacy, Peace-making and Peace-keeping,* published in 1992, articulates some of these convictions about the need to tackle structural violence and nonmilitary sources of instability. The document also introduced the concept of postconflict peacebuilding.

6. For a concise summary of strategic peacebuilding's principal aims and insights, see Lederach and Appleby, "Strategic Peacebuilding," 19–44. See also Schirch, *The Little Book of Strategic Peacebuilding.*

7. Lederach, *Building Peace,* 38–55.

8. Lederach and Appleby note, "The most significant weakness of far too many peace processes has been the gap between elite levels of decision making and the communities that are the recipients and inheritors of those outcomes." See Lederach and Appleby, "Strategic Peacebuilding," 33. Those "wielding high levels of political and social authority ... cannot replace cultural agents who, operating on the local level, interpret agreements and prepare the society for their implementation and the transitions called for by the agreements" (27).

9. Lederach, *The Moral Imagination,* 47.

10. See some of the case studies in Caritas Internationalis, *Peacebuilding.*

11. John XXIII continues, "We ... beg and beseech mankind, and above all the rulers of States, to be unsparing of their labour and efforts to ensure that human affairs follow a rational and dignified course. In their deliberations together, let men of outstanding wisdom and influence give serious thought to the problem of achieving a more human adjustment of relations between States throughout the world." John XXIII, *Pacem in terris,* §§118–19.

12. We saw in chapter 2 that after initial skepticism about the League of Nations from Pius XI, Catholic social teaching on peace has enthusiastically supported the United Nations and called for its reform and strengthening. See Benedict XVI, *Caritas in veritate,* §67. Cahill writes about this deep-seated "predilection of Catholic social teaching to envision the world 'community' on analogy to the family, local community, province, nation-state and regional associations of states. Concentric circles of relationship and authority are united under single heads, constituting together incrementally higher and more comprehensive associations in a common good. Just as family members are united under the *paterfamilias,* so families are united within local communities, organizations and governments; local and state governments are united under a federal government; national states are united in regional alliances; and finally all are united under a 'world political authority.'" See Cahill, "*Caritas in Veritate,*" 306.

13. John Paul II states that, "While peace should be everyone's concern, the building of peace is a task that falls directly and principally to *political*

leaders." See John Paul II, "Peace: A Gift of God Entrusted to Us!," §9; original emphasis.

14. John XXII, *Pacem in terris*, §152.

15. Whitmore, "Peacebuilding and Its Challenging Partners," 179.

16. Shadle, *The Origins of War*, 151.

17. Shadle argues, "For example they [the bishops] say very little about the cultural preconditions for the establishment of just institutions: Does there have to be a generally just culture among states for just international institutions to be established? Nor do they discuss how just international institutions must be maintained through the practices of the states that compose them, or how states can subvert these institutions through their actions." See Shadle, *The Origins of War*, 151.

18. Eli McCarthy identifies a similar gap in Catholic social teaching on peace, arguing its rights-based ethic needs supplementing with attention to virtues. See McCarthy, *Becoming Nonviolent Peacemakers*, 158–86.

19. See Benedict XVI, *Caritas in veritate*, §24: "*Populorum Progressio* assigned a central, albeit not exclusive, role to 'public authorities.' In our own day, the State finds itself having to address the limitations to its sovereignty imposed by the new context of international trade and finance, which is characterized by increasing mobility both of financial capital and means of production, material and immaterial. This new context has altered the political power of States. Today, as we take to heart the lessons of the current economic crisis, which sees the State's *public authorities* directly involved in correcting errors and malfunctions, it seems more realistic to *re-evaluate their role* and their powers, which need to be prudently reviewed and remodelled so as to enable them, perhaps through new forms of engagement, to address the challenges of today's world" (original emphasis).

20. Benedict XVI, *Caritas in veritate*, §67.

21. Cahill argues, "The very premise of global UN control—universal international recognition of and compliance with its ultimate authority—is highly unrealistic. This does not mean that the United Nations does not exercise a vital leadership function, or that its sponsored treaties and goal-setting agreements are ineffectual. But it is unlikely ever to function as the worldwide equivalent of a state's federal government." See Cahill, "*Caritas in veritate*," 306.

22. Leo XIII, *Rerum novarum*, §25.

23. Mary E. Hobgood argues that John Paul II in *Sollicitudo rei socialis* "refuses to locate the origins of poverty in the conflictual nature of any political, social, or economic structures beyond what is created by the selfishness, shortsightedness, mistaken political ideas, or unfortunate cultural values of individuals." See Hobgood, "Conflicting Paradigms in Social Analysis," 178.

24. Himes continues, "The failure to acknowledge the deeply conflictual nature of human reality has permitted Catholic social teaching to remain underdeveloped in strategies of conflict resolution, even though, in practice, the church is deeply engaged in such efforts around the world." See Himes, "Peacebuilding and Catholic Social Teaching," 282–83.

25. Christiansen, "Commentary on *Pacem in Terris*," 233.

26. John XXIII, *Mater et magistra*, §157.

27. John XXIII, *Pacem in terris*, §§98–100.

28. Vatican II, *Gaudium et spes*, §24.

29. Vatican II, *Gaudium et spes*, §24.

30. Vatican II, *Gaudium et spes*, §32.

31. Paul VI, *Populorum progressio*, §17, §67.

32. Christiansen argues that the term is used "at one time to point to the grounds of equality, at another to refer to new obligations, and at still others to speak parenthetically of a spirit of solidarity." See Christiansen, "On Relative Equality," 662. In one sense, this simply reflects Catholic moral theology's tendency to blend claims about human nature with claims about the duties arising from that nature and the telos or fulfillment at which it aims, but Christiansen argues that the resulting conflation of duties, virtues, and ideals is problematic: "Such a confusing mixture of categories under a single term can make the setting of priority rules among competing principles an intractably difficult task" (662–63).

33. This is very clear in Paul VI's Message for the World Day of Peace, 1971, "Every Man Is My Brother": "Peace avails itself of the ever closer network of human relations in the fields of culture, economics, commerce, sport and tourism. We must live together, and it is good to know each other, and to respect and help one another. A fundamental cohesion is taking shape in the world. This favours peace. International relations are increasingly developing, and they form the premise and also the guarantee of a certain concord. The great international and supranational institutions are seen to be providential, at the source as well as at the perfection of humanity's peaceful coexistence." See also his image of human progress as an inexorably incoming tide in *Populorum progressio*, §7: "As the waves of the sea gradually creep farther and farther in along the shoreline, so the human race inches its way forward through history."

34. See *Pacem in terris*, §98 and §107 and *Mater et magistra*, which, after mentioning solidarity, goes on to list "international and regional organizations, national and private societies", "World banking institutes, individual States and private persons" (*Mater et magistra*, §165). This macro-level focus is also

evident in *Sollicitudo rei socialis,* but it is complemented in that encyclical by a stronger account of the midlevel.

35. Wojtyła, *The Acting Person.*

36. Wojtyła always describes common action in terms of acting "together with others" rather than "acting together," and he is clear that the subject of the action is always the persons involved. It is only in a very attenuated sense that Wojtyła refers to the community as a "quasi-subject": "Being and acting together with others does not constitute a new subject of acting but only introduces new relations among the persons who are the real and actual subjects of acting." Wojtyła, *The Acting Person,* 277.

37. *The Acting Person,* 284–85.

38. *The Acting Person,* 286. He adds that this attitude is particularly important in the context of totalism, in which genuine participation is thwarted "by defects in the system according to which the entire human community of acting operates" (272).

39. In another article, Wojtyła writes, "The measure of effort put into the realisation of the common good, the measure of individual sacrifices, including exile, prison and death, has and continues to witness to the magnitude of that good, to its superiority. These situations, especially the extreme ones, convince us of the truth that the common good is in itself a condition of the individual good of the particular members of the community." Quoted in Doran, *Solidarity,* 147.

40. John Paul II's experience of the Solidarity movement in Poland is clearly in the background here. Gerald Beyer's study *Recovering Solidarity* provides an excellent account of the Solidarity movement: see esp. ch. 2, "The Ethic of Solidarity from 1980 to 1989," 11–27.

41. See, e.g., the reference to participation in *Sollicitudo rei socialis,* §15: "It must also be restated that no social group, for example a political party, has the right to usurp the role of sole leader, since this brings about the destruction of the true subjectivity of society and the individual citizens, as happens in every form of totalitarianism. In this situation the individual and the people become 'objects' in spite of all declarations to the contrary and verbal assurances."

42. John Paul II, *Sollicitudo rei socialis,* §39; emphasis added.

43. Examples are colonialism and international debt (see *Sollicitudo rei socialis,* §19). Another example, in the 1987 World Day of Peace message, is the ideological colonization of poorer countries through the use of aid. See John Paul II, "Development and Solidarity, Two Keys to Peace."

44. John Paul II, *Sollicitudo rei socialis,* §40; see also §§9, 26, 36, 39. In *Centesimus annus,* discussing the year 1989, John Paul II gives thanks for the

"heroic witness borne in such difficult circumstances by many Pastors, entire Christian communities, individual members of the faithful, and other people of good will," as they try to transform countries affected by injustice and economic hardship through dialogue and solidarity rather than violence. See John Paul II, *Centesimus annus*, §22.

45. This idea is restated in Pontifical Council for Justice and Peace, *Compendium of the Social Doctrine of the Church*, §193.

46. John Paul II, *Sollicitudo rei socialis*, §39.

47. *Centesimus annus* is the closest Church teaching comes to grappling in a systematic way with the distinctive characteristics of twenty-first-century conflict. John Paul II notes how Cold War tensions played out in various proxy wars (§18) and how the unstable peace following World War II led to a rise in intrastate ("fratricidal") conflicts. He alludes to the consequent rise in nonconventional armed conflict, citing terrorism and increasingly barbaric methods of political and military conflict (§18). He is also aware that the legacy of colonization is bound up in contemporary conflict, noting the lack of social cohesion in those "decolonized" states that are in practice controlled by foreign business interests and divided among various tribal groups (§20).

48. John Paul II, *Centesimus annus*, §22.

49. John Paul II, *Centesimus annus*, §27: "A great effort is needed to rebuild morally and economically the countries which have abandoned Communism. For a long time the most elementary economic relationships were distorted, and basic virtues of economic life, such as trustfulness, trustworthiness and hard work were denigrated. A patient material and moral reconstruction is needed."

50. John Paul II, *Centesimus annus*, §16.

51. John Paul II, *Centesimus annus*, §25.

52. John Paul II, *Sollicitudo rei socialis*, §40.

53. This is not taken further in *Sollicitudo rei socialis*, but Benedict XVI picks it up in the context of reconciliation in *Africae munus* (2011), specifically mentioning John Paul II and the text from *Sollicitudo* just quoted. A spirituality of communion, he writes, includes the ability to see others "within the profound unity of the Mystical Body as being 'a part of me', to recognise their needs, desires and gifts and to 'make room' for them and bear their burdens." See Benedict XVI, *Africae munus*, §35. Benedict sees this Christian communion as building on and preserving diversity and as "the very antithesis of division, tribalism, racism and ethnocentrism (cf. Gal 3:26–28)" (§41). Developing a stronger account of the Church's distinctively ecclesial role in peacebuilding is a key concern of Katongole, *The Journey of Reconciliation*.

54. Rowan Williams, "Saving Time," 321. He continues, "I wonder whether the very ideas of culture, idiom and ethic insist on the tragic in some form. If our salvation is cultural (historical, linguistic, etc.), it is not a return to primordial harmonics, purely innocent difference. We are always already, in history, shaped by privation, living at the expense of each other: important moral choices entail the loss of certain specific goods for certain specific persons, because moral determination, like any 'cultural' determination, recognizes that not all goods for all persons are contingently compatible" (321).

55. Whitmore, "Peacebuilding and Its Challenging Partners," 179.

56. Teresa Whitfield provides a reconstructed account of the events of November 16, 1989, in her *Paying the Price*, 1–14.

57. Sobrino, *Witnesses to the Kingdom*, 77.

58. Sobrino, *Witnesses to the Kingdom*, 75.

59. Puhl, *The Spiritual Exercises of St. Ignatius*, §106.

60. Sobrino, *Witnesses to the Kingdom*, 69.

61. In an address to Santa Clara University on receiving an honorary doctorate, Ellacuría spoke about the purpose of a Christian university: "The university should become incarnate among the poor, it should become science for those who have no science, the clear voice of those who have no voice, the intellectual support of those whose very reality makes them true and right and reasonable, even though this sometimes takes the form of having nothing, but who cannot cite academic reasons to justify themselves." Ignacio Ellacuría, Commencement Address at the University of Santa Clara, 1982, quoted in Sobrino, *Witnesses to the Kingdom*, 84.

62. From the first exercise of the first week. See Puhl, *The Spiritual Exercises of St. Ignatius*, §53.

63. Puhl, *The Spiritual Exercises of St. Ignatius*, §§53–54.

64. Sobrino, *Witnesses to the Kingdom*, 69. See also Whitfield, *Paying the Price*, 44–45.

65. For further analysis of the significance of the *Exercises* in Ellacuría's thought and practice, see Ashley, "Contemplation in the Action of Justice"; and Burke, "Christian Salvation and the Disposition of Transcendence."

66. Sobrino, *Witnesses to the Kingdom*, 73.

67. Sobrino, *Witnesses to the Kingdom*, 96.

68. Whitmore, "Peacebuilding and Its Challenging Partners," 179.

69. Puhl, *The Spiritual Exercises of St. Ignatius*, §§50–52.

70. John Paul II, *Sollicitudo rei socialis*, makes this connection briefly in §40.

71. Augustine, commenting on the verses "No one has greater love than the man who lays down his life for his friends" and "As Christ laid down his

life for us, so we too ought to lay down our lives for our brothers," makes the same point: "And let [us] not [allege that] this has been said in such a way as if, for this reason, we can be equal with the Lord Christ, if for his sake we shall face martyrdom, even to the point of shedding our blood. He had the power of laying down his life and taking it up again; but we do not live as long as we want, and we die even if we do not want to…Finally, although brethren die for brethren, nevertheless the blood of no martyr was poured out for the remission of the sins of the brethren—but this is what he did for us—and in this he has bestowed upon us, not something for us to imitate, but something for us to be thankful for." Augustine, "Tractate 84," 134–35.

72. Rather, Sobrino asks "what we are going to do to bring them [Salvadorans] down from the cross." See Sobrino, *Witnesses to the Kingdom*, 69.

73. MacKinnon, "Subjective and Objective Conceptions of Atonement," 170.

74. MacKinnon, "Subjective and Objective Conceptions of Atonement," 171–72.

75. In *Sollicitudo rei socialis*, John Paul II suggests that solidarity is the remedy for social sin but does not consider how the discernment and action of solidarity can themselves be affected by social sin.

76. MacKinnon argues, "Any presentation of the work of Christ merits rejection as morally trivial, if it does not touch the deepest contradictions which writers of tragedy have not hesitated to recognize, and to recognize without the distorting consolation of belief in a happy ending." MacKinnon, "Subjective and Objective Conceptions of Atonement," 172.

77. "Between the death of a human being, which is by definition the end from which he cannot return, and what we term 'resurrection', there is no common measure." Balthasar, *Mysterium Paschale*, 50.

78. In criticizing a mysticism of suffering, I am criticizing the assumption that all suffering, and all self-sacrifice, is necessarily of spiritual value in and of itself. I am not suggesting that suffering can never be understood or experienced in spiritual terms, nor am I suggesting that all self-sacrifice is necessarily misguided or illegitimate.

79. Lederach, *The Moral Imagination*, 55.

80. Lederach, *The Moral Imagination*, 54.

81. Lederach, *The Moral Imagination*, 55.

82. Consider the degree to which human tragedy is set to one side when Paul VI says, "Notwithstanding everything, peace marches on. There are breaks in continuity, there are inconsistencies and difficulties. But all the same peace marches on and is establishing itself in the world with a certain invincibility." See Paul VI, "Every Man Is My Brother."

Chapter 5

1. This tendency was criticized by Rahner, Lonergan, and Curran, among others. Curran summarizes some of these criticisms in "Natural Law and Moral Theology," 252–79.

2. Jean Porter makes a good case for the flexibility and sophistication of natural law as used by the classic medieval scholastics. See Porter, *Natural and Divine Law*, 63–119.

3. Mahoney, *The Making of Moral Theology*, 31.

4. Kaveney, "The Spirit of Vatican II and Moral Theology," 49.

5. See Keenan, *A History of Catholic Moral Theology in the Twentieth Century*, 30. The papacy was ahead of the curve: Benedict XV and Pius XI did address the horrors of World War I, even if their envisaged solution—basically a return to medieval integralism—was more nostalgic than realistic.

6. Important here was the increased attention to scripture following Vatican II and the directive in the document on the training of priests, *Optatam totius*, that moral theology should be "nourished more on the teaching of the Bible" (§17). See Kristin Heyer's comments on this topic in her "Social Sin and Immigration," 410.

7. O'Malley, comparing the language of Vatican II with that of previous councils, argues that "at stake were almost two different visions of Catholicism: from commands to invitations, from laws to ideals, from definition to mystery, from threats to persuasion, from coercion to conscience, from monologue to dialogue, from ruling to serving, from withdrawn to integrated, from vertical to horizontal, from exclusion to inclusion, from hostility to friendship, from rivalry to partnership, from suspicion to trust, from static to ongoing, from passive acceptance to active engagement, from fault-finding to appreciation, from prescriptive to principles, from behaviour modification to inner appropriation." O'Malley, *What Happened at Vatican II*, 307. Darlene Fozard Weaver explores the significance of Vatican II as "language event" for moral theology in her "Vatican II and Moral Theology," 23–42.

8. For the manualist tendency to view laypeople as incompetent moral agents, see Keenan, *A History of Catholic Moral Theology*, 30.

9. Vatican II, *Gaudium et spes*, §1.

10. Also important in this connection was the increasing importance and development of the concept of dignity in Catholic social teaching. On this point, see Rowlands, *Catholic Social Teaching*, ch. 1.

11. The context was the attempt to retrieve the Lenten penitential practices of the early Church. See Vatican II, *Sacrosanctum concilium*, §109; Pfeil, "Doctrinal Implications," 134.

12. Vatican II, *Gaudium et spes*, §25.

13. See Leo XIII, *Rerum novarum*, §17. Gregory Baum describes this tendency of earlier Catholic social teaching to exhort individuals to conversion as "moralizing." See Baum, "Structures of Sin," 110–11. Structural change is not completely outside the purview of *Rerum novarum*, however: the encyclical does advocate a return to something like the medieval guild system. Marvin Mich argues that the innovation of John XXIII's *Mater et magistra* was its call for *progressive* social change rather than the nostalgia for earlier eras that marked earlier social teaching. See Mich, "Commentary on *Mater et Magistra*," 197.

14. CELAM, "Peace," §§2–5.

15. Although explicit language of social sin or structures of sin is absent, the 1971 Synod of Bishops document sees in the "serious injustices which are building around the human world a network of domination, oppression and abuses which stifle freedom and which keep the greater part of humanity from sharing in the building up and enjoyment of a more just and more loving world." Synod of Bishops, *Justitia in mundo*, §3; quoted in Himes, "Commentary on *Justitia in mundo*," 339. Himes notes, "The bishops were not naïve about the difficulties standing between the poor and development. In particular, they single out 'social structures' that are 'objective obstacles' to progress. There are 'systematic barriers' that 'oppose the collective advance' of the majority of people. . . . Poor people and nations confront 'conditions of life created especially by colonial domination' that leave them 'the victims of the interplay of international economic forces'" (344).

16. In his closing address to the synod of bishops, John Paul II asked, "If one may and must speak in an analogical sense about social sin, and also about structural sin— since sin is properly an act of the person— for us, as pastors and theologians, the following problem arises: Which penance and which social reconciliation must correspond to this *analogical* sin?" John Paul II, "The Value of This Collegial Body," 65. Margaret Pfeil reflects on the relationship between social sin and social reconciliation in Pfeil, "Social Sin: Social Reconciliation?," 171–89.

17. John Paul II, *Reconciliatio et paenitentia*, §16.

18. The *Compendium of the Social Doctrine of the Church* restates the teaching of *Reconciliatio et paenitentia* with only minor changes of wording: see *Compendium*, §§116–19.

19. The document states that in the previous paragraph, however, that "there is nothing so personal and untransferable in each individual as merit for virtue or responsibility for sin." John Paul II, *Reconciliatio et paenitentia*, §16.

20. In this vein, John Paul II refers to "social sins," including the drugs trade, corruption, and racism, in the apostolic exhortation *Ecclesia in America*, §56.

21. John Paul II, *Reconciliatio et paenitentia*, §16. The 1979 U.S. Bishops' 1979 pastoral letter, "Brothers and Sisters to Us," makes the same point in relation to racism but somewhat more boldly: "The structures of our society are subtly racist, for these structures reflect the values which society upholds. They are geared to the success of the majority and the failure of the minority; and members of both groups give unwitting approval by accepting things as they are. Perhaps no single individual is to blame. The sinfulness is often anonymous but nonetheless real. The sin is social in nature in that each of us, in varying degrees, is responsible. All of us in some measure are accomplices." Quoted in O'Keefe, *What Are They Saying about Social Sin?* 66–67.

22. Interestingly, the document adds that such a sense of social sin "can readily be seen to derive from non-Christian ideologies and systems." See John Paul II, *Reconciliatio et paenitentia*, §16.

23. John Paul II, *Reconciliatio et paenitentia*, §16. John Paul II's apologies for sins committed by members of the Church in the past raised an interesting quandary in this respect: *Reconciliatio et paenitentia* states that "there is nothing so personal and untransferable in each individual as merit for virtue or responsibility for sin" and that one cannot repent for the sins of another (§31), but *Tertio millenio adveniente* states that *the Church* undertakes penance (§33) for the sins of her members. As Jeremy Bergen points out, "The irony is that the insistence that sin is only personal appears to render an act like the Day of Pardon to be repentance for sins without agents who committed them. If there is no guilty agent, who is in need of forgiveness?" See Bergen, *Ecclesial Repentance*, 221.

24. The Congregation of the Doctrine of the Faith (CDF) "Instruction on Christian Freedom and Liberation" talks in terms of a "secondary and derived sense" rather than an analogical sense: "The sin which is at the root of unjust situations is, in a true and immediate sense, a voluntary act which has its source in the freedom of individuals. Only in a secondary and derived sense is it applicable to structures, and only in this sense can one speak of 'social sin.'" See CDF, "Instruction on Christian Freedom and Liberation," §75.

25. Pfeil, "Doctrinal Implications," 142. See also John Paul II, *Centesimus annus*, §38.

26. "If the present situation can be attributed to difficulties of various kinds, it is not out of place to speak of 'structures of sin,' which, as I stated in my Apostolic Exhortation *Reconciliatio et Paenitentia*, are rooted in personal

sin, and thus always linked to the concrete acts of individuals who introduce these structures, consolidate them and make them difficult to remove. And thus they grow stronger, spread, and become the source of other sins, and so influence people's behavior." John Paul II, *Sollicitudo rei socialis*, §36.

27. "In this consists the difference between socio-political analysis and formal reference to 'sin' and the 'structures of sin.' According to this latter viewpoint, there enter in the will of the Triune God, his plan for humanity, his justice and his mercy." John Paul II, *Sollicitudo rei socialis*, §36.

28. John Paul II, *Sollicitudo rei socialis*, §37; original emphasis.

29. Pfeil notes one place, in *Ut unum sint*, where John Paul II uses the language of social sin without qualification, but it is worth noting that here, too, "social sin" is parsed in terms of "structures of sin": "Not only personal sins must be forgiven and left behind, but also social sins, which is to say the sinful 'structures' themselves which have contributed and can still contribute to division and to the reinforcing of division." *Ut unum sint*, §34. Pfeil argues, "He pointedly speaks of 'social sins' as distinguished from 'personal sins' and then specifies 'social sins' as 'the sinful structures' themselves. Even keeping in mind John Paul II's insistence in *Reconciliatio et paenitentia* that 'social sin' is an analogous concept, the fact remains that in his own usage, the language of social sin functions to signify a particular aspect of sin that is not adequately named by the term 'personal sins' alone." See Pfeil, "Correlating Social Sin," 99–100.

30. As Mahoney observes, "The Church's individualistic moral tradition has experienced considerable difficulty in adapting its thinking to such issues of macro-ethics." Mahoney, *The Making of Moral Theology*, 34.

31. Aquinas, for example, states that the image of God in human beings is their intellectual nature. Human beings are like God in their capacity for loving and understanding, and like God according to the degree to which, knowing and loving God, they come to resemble him in the "conformity of grace" (*Summa Theologica* I.93.4). This naturally involves the exercise of free will: while human desire for happiness is natural "and not subject to free will," the pursuit of that naturally desired good is an act of the free will as "appetitive power" (*Summa Theologica* I.83.3). See the discussion of dignity in the Catholic social teaching tradition in Rowlands, *Catholic Social Teaching*.

32. One of the difficulties, as Daniel Finn points out, is that while Church teaching has the concepts of social sin and structures of sin, "Catholic social thought has no coherent account of what a structure is, presumably a prerequisite for considering what it means to apply the descriptor 'sinful' to one." See Finn, "What Is a Sinful Social Structure?," 138.

33. John Paul II, *Reconciliatio et paenitentia*, §16.

34. The *Compendium of the Social Doctrine of the Church* states, "At the bottom of every situation of sin there is always the individual who sins" (§117). Fair enough, but it is not the *only* thing that is at the bottom.

35. Finn argues that John Paul's vision of society in *Centesimus annus* is not individualist, in the libertarian sense of a collection of individuals who band together only to achieve certain goals: "On the contrary, John Paul is aware that groups and societies are organic wholes and actually have a life of their own that not only arises out of the self-understanding of their members but reciprocally has influence on those members' understanding of themselves and their world." See Finn, "Commentary on *Centesimus Annus*," 450–51. It is true that Catholic social teaching in general, and John Paul II in particular, has an understanding of the social as an organic whole and of the role of intermediate groups within it. Catholic social teaching is resolutely not individualist in this sense, and I note Karol Wojtyła's early writing against this view of society in chapter 5. The difficulty is that while Catholic social teaching on solidarity argues against social atomism, Catholic teaching on social sin tends to imply it, and the tension between the two views is simply left unresolved.

36. A tendency visible in CDF, "Instruction on Christian Freedom and Liberation," §15: "Structures, whether they are good or bad, are the result of man's actions and so are consequences more than causes." Finn comments, "If your parish, the college you attended, Stalin's government, and the Wednesday night bowling league are all social structures, is it really helpful to describe them as consequences more than causes? Surely they are both. And the incommensurability of the ways they are cause and consequence renders any judgement of 'more' or 'less' deeply questionable." See Finn, "What Is a Sinful Social Structure?," 142.

37. Mary E. Hobgood strongly criticizes *Sollicitudo rei socialis* for its focus on the individual and its "moral atomism" in her "Conflicting Paradigms in Social Analysis." She argues that the encyclical departs from Paul VI's structural analysis of the causes of poverty in *Populorum progressio* (175) and states that the encyclical is "devoid of analysis that can be aligned with the liberation model" and that "selective normative values have been abstracted from the liberation model and are radically transfigured into individual charitable acts that support rather than challenge the status quo" (181).

38. Bhaskar, *The Possibility of Naturalism*, 35; original emphasis.

39. It is for this reason that I consider treatments of social sin that attempt to establish the possibility of nondistributive collective responsibility (e.g., formal sin that can be attributed to the group but not specifically to any of the individuals comprising it) a red herring. For discussion of this approach, see Himes, "Social Sin and the Role of the Individual," 199–207.

40. Ignacio Martín-Baró S.J., quoted in Pfeil, "Social Sin: Social Reconciliation?," 184. Pfeil discusses another good example from Cornel West's *Race Matters*, in which he relates an incident in New York when ten successive cab drivers refused to pick him up: "We might analyze the decision-making process of any one of the ten cabdrivers who refused to stop for West, but against a larger horizon, we must also ask how the same choice on the part of ten consecutive cabdrivers might reflect a systemic disorder, namely a combination of race-based prejudice and power that constitutes racism. Certainly, we may hold each of the ten drivers accountable as moral agents; but, to limit our ethical analysis to the individual level alone would not permit us to address the moral significance of the *pattern* of wrongly ordered behavior in evidence here. These cabdrivers, perhaps with varying degrees of awareness, seem to have been participating in a larger structure that effectively institutionalized racism." The social structures have themselves become damaged by sin. See Pfeil, "Correlating Social Sin," 96.

41. For more on this theme from a critical realist perspective, see Finn, "What Is a Sinful Social Structure?," 149–51.

42. Bhaskar, *The Possibility of Naturalism*, 42.

43. Catholic social teaching on social sin clearly has the alternative possibility in view, e.g., that imputing sin to impersonal societal structures or collectives allows individuals to deny responsibility. On this, see John Paul II, *Reconciliatio et paenitentia*, §16; and especially CDF, "Instruction on Christian Freedom and Liberation," §§74–75.

44. Finn writes, "There is never a bright line between the causal structures of influence and free choice, since structural influence occurs through the exercise of freedom." Finn, "What Is a Sinful Social Structure?," 158.

45. Liechty and Clegg, *Moving beyond Sectarianism*, 9.

46. Liechty and Clegg, *Moving beyond Sectarianism*, 14.

47. For the analogical character of original sin, see Catholic Church, *Catechism of the Catholic Church*, §404. For the connection between original sin and social sin, see John Paul II, *Reconciliatio et paenitentia*, §2; Benedict XVI, *Caritas in veritate*, §34.

48. The image of the "rough ground" is Wittgenstein's: "We have got onto slippery ice where there is no friction and so in a certain sense the conditions are ideal, but also, because of that, we are unable to walk. We want to walk: so we need *friction*. Back to the rough ground!" See Wittgenstein, *Philosophical Investigations*, §107.

49. The anthropologist Timothy Jenkins makes the connection between ethnographic fieldwork and the perception of everyday life to explore the nature of anthropological knowledge. See Jenkins, "Fieldwork and the Perception of Everyday Life."

50. Hastrup, "Social Anthropology," 140.

51. Hastrup, "Social Anthropology," 140.

52. The importance of *practice* to social life means that we cannot see social rules as an objective, inflexible map determining individuals' actions and responses. Jenkins argues, "If much social life is practical rather than theoretical, embodied in habits and 'dispositions', behaviour is not made up of rule-governed responses to stimuli, but rather is constructed or improvised upon the basis of these habits that enable actors to generate an infinite number of practices adapted to endlessly changing situations, without this basis ever being constituted as explicit principles.... It is upon these grounds that Bourdieu opposes all attempts to objectify social life, to construct theoretical, language-based accounts which refer to rules or structures in a timeless order, and so both ignore the work of the actors in constructing their own practice and also lend themselves to—as well as feeding upon—the ability of the actors themselves to objectify and to give an abstract account of their own practice." See Jenkins, "Fieldwork and the Perception of Everyday Life," 439–40. In this sense, good social theory, as well as good Catholic moral theology, demands appropriate concern for the personal.

53. Mary McClintock Fulkerson, *Places of Redemption*, discusses how the "wound" of ongoing racial segregation in U.S. society is reflected in church communities. As part of Fulkerson's ethnographic study of the Good Samaritan Methodist Church she notes her *bodily* discomfort at worshipping with a greater proportion of nonwhite people than she was accustomed to. Although she describes herself as "feminist, race-conscious, progressive" (3), she finds herself on her first visit to Good Samaritan "aware of the paleness of my skin[,] ... trying to hide any signs that I am not used to worshipping with more than a few token black people" (4–5). The racial segregation of U.S. society is something to which she is *habituated*, in spite of her best intentions and conscious attitudes. See Fulkerson, *Places of Redemption*, 3–24. Again, we are dealing here with a bodily reaction of discomfort that could not be described as sin, but which is an integral part of a social fabric characterized by inequality and injustice.

54. Liechty and Clegg, *Moving beyond Sectarianism*, 10.

55. Jenkins writes, "The 'real' persists far longer than events, personalities or interpretations, and exists at this obscure level: moral or social facts are situated in the constraints and compulsions experienced as humans make sense of themselves and others, in the constancies of mutual interpretation and the patterns of understanding." See Jenkins, *Religion in English Everyday Life*, 12.

56. This is not to deny that the social is real but simply to establish the kind of reality that it has. On this point, Clifford Geertz observes, "Just why

this idea, that cultural description is fashioned knowledge, second hand, so bothers some people is not entirely clear to me.... Perhaps it is the result of a fear that to acknowledge that one has put something together rather than found it on a beach is to undermine its claim to true being and actuality. But a chair is culturally (socially, historically ...) constructed, a product of acting persons informed of notions not wholly their own, yet you can sit in it, it can be made well or ill, and it cannot, at least in the present state of the art, be made out of water or— this for those haunted by 'idealism'— thought into existence." Geertz, *After the Fact*, 62.

57. See Hastrup, "Getting It Right," 458; see also Hastrup, "Social Anthropology," 139; Jenkins, "Fieldwork and the Perception of Everyday Life," 442–43.

58. Hastrup argues that social space can only be perceived from the inside, "when anthropologists place themselves in the field of tension between the individual and the social in the same way as local protagonists." This means that the anthropologist has to take up one of the roles offered to her by the community. See Hastrup, "Social Anthropology," 143. It is the experience of playing different roles, misinterpreting offers, gaining particular knowledge, and encountering resistance from informants that allows the ethnographer to understand social life from the inside.

59. Cahill argues that Church teaching has struggled to see the ways in which human beings "are in important ways *constituted* as persons and as moral agents by the social relationships in which they participate.... [I]t is a mistake to see persons as if they were autonomous 'units' who are within but not integrally part of a fabric of social relationships that define their identities and the ways in which they are able to exercise choice and agency." See Cahill, "A Theology for Peacebuilding," 305–6 (original emphasis). The idea of individual and social as not being "side effects" of one another comes from Hastrup, "Social Anthropology," 140.

60. *Gaudium et spes* acknowledges this in §25, as noted above.

61. Liechty and Clegg, *Moving beyond Sectarianism*, 13–14.

62. And not just narration, but potentially by or involving an outsider or interlocutor. Jenkins points out, "Without the presence of an outsider asking questions, the actors do not need to give any account of what is going on; indeed, it may be that, as Bourdieu suggests, successful practice normally excludes knowledge of its own logic." See Jenkins, "Fieldwork and the Perception of Everyday Life," 440. Robert Schreiter has some insightful comments on the human need to narrate identity and violence as the "narrative of the lie" in his *Reconciliation*, 29–36.

63. Himes, "Social Sin and the Role of the Individual," 213–14.

64. Here, the recipe for transformation of the situation of sin is also a recipe for dealing with the conceptual headache it presents: social sin emerges as personal sin. That is, to the extent that my actions in a given context are unaware, unwilling, or constrained—those social complexities to which I have drawn attention—then to that extent I am not culpable for them. As soon as I become aware of the situation as evil, my action as harmful, and my freedom and ability to act otherwise, I am then committing formal sin if I persist.

65. Himes's account of the relationship between the individual and the social draws on game theory to good effect: "There is a synergy in groups that can add up to more than the sum of the parts. But to admit that a group produces consequences is not to claim that a group intends the consequences. . . . [C]orporations and governments . . . produce outcomes impossible to achieve by individual effort; but the intending of those outcomes is in the mind of discrete individuals." See Himes, "Social Sin and the Role of the Individual," 206–7.

66. Himes argues, "One, a person must become aware of the social evil, sensitized to its deleterious effects and its manifestations. Often this may entail an experiential strategy, exposing a person to the suffering of those victimized by social sin. Then, once a person is aware of the social ill, the second task becomes important, namely, to help someone see how their active, or even passive, support for a given institution, societal attitude or cultural value helps to maintain social sin. This stage requires critical awareness where a person understands the nature and dynamics of social existence and appreciates how societal structures affect our individual lives. Until a person moves beyond the stage of uncritical naivete to the threshold of critical consciousness it is not possible to enter into the world of mature moral reflection." Himes, "Social Sin and the Role of the Individual," 192–93.

67. Gaita, *A Common Humanity*, xvii; original emphasis.

68. Or as John Paul II puts it in *Reconciliatio et paenitentia*, "moral responsibility for evil . . . and therefore sin" (§16).

69. Narrative verdicts have been an option available to coroners in England and Wales since 2004, and they allow a verdict to be delivered in the form of a summary of the facts of the case. They are often used in cases in which responsibility for a given event (e.g., a suicide or death by misadventure) is diffuse or hard to establish.

70. Liechty and Clegg, *Moving beyond Sectarianism*, 18.

71. Liechty and Clegg, *Moving beyond Sectarianism*, 18, 21.

72. Liechty and Clegg, *Moving beyond Sectarianism*, 14–15.

73. Liechty and Clegg, *Moving beyond Sectarianism*, 16.

74. This is not to deny the possibility of an objectively true and complete view of any situation; it is simply to reserve that to God, and to acknowledge the approximate nature of all human attempts *in via*.

75. Karl Rahner writes, "We discover the personal only as we go out to encounter that image of ourselves which God has made for himself, the picture of which he holds before us, and by which we, imperfect as we are, are always simultaneously cast down and delighted, because we recognise in it both ourselves and our God. We can do no more than move towards it; it is only slowly revealed, and never wholly in this life. While we are still pilgrims, it is not only God but also ourselves that we know only in reflections and likenesses; it is only *then* that we shall know ourselves, too, even as we are known." Rahner, "Ignatian Spirituality," 205–6; original emphasis.

76. Rahner, "The Theological Concept of Concupiscentia," 378.

77. Rahner, "The Theological Concept of Concupiscentia." There is no need, for example, for "a dogmatic consideration of concupiscentia . . . immediately to concern itself with the tendency of the sensitive appetite to what is morally *forbidden*" (351) or to understand concupiscence as a purely sensitive power (352) (original emphasis).

78. Rahner, "The Theological Concept of Concupiscentia," 354–55; for the common experience of concupiscence as the resistance of the sensitive to the spiritual, see 364, 369.

79. Rahner, "The Theological Concept of Concupiscentia," 365.

80. Rahner, "The Theological Concept of Concupiscentia," 352–53, 359. "In virtue of man's metaphysical structure it will be fundamentally impossible from the start for there ever to be an act of sensitive cognition which is not also *eo ipso* an act of spiritual cognition" (353).

81. "There is much in man which always remains in concrete fact somehow impersonal; impenetrable and unilluminated for his existential decision; merely endured and not freely acted out." Rahner, "The Theological Concept of Concupiscentia," 369.

82. Rahner, "The Theological Concept of Concupiscentia," 365–66.

83. Rahner, "The Theological Concept of Concupiscentia," 369.

84. Rahner, "The Theological Concept of Concupiscentia," 365.

85. Rahner, "The Theological Concept of Concupiscentia," 369. Sebastian Moore, commenting on Rahner, puts it less technically and more frankly: "The refusal of God's call to wholeness is the tendency of decision and spontaneity to stay apart. We prefer them apart. Faced with any decision, we strive to leave part of ourselves out of it. We resist a temptation, but we keep it going. We make a decision, but we look for the escape clause. Nothing is final in this

life—and by God we want it that way. We are inveterate two-timers. I absolutely dread the thought of the whole of me coming together in a 'yes' to somebody or something, with nothing of myself left out, and therefore no possibility of retreat. Yes, I *want* it too, I know. Sometimes I sort of feel for it in prayer. But the dread and the desire are inextricably intertwined." Moore, *The Crucified Is No Stranger*, 46; original emphasis.

86. Rahner, "The Theological Concept of Concupiscentia," 366.

87. Katongole, *The Journey of Reconciliation*, 78.

88. We can see a version of this in the thought of Wojtyła on solidarity as I explored it earlier— the need for "acting together with others" to be a self-conscious undertaking. See ch. 4.

89. Hastrup gives the example of "society" and "religion": "It applies to Durkheim's concept of society as a moral whole. It began as an invention, or an analytical framework for understanding the connections and interdependencies of certain social phenomena, but it almost immediately came to be viewed as a 'thing' in the world. . . . In other words, an epistemological relationship, that is a way of comprehending the world, was transformed into an ontological entity, or an objectively existing phenomenon, whose nature successive generations of scholars have had to explore." Hastrup, "Religion in Context," 258.

90. On the emergence of "society" as a "thing out there" in Durkheim's work, Hastrup writes, "The important issue is that in the process of understanding the nature of social integration, a new *object* was born into the world. The object was to be studied empirically through its symptoms, and gradually the invisible and intangible 'society' achieved logical and historical priority over those empirical symptoms it was designed to organize in a comprehensive form in the first place." Hastrup, "Religion in Context," 257. She continues, "If notions such as 'society' or 'religion' start as attempts at understanding specific and very varied phenomena, they end up as 'things' or ontological entities, that scholars have a hard time dissolving afterwards" (259).

91. John Paul II, *Reconciliatio et paenitentia*, §16.

92. Rahner, "The Theological Concept of Concupiscentia," 382; original emphasis.

Chapter 6

1. In Guatemala in 1994, the Human Rights Office of the Archdiocese of Guatemala created the Project for the Recovery of Historical Memory (REMHI) following Guatemala's thirty-six-year civil war. Clergy and laypeople traveled around Guatemala taking testimony from thousands of survivors and victims of violence, which the report presents along with analysis

of the military, social, and political context. The project issued its report in 1998, after which the head of the project, Bishop Juan Gerardi, was murdered. The REMHI final report was translated into English: see Quigley, *Guatemala, Never Again!* In El Salvador, Archbishop Óscar Romero established a human rights office, Socorro Jurídico, which issued regular reports on human rights abuses during the course of the Salvadoran Civil War. Socorro Jurídico became Tutela Legal, whose ongoing work in documenting human rights abuses laid important groundwork for the official report of the UN Truth Commission, "'From Madness to Hope': The 12-Year War in El Salvador."

2. Francis, "Nonviolence, a Style of Politics for Peace," §6, §1.

3. The word *reconciliation* appears most frequently in *Unitatis redintegratio*, where it refers to the reconciliation of East and West (§11) and of all Christians (§24); it appears in *Gaudium et spes*, §22 and §78, in connection with peace; it appears in *Lumen gentium*, §11 and §28, in connection with the sacrament of reconciliation.

4. In *Pacem in terris* the word appears only three times: twice in connection with the reconciliation of opposing parties (§93, §162) and once in connection with the prayer "to Him who shed His blood to reconcile the human race to the heavenly Father" and the quotation of Eph 1:14, 17.

5. Vatican II, *Lumen gentium*, §7, §§9–17.

6. John Paul II, *Reconciliatio et paenitentia*, §8; the same paragraph quotes Vatican II, *Lumen gentium*, §1.

7. John Paul II, *Reconciliatio et paenitentia*, §§10–11.

8. John Paul II, *Reconciliatio et paenitentia*, §§15–14.

9. John Paul II, *Reconciliatio et paenitentia*, §16. For a fuller summary and discussion of this material, see ch. 5 above.

10. John Paul II, *Reconciliatio et paenitentia*, §25.

11. John Paul II, *Reconciliatio et paenitentia*, §1.

12. "To acknowledge one's sin, indeed—penetrating still more deeply into the consideration of one's own personhood—to recognize oneself as being a sinner, capable of sin and inclined to commit sin, is the essential first step in returning to God." John Paul II, *Reconciliatio et paenitentia*, §13.

13. See John Paul II, *Reconciliatio et paenitentia*, §16 and §4: "The synod at the same time spoke about the reconciliation of the whole human family and of the conversion of the heart of every individual, of his or her return to God: It did so because it wished to recognize and proclaim the fact that there can be no union among people without an internal change in each individual. Personal conversion is the necessary path to harmony between individuals."

14. As is often the case in Catholic social teaching more widely, use of scripture is illustrative of rather than integral to the points being made. For

this observation regarding use of scripture in modern Catholic social teaching, see Curran, *Catholic Social Teaching*, 45.

15. John Paul II, *Reconciliatio et paenitentia*, §8, §26.

16. John Paul II, *Reconciliatio et paenitentia*, §§28–34.

17. See John Paul II, *Tertio millennio adveniente*, §§33–36. On separate occasions John Paul II asked forgiveness from contemporary groups representing the Moravians, the indigenous peoples of Latin America, and Africans deported as slaves: see ITC, *Memory and Reconciliation*, n. 19. See also John Paul II's *Incarnationis mysterium*, which expresses a desire that the Church should "kneel before God and implore forgiveness for the past and present sins of her sons and daughters."

18. *Memory and Reconciliation* does interact with some biblical material in section 2.1.

19. ITC, *Memory and Reconciliation*, 5.1, drawing on John Paul II, *Incarnationis mysterium*, §11.

20. ITC, *Memory and Reconciliation*, 3.4.

21. ITC, *Memory and Reconciliation*, 1.3.

22. ITC, *Memory and Reconciliation*, 5.1: "Objective responsibility refers to the moral value of the act in itself, insofar as it is good or evil, and thus refers to the imputability of the action. Subjective responsibility concerns the effective perception by individual conscience of the goodness or evil of the act performed. Subjective responsibility ceases with the death of the one who performed the act; it is not transmitted through generation; the descendants do not inherit (subjective) responsibility for the acts of their ancestors. In this sense, asking for forgiveness presupposes a contemporaneity between those who are hurt by an action and those who committed it. The only responsibility capable of continuing in history can be the objective kind, to which one may freely adhere subjectively or not." Jeremy Bergen argues that *Memory and Reconciliation*'s account of how the Church can assume the personal sins of its members is ambiguous. See Bergen, *Ecclesial Repentance*, 128.

23. ITC, *Memory and Reconciliation*, 4. Christopher Bellitto points out a difficulty here: can historians really be asked to determine the subjective culpability of people no longer alive? He notes that historians might be more sensibly able to comment on the objective failings of the corporate Church, but this is something for which, for theological reasons, *Memory and Reconciliation* is much less ready to apologize. It is not clear that all of John Paul II's apologies pertain to situations where the offenders could have understood their action as wrong and avoided it—the Crusades and the persecution of non-Catholic Christians included. See Bellitto, "Teaching the Church's Mistakes," 129, 134.

24. Analyzing *Memory and Reconciliation*, Bergen argues, "An embodied account of the truth that reconciles will take seriously the perspective on the past that can only be given by those who have been hurt by it. If the church confesses sin in its past, it must recognize that this sin may also obscure the account that may be given of that sin. . . . [T]he propositional account of truth assumes that the perspective of those (non-Catholic Christians, Jews, Aboriginal people) sinned against is not essential for arriving at the truth. Once this truth is determined, only then is reconciliation sought. By contrast, engaging dialogically with their interpretation of the past would not only provide a more comprehensive picture of what 'really happened', the process of jointly owning a new account of the past and the mutuality and respect presupposed by it, will already contribute to a healing of relationships." See Bergen, *Ecclesial Repentance*, 125.

25. For relevant comment on this "additive" problem in the context of social sin, see ch. 5 above.

26. Benedict XVI, *Africae munus*, §6, §15, §20.

27. Benedict XVI, *Africae munus*, §20.

28. Benedict XVI, *Africae munus*, §33, §§155–58, §169. The document focuses in particular on the Church's role as a "sentinel" (§30, §81) and in education (§23, §§75–78. This sense of the full scope of the reconciling activity of the Church is clearer still in the *instrumentum laboris* for the synod, which draws attention to the role of church leaders (§67, §107), the Church's involvement in national reconciliation processes (§90), and the reconciling activities of small Christian communities on a local level (§90). See Synod of African Bishops, *The Church in Africa*.

29. There is little recognition in the document that the Church's claim to exist as a "reconciled and reconciling" community might be undermined or mitigated by her failures to live as a reconciled body.

30. See also John Paul II, "Offer Forgiveness and Receive Peace": "Believers know that *reconciliation comes from God*, who is always ready to forgive those who turn to him and turn their back on their sins" (§6).

31. Benedict XVI, *Africae munus*, §20.

32. Benedict XVI, *Africae munus*, §20.

33. Schreiter, *Reconciliation*, 44–45.

34. Benedict XVI, *Africae munus*, §19.

35. Benedict XVI, *Africae munus*, §19.

36. Benedict XVI, *Africae munus*, §26.

37. Katongole, *The Journey of Reconciliation*, 148–49.

38. Benedict XVI, *Africae munus*, §22, §23, §26.

39. Benedict XVI, *Africae munus*, §53, §23.

40. Benedict XVI, *Africae munus*, §102, §108; on laypeople, §131.

41. For involvement in national reconciliation processes, see Synod of African Bishops, *The Church in Africa*, §67; for the role of bishops, see §107: "The voice of bishop-servants of the Word, raised and heard in times of social crisis is like that of a sentinel of a city. In facing political problems concerning constitutions, elections, injustices, violations of human rights, etc., a prophetic word from the bishop is a response to the people's thirst for justice and peace. The courage and boldness of bishops make them living examples of the 'salt of the earth' and the 'light of the world.'"

42. Katongole, *The Journey of Reconciliation*, 149.

43. Benedict XVI, *Address of His Holiness Benedict XVI during Luncheon with Synod Fathers* (24 October 2009), quoted in Katongole, *The Journey of Reconciliation*, 149.

44. Katongole, *The Journey of Reconciliation*, 148.

45. Benedict XVI, *Africae munus*, §21.

46. Webster, "The Ethics of Reconciliation," 118.

47. Benedict XVI, *Africae munus*, §§34–36, §§39–41, §26.

48. In §23, *Africae munus* states, "It is worth repeating that, while a distinction must be made between the role of pastors and that of the lay faithful, the Church's mission is not political in nature." It is not made clear what this means, though it may mean that laypeople, while encouraged to engage in politics, are not to seek state power in the name of the Church.

49. For ease of expression, I refer throughout to what "Paul" writes in Colossians and Ephesians, but this should not be read as a firm position about the authorship of these letters. Given the density of scriptural quotation in this chapter, I give scriptural references in the text.

50. See Dunn, *Romans 1–8*, 259; Schwöbel, "Reconciliation," 16.

51. Five out of six uses of the word are in reference to divine-human relationships. See Schwöbel, "Reconciliation," 15.

52. Schwöbel, "Reconciliation," 28.

53. Indeed, there may be good reasons *not* to do so. Dunn points out that Paul's language of "gaining access to this grace in which we stand" in Romans 5:2 appears to draw on courtly language of access to imperial or kingly favor rather than on sacrificial imagery (248–49). He argues also that Paul's sacrifice language may be intended to refer to the Maccabean martyr tradition of people dying for law or nation, in the context of which his claim that Jesus died "for the ungodly" is a pointed contrast. See Dunn, *Romans 1–8*, 255, 259. While Dunn nevertheless still argues for an emphasis on sacrifice, Fitzmyer suggests that references to Jesus's death need not be pressed in this direction: "Reference neither to 'death' nor to 'blood' per se connotes anything sacrificial

or cultic; death connotes the giving up of one's life, and blood refers to that." See Fitzmyer, *Romans*, 401. For the possible blending in the Maccabean tradition of sacrifice and reconciliation language, see Dunn, *Romans 1–8*, 259.

54. Schwöbel, "Reconciliation," 19.

55. Schwöbel, "Reconciliation," 21.

56. "From the broader context, provided for us by Greco-Roman literature of the period, we know that *just these observances were widely regarded as characteristically and distinctively Jewish*. . . . [J]ust these observances in particular functioned as identity markers, they served to identify their practitioners as Jewish in the eyes of the wider public, they were the peculiar rites which marked out the Jews as that peculiar people. . . . These identity markers identified Jewishness because they were seen by the Jews themselves as fundamental observances of the covenant. They functioned as badges of covenant membership." Dunn, "The New Perspective on Paul," 191–92; original emphasis.

57. Dunn, "The New Perspective on Paul," 194.

58. Dunn, *The Theology of Paul*, 198.

59. Schreiter emphasizes the same point in "A Practical Theology of Healing, Forgiveness and Reconciliation," 374–75.

60. Dunn, *The Theology of Paul*, 230 n. 132.

61. John Paul II, *Reconciliatio et paenitentia*, §10.

62. ITC, *Memory and Reconciliation*, 2.2, states that "the believer must count on the death and resurrection of the Lord Jesus . . . to be part of the history in which 'grace overflows' (cf. Rom 5:12–21)."

63. I am indebted here to an unpublished paper by James Crampsey S.J., "Overtures to Ministry."

64. Mt 16:19 and 18:18 are often key here, along with themes of Christ the high priest from the Letter to the Hebrews.

65. Kaur, "Guatemala," 35–66.

66. Katongole comments interestingly on silence in Rwanda in "The End of Words" in *The Journey of Reconciliation*, 34–44.

67. Kaur notes that Fr. Melchior Fraj assisted the local Achí population by compiling a list of the dead: "Survivors would appear at the church under the pretext of asking for confession to add the names of their dead. . . . The list was drawn up shortly after the amnesties, but compiling it was still dangerous." Kaur, "Guatemala," 49.

68. Schreiter, *Reconciliation*, 44–45.

69. Benedict XVI in *Africae munus* acknowledges the demands of justice and charity and calls for Christians to become exemplary in both. See *Africae munus*, §18.

70. See Raimond Gaita on "severe pity" in the Oedipus cycle in ch. 5 above.

71. Rutikanga, "Rwanda," 163.

72. They can also contribute in problematic ways to the maintenance of structural inequalities, as when, for example, the best hospitals and schools in a country are run by Christians, who are perceived as making up the cultural and political elite.

73. Pope Francis, "Nonviolence, a Style of Politics for Peace," §3; original emphasis.

74. Pope Francis, "Nonviolence, a Style of Politics for Peace," §3; original emphasis.

75. This is a key emphasis for Katongole, *The Journey of Reconciliation*, 4–8.

76. John Paul II, *Reconciliatio et paenitentia*, §§8–9.

77. ITC, *Memory and Reconciliation*, 3.4.

78. Cejka and Bamat, "Introduction," 17; original emphasis.

79. Cejka and Bamat, "Introduction," 13.

80. Lederach, *The Moral Imagination*, 5.

81. John Paul II, *Reconciliatio et paenitentia*, §4, §8; Francis, *Laudato sí*, §66.

82. Reichberg, *Thomas Aquinas on War and Peace*, 3.

83. In fairness, the document's focus is intraecclesial, so this emphasis on reconciliation as a return to the communion of the Church is to be expected.

84. This is part of Paul's argument in Romans 11.

85. Dunn, "The New Perspective on Paul," 198.

86. This is the point of the parable of the Good Samaritan. The lawyer asks, "Who is my neighbor?," in the sense of "How far does my obligation extend?" Jesus's reply turns the question on its head: being a neighbor is showing mercy to all in need of it (Lk 10:25–37). Thanks to Nick Austin S.J. for this example.

87. Benedict XVI, *Africae munus*, §152: "The table of the Lord gathers together men and women of different origins, cultures, races, languages and ethnic groups. Thanks to the Body and Blood of Christ, they become truly one. In the eucharistic Christ, they become blood relations and thus true brothers and sisters, thanks to the word and to the Body and Blood of the same Jesus Christ. This bond of fraternity is stronger than that of human families, than that of our tribes."

88. Benedict XVI, *Africae munus*, §26, §19.

89. "A pastor's language must be realistic, it must touch upon reality, but within the perspective of God and His Word. Therefore this mediation

involves, on one hand being truly tied to reality, taking the care to talk about what is, and on the other hand, not falling into technically political solutions: this means to demonstrate a concrete but spiritual world." *Address of His Holiness Benedict XVI during Luncheon with the Synod Fathers*, quoted in Katongole, *The Journey of Reconciliation*, 149.

90. Cavanaugh, *Torture and Eucharist*.

91. Cavanaugh gives a condensed summary in "The Church in the Streets."

92. Katongole, *The Journey of Reconciliation*, 159–66.

93. Cavanaugh, "The Church in the Streets," 400–401; quoted in Katongole, *The Journey of Reconciliation*, 160.

94. Katongole, *The Journey of Reconciliation*, 146.

95. On Maggy Barankitse, see Katongole, *The Journey of Reconciliation*, 164–66; on Buta seminary, see 83–85. Katongole also offers a number of examples of prophetic leadership by African bishops, whose style of leadership offers a critique of political misuse of power and a concrete example of an alternative. Writing about Archbishop Emmanuel Kataliko of Bukavu, he states: "[Kataliko's] project involved nothing less than a redefinition of politics from the vantage point of the story of God's nonviolent and reconciling love. The immediate social and practical implication of this redefinition was that for Kataliko politics was not about power in the sense of domination, force, and plunder, but power as self-sacrificing service on behalf of others" (155).

96. I do not intend here to align myself with an Augustinian view of politics as a necessary evil but to point out the incompatibility of a certain kind of nationalism/identity politics with Catholic social teaching, which affirms that the good of each state cannot be pursued in isolation from or over against others. See John XXIII, *Pacem in terris*, §§130–31: "And finally, each country's social progress, order, security and peace are necessarily linked with the social progress, order, security and peace of every other country. From this it is clear that no State can fittingly pursue its own interests in isolation from the rest, nor, under such circumstances, can it develop itself as it should. The prosperity and progress of any State is in part consequence, and in part cause, of the prosperity and progress of all other States."

97. Budde, *Beyond the Borders of Baptism*, 7; quoted in Katongole, *The Journey of Reconciliation*, 79.

98. Levertov, "Misnomer," in *Evening Train*, 79, copyright ©1992 by Denise Levertov, reprinted by permission of New Directions Publishing Corp.

99. See Vladisavljevic, "Austria Church Bans Mass at Bleiburg Commemoration."

100. De Chergé, "Testament." I have written more extensively about the Cistercian monks of Tibhirine in Hawksley, "Of Gods and Men: Peacebuilding and Catholic Social Teaching."

101. Benedict XVI, *Africae munus*, §152; see also §41; Katongole, *The Journey of Reconciliation*, 67.

102. De Chergé, "Testament."

Chapter 7

1. Augustine, *City of God* XIX.12.

2. It is important to note that true order as Augustine understands it is not a state of rigid stasis, the order of everything fixed unchanging in its position. Creation is changeable, and its perfection involves development: true order means a dynamic order in which things develop, interact, and change but always in accordance with their God-given "measure, weight, and order." Disorder—again, the example of the upside-down man—involves somehow straining against these inbuilt principles of movement, interaction, and development. See Williams, "Good for Nothing?," 11–13. See also Augustine, *Confessions* V.4.

3. Augustine, *City of God* XIX.12.

4. Augustine, *City of God* XIX.12.

5. See also Augustine, *Concerning the Nature of the Good*, ch. 6, 17.

6. Augustine says the same of grief in *City of God* XIX.13: a man's grief over the loss of his nature's peace "arises from some remnants of that peace, whereby his nature befriends itself."

7. Augustine, *City of God* XIX.17, 26–27.

8. Augustine states that a people estranged from God, though it has a peace of its own, "will not, indeed, possess it in the end, because it does not make good use of it before the end." *City of God* XIX.26; see also XIX.13.

9. Augustine, *City of God* XIX.12.

10. John XXIII, *Pacem in terris*, §115.

11. John XXIII, *Pacem in terris*, §113, §114.

12. This is connected to Aquinas's definition of sin in *Summa Theologica* I–II.71.6. There Aquinas picks up Augustine's definition of sin as an act contrary to the eternal law and unpacks it by stating that the eternal law is contained primarily in natural law and secondarily in human reason. Therefore sin is also contrary to human reason. Carried forward into *Pacem in terris*, with its positive neo-scholastic account of human beings' ability to grasp the natural law, it results in an understanding of war as *contrary* to human reason and peace as being in accord with human reason.

13. John XXIII, *Pacem in terris*, §167.

14. John XXIII, *Pacem in terris*, §46, §168.

15. Vatican II, *Gaudium et spes*, §78.

16. Vatican II, *Gaudium et spes*, §13, §25, §§37–38.

17. John Paul II, "Development and Solidarity, Two Keys to Peace," §10.

18. Paul VI, "Every Man Is My Brother."

19. I quoted earlier Kenneth Himes, who argues that this communitarian vision means that "conflict is viewed as more apparent than real; the organic metaphor of society, so prevalent in Catholic social teaching, induces a belief that harmony and cooperation are easier to achieve than is the case." See Himes, "Peacebuilding," 282–83.

20. Whitmore, "Peacebuilding and Its Challenging Partners," 179.

21. Lash, "Not Exactly Politics or Power," 363.

22. To say that the resurrection produces a kind of transformation from within in this way is not to say that the kingdom of God comes only to the extent that we get our act together. As with the growth of a seed, happening out of sight, the transformation to which we are called does not lie within our power. God's victory does not *depend* on our transformation, but it does include it, it does go by way of it.

23. Williams, *The Truce of God*, 7–8.

24. Williams, *The Truce of God*, 8.

25. One 2012 survey reported that 31 percent of respondents believed in God, but 49 percent believed in life after death. See Sullivan, Voas, and Brown, *The Art of Asking Questions about Religion*. See also the Theos study, *The Spirit of Things Unseen*.

26. Katongole discusses Julia Esquivel's poem "Threatened with Resurrection" in *The Journey of Reconciliation*, 106–8.

27. MacKinnon, "Subjective and Objective Conceptions of Atonement," 173.

28. Consider the account of the piercing of Jesus's side in John's gospel, which is immediately followed by the insistence of the eyewitness to this that "his testimony is true, and he knows that he tells the truth" (Jn 19:34–35). The narration of the arrangements to have the tomb guarded in Mt 27:62–65 performs a similar function, both refuting rumors about the disciples removing the body and establishing the real deadness of Jesus.

29. Mt 28:10; Mk 16:6; Lk 24:36; Jn 20:19, 21, 26. The angel also greets the first arrivals at the tomb with "Do not be afraid" in Mt 28:5 and Mk 16:6.

30. Lederach, "The Mystery of Transformative Times and Spaces," 265.

31. Moore, *The Crucified Is No Stranger*, 80.

32. "Do you not know that all of us who were baptised into Christ Jesus were baptised into his death? Therefore we have been buried with him in baptism, so that, just as Christ was raised from the dead, so we too might walk in newness of life." Romans 6:4.

33. Augustine, *City of God* XIV.15.

34. See Augustine, *City of God* XIX.15: God did not intend that people should have lordship over one another, but only over animals. Slavery, both to sin and to one another, is the punishment for sin. Pride hates the "fellowship of equality under God, and wishes to impose its own dominions upon its equals, in place of God's rule." See also XIX.12.

35. Augustine, *City of God* XIV.14.

36. Augustine states that human beings were "divested, that is, of the grace that made the nakedness of their bodies of no concern to them, so that it became a source of shame to them when the law of sin warred against their mind. Thus, they learned what they would have been happier not knowing, had they believed in God and obeyed Him, and so not committed the act which compelled them to learn by experience the harm done by infidelity and disobedience. Therefore, dismayed by the disobedience of their flesh—by the punishment which bore witness, as it were, to their own disobedience—'they sewed fig-leaves together, and made themselves *campestrina*', that is, loincloths, which is the expression that some translators use." Augustine, *City of God* XIV.17.

37. John Paul II, *Sollicitudo rei socialis*, §19; "Development and Solidarity, Two Keys to Peace."

38. Williams, *Resurrection*, 18; original emphasis.

39. Williams makes the same point about the kind of judgment that creates a relationship of oppressor-victim: "We are not dealing here with law or morality; there are other kinds of judgement-as-discernment, discrimination and responsibility, which would require a different treatment. What is at issue is simply the transaction that leads to exclusion, to the severance of any relation of reciprocity." Williams, *Resurrection*, 10.

40. On an individual level, too, some division or "cutting off" from others can be necessary. Some kinds of "covering," too, become necessary in a fallen creation. Williams observes, "Since the Fall, concealment is necessary and good in the sense that there is plenty in human thought, feeling, and experience that *should not* be part of shared discourse. We are alienated, divided, and corrupted; but to bring this into speech (and to assume we thereby tell a better or fuller truth) is to collude with sin." Williams, "The Suspicion of Suspicion," 44; original emphasis.

41. Thus, sinful disorder is not always, indeed perhaps only seldom, a matter of conscious rebellion against God and the divine order. Augustine observes that "many sins are committed through pride; but yet not all things which are wrongly done are done proudly—at any rate, not by the ignorant, not by the infirm, and not, generally speaking, by the weeping and sorrowful." Augustine, *On Nature and Grace* XXIX.33.

42. Power can be seized; authority can only be freely acknowledged, so "seizing authority" is a contradiction in terms, and the means destroys the end. See Zechmeister, "The Authority of Those Who Suffer."

43. Williams, "Saving Time," 322.

44. Augustine, *City of God* XIX.6.

45. Lederach, "The Long Journey Back to Humanity," 34.

46. Williams, "Saving Time," 322.

47. Commenting on Augustine's distinction, Williams observes, "Insofar as the commonwealth is just and orderly, it is worth preserving, and its ruler will take steps to preserve it; that is, insofar as it is *imperfectly* just and orderly, it justifies defensive action. True justice and orderliness cannot be defended by such means, because they participate in the city of God, which depends upon defenceless trust in the continuance of God's *ordo.*" Williams, "Politics and the Soul," 66; original emphasis.

48. Moore, *The Crucified Is No Stranger*, 13.

49. Moore, *The Crucified Is No Stranger*, 13.

50. Moore, *The Crucified Is No Stranger*, 21; original emphasis.

51. Moore warns that we can easily miss this moment of realization, the beginning of our healing, either by failing to reach it or by overshooting it. A person can fail to reach it if he treats God as "his ally in the struggle with his inner chaos. The God who loves him is and will remain the projection of his optimism until he is somehow brought by God to turn about and face the chaos and—far more than this—to recognize that the chaos has a name, a form of its own, a force: the name is sin, the evil of man that resists the love of God. When man praises this love, sin does not contradict him but simply goes underground and continues to belie in hidden ways his belief in God's love." Moore, *The Crucified Is No Stranger*, 6. A person can also overshoot it if he succumbs to the "almost insuperable temptation to claim this realization 'for himself', to appropriate it in terms of the ego. . . . For the wise, on the contrary, the coming into self is expressed only in silent contemplation, in humility, and in the indefinable benefits which the wise confer on the less aware" (11).

52. See Alison, *Knowing Jesus*, 16: "The resurrection is forgiveness: not a decree of forgiveness, but the presence of gratuity as a person."

53. Williams, *Resurrection*, 3.

54. Williams, *Resurrection*, 8.

55. Alison, *Knowing Jesus*, 16. Williams makes the same point: "God as gracious 'occurs', is manifest, only in the resurrection of the crucified." Williams, *Resurrection*, 16.

56. See Alison on the "intelligence of the victim": "The intelligence of the victim [in the gospels] is not seen as something only related to the person of Jesus, though he reveals it fully; it is seen as something that has always been present. Jesus is revealing something that has always been true about human society.... Human society is a violent place, which makes victims, and the revelation of God is to be found in the midst of that violence, on the side of the victims." Alison, *Knowing Jesus*, 43.

57. Williams, *Resurrection*, 6.

58. Williams, *Resurrection*, 11: "I 'atone' for my primal sin of oppression by according a superior instead of an inferior place to my victims, placing a moral scourge in their hands to beat me as I once beat them; and this is a travesty of the process of human reconciliation and restoration: my imagination is still trapped in the illusion that the basic and ultimate form of human relation is that between the powerful and the powerless. Even if this is translated into terms of moral superiority and inferiority, the structure remains the same, a 'master-slave' relationship in which one partner is defined by the other."

59. Williams, *Resurrection*, 6.

60. Alison makes a similar point in his *On Being Liked*, 40–41: "After the resurrection of Jesus made available what his life and death had been about as forgiveness, the apostolic witnesses began to be able to perceive that what had enabled Jesus to give himself up to death was that he was already deliberately involved, as a terrestrial human being, with a set purpose, making of his death a 'losing to death' so that we could be shown that we too can live as if death were not."

61. Williams, *Resurrection*, 9.

62. Williams, *Resurrection*, 4, 6; original emphasis. Schreiter's exploration of reconciliation in Paul leads to the same conclusion. God takes the initiative in reconciling sinful creation, and therefore the initiative for reconciliation lies with the victim: "For there to be reconciliation, the victims must forgive; the perpetrators cannot forgive themselves. And that forgiveness must carry something of the unboundedness of grace that God gives. We must not 'count trespasses' any more than God has." Schreiter, *Reconciliation*, 44–45.

63. De Chergé, "Testament."

64. Judith Butler's brief comments on a politics of vulnerability in a 2003 interview give some idea of what a politics of true peace might mean. See Stauffer, "Interview with Judith Butler."

65. Schreiter has some scriptural reflections along these lines in part 1 of his *Ministry of Reconciliation*, which explores reconciliation through the lens of postresurrection encounters between Jesus and the disciples.

66. For a discussion of the events of Acts 10–11 along these lines, see Alison, *On Being Liked*, vii–xii.

67. The old division of social class rears its head in 1 Corinthians 11, for example, and enduring tensions between Hebrews and Hellenists are behind the appointment of seven men as *diakonoi* in Acts 6:1.

68. I am reminded of a comment made by (now) Archbishop Charles Scicluna at a conference on the clerical sexual abuse crisis, held at St Mary's University, Twickenham, in 2012. In a discussion about power and the Church, Scicluna defended the Church's need to exercise coercive power: this is how offenders are disciplined and victims protected.

69. This is an important emphasis in Katongole, *The Journey of Reconciliation*.

70. See, e.g., Cavanaugh, "The Church in the Streets."

71. "Christians do not construct out of whole cloth, or from the bottom up, what they say about God and Jesus or the nature of things in relation to God; instead, they use in odd ways whatever language-games they happen to speak." Tanner adds that the same holds true for Christian practices: "While Christians cannot do everything that non-Christians do—since not all practices can be made Christian (for instance, slavery)—Christian practices are always the practices of others made odd." Tanner, *Theories of Culture*, 113. See also her remarks on Christian "style," 145–55.

72. Williams, "Saving Time," 322.

73. Fulkerson, *Places of Redemption*, 20.

74. Fulkerson, *Places of Redemption*, 224.

75. Fulkerson, *Places of Redemption*, 253.

76. Fulkerson, *Places of Redemption*, 229.

77. John XXIII, *Pacem in terris*, §162.

BIBLIOGRAPHY

Alberigo, Giuseppe, and Joseph A. Komonchak. *History of Vatican II*. Vol. 4. Leuven: Peeters, 2003.

Alison, James. *Knowing Jesus*. London: SPCK, 1993.

———. *On Being Liked*. London: Darton, Longman and Todd, 2003.

Allen, John L., Jr. "'Trauma Forms the Invisible Ruins ISIS Left Behind on the Nineveh Plains." *Crux*, 15 June 2018. https://cruxnow.com/crux-nineveh/2018/06/15/trauma-forms-the-invisible-ruins-isis-left-behind-on-the-nineveh-plains/.

Appleby, R. Scott. "Peacebuilding and Catholicism: Affinities, Convergences, Possibilities." In *Peacebuilding: Catholic Theology, Ethics and Praxis*, edited by Robert J. Schreiter, R. Scott Appleby, and Gerard F. Powers, 3–22. Maryknoll, NY: Orbis Books, 2010.

Aquinas, Thomas. *De Regno*. Translated by Gerard B. Phelan. Toronto: Pontifical Institute of Medieval Studies, 1949. Online edition at http://dhspriory.org/thomas/english/DeRegno.htm.

———. *Summa Theologica*. Translated by the Fathers of the English Dominican Province. Online edition (2017) at www.newadvent.org/summa/.

Ashley, J. Matthew. "Contemplation in the Action of Justice: Ignacio Ellacuría and Ignatian Spirituality." In *Love That Produces Hope: The Thought of Ignacio Ellacuría*, edited by Kevin F. Burke and Robert Lassalle-Klein, 144–65. Collegeville, MN: Liturgical Press, 2006.

Associated Press. "Catholic Priest Murdered in Mexico." *Catholic Herald*, 29 March 2017. www.catholicherald.co.uk/news/2017/03/29/catholic-priest-murdered-in-mexico/.

Augustine. *Answer to Faustus, a Manichean (Contra Faustum Manicheum)*. Translated by Roland Teske. New York: New City Press, 2007.

———. *The City of God against the Pagans*. Translated by R. W. Dyson. Cambridge: Cambridge University Press, 1998.

———. *Confessions.* Translated by R. S. Pine-Coffin. London: Penguin Books, 1969.

———. *On Free Choice of the Will.* Translated by Thomas Williams. Indianapolis, IN: Hackett, 1993.

———. *Letter to Boniface* (Letter 189). In Augustine, *Letters 156–210.* Translated by Roland Teske S.J., 259–62. New York: New City Press, 2004.

———. *Letter to Publicola* (Letter 47). In Augustine, *Letters 1–99.* Translated by Roland Teske S.J., 187–91. New York: New City Press, 2001.

———. *The Nature of the Good.* In Augustine, *Against the Manicheans,* edited and translated by Roland Teske, 325–45. New York: New City Press, 2006.

———. *On Nature and Grace.* In Augustine, *Selected Writings on Grace and Pelagianism,* edited by Boniface Ramsey, 319–77. Translated by Roland Teske. New York: New City Press, 2011.

———. "Tractate 84." In *Tractates on the Gospel of John 55–111,* 134–35. Translated by John W. Rettig. Washington, DC: Catholic University of America Press, 1994.

Autesserre, Séverine. *Peaceland: Conflict Resolution and the Everyday Politics of International Intervention.* New York: Cambridge University Press, 2014.

Balthasar, Hans Urs von. *Mysterium Paschale.* Translated by Aidan Nichols. Edinburgh: T.&T. Clark, 1990.

Barstad, Hans M. *The Babylonian Captivity of the Book of Isaiah: "Exilic" Judah and the Provenance of Isaiah 40–55.* Oslo: Novus, 1997.

Basset, Lytta. *Holy Anger: Jacob, Job, Jesus.* Translated by Bruce Henry and Monica Sandor. London: Continuum, 2007.

Baum, Gregory. "Structures of Sin." In *The Logic of Solidarity: Commentaries on Pope John Paul II's Encyclical "On Social Concern,"* edited by Gregory Baum and Robert Ellsberg, 110–26. Maryknoll, NY: Orbis Books, 1989.

BBC News. "Pope Francis Kisses Feet of Rival South Sudan Leaders." *BBC News,* 11 April 2019. www.bbc.co.uk/news/av/world-africa-47903916/pope-francis-kisses-feet-of-rival-south-sudan-leaders.

———. "Pope Francis Warns on 'Piecemeal World War III.'" BBC News, 13 September 2014. www.bbc.co.uk/news/world-europe-29190890.

Beck, Ashley. "How Catholic Teaching about War Has Changed: The Issues in View." *New Blackfriars* 96, no. 1062 (March 2015): 130–46.

Bellitto, Christopher M. "Teaching the Church's Mistakes: Historical Hermeneutics in *Memory and Reconciliation: The Church and the Faults of the Past.*" *Horizons* 32, no. 1 (Spring 2005): 123–35.

Benedict XV. *Ad beatissimi apostolorum.* Encyclical Letter, 1914. www.vatican.va.

———. *Allorché fummo chiamati.* Encyclical Letter, 1915. www.vatican.va.

————. *Pacem Dei munus pulcherrimum.* Encyclical Letter, 1920. www.vatican .va.

Benedict XVI. *Africae munus.* Post-Synodal Apostolic Exhortation, 2007. www.vatican.va.

————. *Caritas in veritate.* Encyclical Letter, 2009. www.vatican.va.

————. "Midday Angelus." 18 February 2007. www.vatican.va.

Bergen, Jeremy. *Ecclesial Repentance: The Churches Confront Their Sinful Pasts.* London: Continuum, 2011.

Beyer, Gerald John. *Recovering Solidarity: Lessons from Poland's Unfinished Revolution.* Notre Dame, IN: University of Notre Dame Press, 2010.

Bhaskar, Roy. *The Possibility of Naturalism: A Philosophical Critique of the Contemporary Human Sciences.* Brighton: Harvester Press, 1979.

Boutros-Ghali, Boutros. "An Agenda for Peace: Preventative Diplomacy, Peace-making and Peace-keeping." UN Documents, 17 June 1992. www .un-documents.net/a47-277.htm.

Brown, P. R. L. "Saint Augustine and Political Society." In *The City of God: A Collection of Critical Essays*, edited by Dorothy F. Donnelly, 17–36. New York: Peter Lang, 1995.

Burke, Kevin F. "Christian Salvation and the Disposition of Transcendence: Ignacio Ellacuría's Historical Soteriology." In *Love That Produces Hope: The Thought of Ignacio Ellacuría*, edited by Kevin F. Burke and Robert Lassalle-Klein, 169–86. Collegeville, MN: Liturgical Press, 2006.

Bushlack, Thomas J. "The Return of Neo-Scholasticism? Recent Criticism of Henri de Lubac on Nature and Grace and Their Significance for Moral Theology, Politics, and Law." *Journal of the Society of Christian Ethics* 35, no. 2 (Fall–Winter 2015): 83–100.

Butler, Judith. *Frames of War: When Is Life Grievable?* London: Verso, 2016.

Cahill, Lisa Sowle. "*Caritas in Veritate*: Benedict's Global Reorientation." *Theological Studies* 71, no. 2 (May 2010): 291–319.

————. *Love Your Enemies: Discipleship, Pacifism, and Just War Theory.* Minneapolis, MN: Fortress Press, 1993.

————. "Peacebuilding: A Practical Strategy of Hope." *Journal of Catholic Social Thought* 11, no. 1 (Winter 2014): 47–66.

————. "A Theology for Peacebuilding." In *Peacebuilding: Catholic Theology, Ethics and Praxis*, edited by Robert J. Schreiter, R. Scott Appleby, and Gerard F. Powers, 300–331. Maryknoll, NY: Orbis Books, 2010.

Caritas Internationalis. *Peacebuilding: A Caritas Training Manual.* Vatican City: Caritas Internationalis, 2002.

Catholic Church. *The Catechism of the Catholic Church.* London: Burns & Oates, 2003.

Cavanaugh, William T. "The Church in the Streets: Eucharist and Politics." *Modern Theology* 30, no. 2 (2014): 384–402.

———. *The Myth of Religious Violence: Secular Ideology and the Roots of Modern Conflict.* Oxford: Oxford University Press, 2009.

———. *Torture and Eucharist.* Oxford: Blackwell, 1998.

Cejka, Mary Ann, and Thomas Bamat. Introduction to *Artisans of Peace: Grassroots Peacemaking among Christian Communities,* edited by Mary Ann Cejka and Thomas Bamat, 1–18. Maryknoll, NY: Orbis Books, 2003.

———, eds. *Artisans of Peace: Grassroots Peacemaking among Christian Communities.* Maryknoll, NY: Orbis Books, 2003.

Childs, Brevard. *Isaiah.* London: Westminster John Knox Press, 2001.

Christiansen, Drew. "Catholic Peacemaking, 1991–2005: The Legacy of Pope John Paul II." *Review of Faith and International Affairs* 4, no. 2 (2006): 21–28.

———. "Commentary on *Pacem in Terris.*" In *Modern Catholic Social Teaching: Commentaries and Interpretations,* edited by Kenneth R. Himes, Lisa Sowle Cahill, Charles E. Curran, David Hollenbach, and Thomas Shannon, 217–43. Washington, DC: Georgetown University Press, 2005.

———. "On Relative Equality: Catholic Egalitarianism after Vatican II." *Theological Studies* 45, no. 4 (1984): 651–75.

Congregation for the Doctrine of the Faith (CDF). "Instruction on Certain Aspects of the 'Theology of Liberation.'" Instruction, 1984. www.vatican.va.

———. "Instruction on Christian Freedom and Liberation." Instruction, 1986. www.vatican.va.

Crampsey, James. "Overtures to Ministry." Paper presented at the conference of the Catholic Theological Association of Great Britain, September 2018.

Curran, Charles E. *Catholic Social Teaching, 1891–Present: A Historical, Theological, and Ethical Analysis.* Washington, DC: Georgetown University Press, 2002.

———. "Natural Law and Moral Theology." In *Natural Law and Theology,* edited by Charles E. Curran and Richard A. McCormick, 247–95. Mahwah, NJ: Paulist Press, 1991.

De Chergé, Christian. "Testament." 1 January 1994. www.ocso.org/history /saints-blesseds-martyrs/testament-of-christian-de-cherge/.

De Lubac, Henri. *Mémoire sur l'occasion de mes écrits.* Namur: Culture et vérité, 1989.

———. *The Mystery of the Supernatural.* Translated by Rosemary Sheed. London: Geoffrey Chapman, 1967.

———. *Surnaturel: Etudes historiques.* Paris: Desclée de Brouwer, 1991.

Donahue, John R. "The Bible and Catholic Social Teaching." In *Modern Catholic Social Teaching: Commentaries and Interpretations*, edited by Kenneth R. Himes, Lisa Sowle Cahill, Charles E. Curran, David Hollenbach, and Thomas Shannon, 9–40. Washington, DC: Georgetown University Press, 2005.

Doran, Kevin P. *Solidarity: A Synthesis of Personalism and Communalism in the Thought of Karol Wojtyła/John Paul II*. New York: Peter Lang, 1996.

Dunn, James D. G. "The New Perspective on Paul." In *Jesus, Paul and the Law: Studies in Mark and Galatians*, 183–206. London: SPCK, 1990.

———. *Romans 1–8*. Word Biblical Commentary Series, vol. 38A. Dallas, TX: Word Books, 1988.

———. *The Theology of Paul the Apostle*. London: T.&T. Clark, 2003.

Episcopal Conference of Latin America (CELAM). "Peace." In *The Church in the Present Day Transformation of Latin America in the Light of the Council*, vol. 2: *Conclusions*, edited by Frederick A. McGuire, 53–66. Washington, DC: United States Conference of Catholic Bishops, Division for Latin America, 1973.

Fabry, Heinz-Joseph. "Nḥm." In *Theological Dictionary of the Old Testament*, vol. 4, edited by G. Johannes Botterweck, Helmer Ringgren, and Heinz-Joseph Fabry, 340–55. Translated by David E. Green. Grand Rapids, MI: Eerdmans, 1998.

Feingold, Laurence. *The Natural Desire to See God According to St. Thomas Aquinas and His Interpreters*. Ave Maria, FL: Sapientia Press, 2010.

Finn, Daniel K. "Commentary on *Centesimus Annus*." In *Modern Catholic Social Teaching: Commentaries and Interpretations*, edited by Kenneth R. Himes, Lisa Sowle Cahill, Charles E. Curran, David Hollenbach, and Thomas Shannon, 436–66. Washington, DC: Georgetown University Press, 2005.

———. "What Is a Sinful Social Structure?" *Theological Studies* 77, no. 1 (2016): 136–64.

Fitzmyer, Joseph A. *Romans: A New Translation with Commentary*. Anchor Bible Commentary Series. New York: Doubleday, 1993.

Francis. *Laudato si'*. Encyclical Letter, 2015. www.vatican.va.

———. "Nonviolence, a Style of Politics for Peace." Message for the World Day of Peace, 2017. www.vatican.va.

Fulkerson, Mary McClintock. *Places of Redemption: Theology for a Worldly Church*. Oxford: Oxford University Press, 2007.

Gaita, Raimond. *A Common Humanity: Thinking about Love and Truth and Justice*. London: Routledge, 2002.

Geertz, Clifford. *After the Fact: Two Countries, Four Decades, One Anthropologist*. Cambridge, MA: Harvard University Press, 1995.

Glatz, Carol. "Vatican: 13 Priests, 1 Religious Brother, 1 Nun and 8 Lay Workers Killed in 2017." *America Magazine*, 29 December 2017. www .americamagazine.org/faith/2017/12/29/vatican-13-priests-1-religious -brother-1-nun-and-8-lay-workers-killed-2017.

Gomes, Robin. "Forty 'Missionaries' Killed Worldwide in 2018." *Vatican News*, 4 January 2019. www.vaticannews.va/en/church/news/2019-01 /missionaries-killed-2018-fides.html.

Harnack, Adolf. *Militia Christi: The Christian Religion and the Military in the First Three Centuries.* Translated by David McInnes Gracie. Philadelphia: Fortress Press, 1981.

Hastrup, Kirsten. "Getting It Right: Knowledge and Evidence in Anthropology." *Current Anthropology* 4, no. 4 (2004): 455–72.

———. "Religion in Context: A Discussion of Ontological Dumping." In *New Approaches to the Study of Religion*, vol. 1: *Regional, Critical and Historical Approaches*, edited by Peter Antes, Armin W. Geertz, and Randi R. Warne, 253–70. New York: Walter de Gruyter, 2004.

———. "Social Anthropology. Towards a Pragmatic Enlightenment?" *Social Anthropology* 13, no. 2 (2005): 133–49.

Hawksley, Theodora. "Drawings for Projection: Proposing Peacebuilding through the Arts." In *Peacebuilding and the Arts*, edited by Jolyon Mitchell, Giselle Vincett, Hal Culbertson, and Theodora Hawksley, 119–35. London: Palgrave Macmillan, 2019.

———. "How Critical Realism Can Help Catholic Social Teaching." In *Moral Agency within Social Structures and Culture: A Primer on Critical Realism for Christian Ethics*, edited by Daniel K. Finn, 9–17. Washington, DC: Georgetown University Press, 2020.

———. "Of Gods and Men: Peacebuilding and Catholic Social Teaching." In *Wiley Blackwell Companion to Religion and Peace*, edited by Jolyon Mitchell, Martyn Percy, Lesley Orr, and Francesca Po. Oxford: Wiley Blackwell, forthcoming.

Hehir, J. Bryan. "Catholicism and Democracy." In *Change in Official Catholic Moral Teachings*, edited by Charles E. Curran, 20–37. Mahwah, NJ: Paulist Press, 2003.

Henao Gaviria, Héctor Fabio. "'And They Shall Make War No More': Lessons about Peacebuilding and Overcoming Conflict from Colombia." *New Blackfriars* 96, no. 1062 (2015): 177–91.

———. "Lessons Learned in Peacebuilding in Colombia." Catholic Peacebuilding Network, June 2007. https://cpn.nd.edu/assets/243414 /2008_hector_fabio_henao_lessons_learned_in_peacebuilding_in _colombia.pdf.

Heyer, Kristin. "Social Sin and Immigration: Good Fences Make Bad Neighbors." *Theological Studies* 71, no. 2 (2010): 410–36.

Himes, Kenneth R. "Commentary on *Justitia in mundo* (*Justice in the World*)." In *Modern Catholic Social Teaching: Commentaries and Interpretations*, edited by Kenneth R. Himes, Lisa Sowle Cahill, Charles E. Curran, David Hollenbach, and Thomas Shannon, 333–62. Washington, DC: Georgetown University Press, 2005.

———. "Pacifism and the Just War Tradition in Roman Catholic Social Teaching." In *One Hundred Years of Catholic Social Thought: Celebration and Challenge*, edited by John A. Coleman, 329–44. Maryknoll, NY: Orbis Books, 1991.

———. "Papal Thinking about Peace since *Pacem in Terris*: The World Day of Peace Messages 1967–2013." *Journal of Catholic Social Thought* 11, no. 1 (2014): 9–32.

———. "Peacebuilding and Catholic Social Teaching." In *Peacebuilding: Catholic Theology, Ethics and Praxis*, edited by Robert J. Schreiter, R. Scott Appleby, and Gerard F. Powers, 265–99. Maryknoll, NY: Orbis Books, 2010.

———. "Social Sin and the Role of the Individual." *Annual of the Society of Christian Ethics* 6 (1986): 183–218.

Hobgood, Mary E. "Conflicting Paradigms in Social Analysis." In *The Logic of Solidarity: Commentaries on Pope John Paul II's Encyclical "On Social Concern,"* edited by Gregory Baum and Robert Ellsberg, 167–85. Maryknoll, NY: Orbis Books, 1989.

Hollenbach, David. "Commentary on *Gaudium et spes*." In *Modern Catholic Social Teaching: Commentaries and Interpretations*, edited by Kenneth R. Himes, Lisa Sowle Cahill, Charles E. Curran, David Hollenbach, and Thomas Shannon, 266–91. Washington, DC: Georgetown University Press, 2005.

———. "Social Ethics under the Sign of the Cross." *Annual of the Society of Christian Ethics* 16 (1996): 3–18.

Hopkins, Gerard Manley. *God's Grandeur and Other Poems*. Edited by Thomas Crofts. New York: Dover Thrift Editions, 1995.

Horowitz, Jason. "Pope Francis, in Plea for South Sudan Peace, Stuns Leaders by Kissing Their Shoes." *New York Times*, 11 April 2019. www.nytimes.com/2019/04/11/world/europe/pope-francis-south-sudan.html.

Hunter, David G. "A Decade of Research on Early Christians and Military Service." *Religious Studies Review* 18, no. 2 (1992): 87–94.

International Theological Commission (ITC). *Memory and Reconciliation*. 1999. www.vatican.va.

Iraqi Christians in Need (ICIN). "New Hope Trauma Centre of Iraq." Iraqi Christians in Need, 2019. https://icin.org.uk/new-hope-trauma-centre -of-iraq/.

Jenkins, John I. *Knowledge and Faith in Thomas Aquinas*. Cambridge: Cambridge University Press, 1997.

Jenkins, Timothy. "Fieldwork and the Perception of Everyday Life." *Man* 29, no. 2 (1994): 433–55.

———. *Religion in English Everyday Life: An Ethnographic Approach*. Oxford: Berghahn Books, 1999.

John XXIII. *Mater et magistra*. Encyclical Letter, 1961. www.vatican.va.

———. *Pacem in terris*. Encyclical Letter, 1963. www.vatican.va.

John Paul II. *Centesimus annus*. Encyclical Letter, 1991. www.vatican.va.

———. "Development and Solidarity, Two Keys to Peace." Message for the World Day of Peace, 1987. www.vatican.va.

———. *Ecclesia in America*. Post-Synodal Apostolic Exhortation, 1999. www .vatican.va.

———. *Evangelium vitae*. Encyclical Letter, 1995. www.vatican.va.

———. "Homily at Drogheda." 29 September 1979. www.vatican.va.

———. *Incarnationis mysterium*. Bull of Indiction, 1998. www.vatican.va.

———. "Offer Forgiveness and Receive Peace." Message for the World Day of Peace, 1997. www.vatican.va.

———. "Peace: A Gift of God Entrusted to Us!" Message for the World Day of Peace, 1982. www.vatican.va.

———. *Reconciliatio et paenitentia*. Post-Synodal Apostolic Exhortation, 1984. www.vatican.va.

———. *Sollicitudo rei socialis*. Encyclical Letter, 1987. www.vatican.va.

———. *Tertio millenio adveniente*. Encyclical Letter, 1994. www.vatican.va.

———. "The Value of This Collegial Body." In *Penance and Reconciliation in the Mission of the Church*. National Conference of Catholic Bishops. Washington DC: U.S. Conference of Catholic Bishops, 1984.

Johnson, James T. *Ideology, Reason, and the Limitation of War: Religious and Secular Concepts, 1200–1740*. Princeton, NJ: Princeton University Press, 1975.

———. "Just War, as It Was and Is." *First Things*, January 2005. www.firstthings .com/article/2005/01/just-war-as-it-was-and-is.

———. *Just War Tradition and the Restraint of War: A Moral and Historical Inquiry*. Princeton, NJ: Princeton University Press, 1981.

———. *The Quest for Peace: Three Moral Traditions in Western Cultural History*. Princeton, NJ: Princeton University Press, 1987.

Kaveney, M. Cathleen. "The Spirit of Vatican II and Moral Theology: *Evangelium Vitae* as a Case Study." In *After Vatican II: Trajectories and*

Hermeneutics, edited by James L. Heft and John O'Malley, 43–67. Grand Rapids, MI: Eerdmans, 2012.

Katongole, Emmanuel. *The Journey of Reconciliation: Groaning for a New Creation in Africa*. Maryknoll, NY: Orbis Books, 2017.

Kaur, Kuldip. "Guatemala: The Challenge of Peacebuilding in Fragmented Communities." In *Artisans of Peace: Grassroots Peacemaking among Christian Communities*, edited by Mary Ann Cejka and Thomas Bamat, 35–66. Maryknoll, NY: Orbis Books, 2003.

Keenan, James F. *A History of Catholic Moral Theology in the Twentieth Century: From Confessing Sins to Liberating Consciences*. London: Continuum, 2010.

Komonchak, Joseph A. "Theology and Culture at Mid-Century: The Example of Henri de Lubac." *Theological Studies* 51, no. 4 (1990): 579–602.

Langan, John A. "The Elements of St. Augustine's Just War Theory." *Journal of Religious Ethics* 12, no. 1 (1984): 19–38.

Lash, Nicholas. "Not Exactly Politics or Power?" *Modern Theology* 8, no. 4 (1992): 353–64.

Lederach, John Paul. *Building Peace: Sustainable Reconciliation in Divided Societies*. Washington, DC: United States Institute of Peace Press, 1997.

———. "The Long Journey Back to Humanity: Catholic Peacebuilding with Armed Actors." In *Peacebuilding: Catholic Theology, Ethics and Praxis*, edited by Robert J. Schreiter, R. Scott Appleby, and Gerard F. Powers, 23–55. Maryknoll, NY: Orbis Books, 2010.

———. *The Moral Imagination: The Art and Soul of Building Peace*. Oxford: Oxford University Press, 2005.

———. "The Mystery of Transformative Times and Spaces: Exploring a Theology of Grassroots Peacebuilding." In *Artisans of Peace: Grassroots Peacemaking among Christian Communities*, edited by Mary Ann Cejka and Thomas Bamat, 256–67. Maryknoll, NY: Orbis Books, 2003.

Lederach, John Paul, and R. Scott Appleby. "Strategic Peacebuilding: An Overview." In *Strategies of Peace: Transforming Conflict in a Violent World*, edited by Daniel Philpott and Gerard F. Powers, 19–44. Oxford: Oxford University Press, 2010.

Leo XIII. *Rerum novarum*. Encyclical Letter, 1891. www.vatican.va.

Levertov, Denise. *Evening Train*. New York: New Directions, 1992.

Liechty, Joseph, and Cecelia Clegg. *Moving beyond Sectarianism: Religion, Conflict and Reconciliation in Northern Ireland*. Dublin: Columba Press, 2001.

MacKinnon, Donald. "Some Notes on the Irreversibility of Time." In *Explorations in Theology 5: Donald MacKinnon*, 90–98. London: SCM, 1979.

———. "Subjective and Objective Conceptions of Atonement." In *Prospect for Theology: Essays in Honour of H. H. Farmer*, edited by F. G. Healey, 167–82. Welwyn: James Nisbet & Co., 1996.

Mahoney, John A. *The Making of Moral Theology: A Study of the Roman Catholic Tradition*. Oxford: Clarendon Press, 1987.

Markus, Robert A. *Saeculum: History and Society in the Theology of St Augustine*. Cambridge: Cambridge University Press, 1970.

McCarthy, Eli Sarasan. *Becoming Nonviolent Peacemakers: A Virtue Ethic for Catholic Social Teaching and U.S. Policy*. Eugene, OR: Pickwick Publications, 2012.

Mich, Marvin. "Commentary on *Mater et Magistra (Christianity and Social Progress)*." In *Modern Catholic Social Teaching: Commentaries and Interpretations*, edited by Kenneth R. Himes, Lisa Sowle Cahill, Charles E. Curran, David Hollenbach, and Thomas Shannon, 191–216. Washington, DC: Georgetown University Press, 2005.

Merton, Thomas. *Redeeming the Time*. London: Burns & Oates, 1966.

Milbank, John. *Theology and Social Theory: Beyond Secular Reason*. Oxford: Wiley, 1993.

Miller, Richard Brian. *Interpretations of Conflict: Ethics, Pacifism, and the Just-War Tradition*. Chicago: University of Chicago Press, 1991.

Moeller, Charles. "History of the Constitution." In *Commentary on the Documents of Vatican II*, vol. 5: *Pastoral Constitution on the Church in the Modern World*, edited by Herbert Vorgrimler, 1–76. London: Burns & Oates, 1969.

Moltmann, Jürgen. *The Crucified God: The Cross of Christ as the Foundation and Criticism of Christian Theology*. London: SCM, 1974.

Moore, Sebastian. *The Crucified Is No Stranger*. London: Darton, Longman and Todd, 1977.

Musto, Ronald G. *Catholic Peacemakers: A Documentary History*, vol. 1: *From the Bible to the Era of the Crusades*. New York: Garland, 1993.

———. *The Catholic Peace Tradition*. Maryknoll, NY: Orbis Books, 1986.

National Catholic Reporter. "World at War Is a Common View for Francis." *National Catholic Reporter*, 28 July 2016. www.ncronline.org/blogs/ncr-today/world-war-common-view-francis.

Neuhaus, David. "Fr. David Neuhaus S.J.: Witness Interview." Salt and Light TV, 24 April 2016. https://saltandlighttv.org/witness/?f=fr-david-neuhaus.

O'Brien, David J. "Stories of Solidarity: The Challenges of Catholic Peacebuilding." In *Peacebuilding: Catholic Theology, Ethics and Praxis*, edited by Robert J. Schreiter, R. Scott Appleby, and Gerard F. Powers, 398–420. Maryknoll, NY: Orbis Books, 2010.

O'Donovan, Oliver. "Augustine's *City of God XIX* and Western Political Thought." In *The City of God: A Collection of Critical Essays*, edited by Dorothy F. Donnelly, 135–49. New York: Peter Lang, 1995.

O'Keefe, Mark. *What Are They Saying about Social Sin?* Mahwah, NJ: Paulist Press, 1990.

O'Malley, John. *What Happened at Vatican II*. Cambridge, MA: Belknap Press of Harvard University Press, 2008.

Origen. *Contra Celsum*. Translated by Henry Chadwick. Cambridge: Cambridge University Press, 1980.

Paul VI. *Evangelii nuntiandi*. Encyclical Letter, 1975. www.vatican.va.

———. "Every Man Is My Brother." Message for the World Day of Peace, 1971. www.vatican.va.

———. *Octogesima adveniens*. Apostolic Letter, 1971. www.vatican.va.

———. *Populorum progressio*. Encyclical Letter, 1967. www.vatican.va.

Peterson, Brandon. "Critical Voices: The Reactions of Rahner and Ratzinger to 'Schema XIII' (*Gaudium et spes*)." *Modern Theology* 31, no. 1 (2015): 1–26.

Pfeil, Margaret R. "Correlating Social Sin and Social Reconciliation: Racism as a Test Case." *Journal for Peace and Justice Studies* 12, no. 1 (2002): 95–113.

———. "Doctrinal Implications of Magisterial Use of Language of Original Sin." *Louvain Studies* 27, no. 2 (2002): 132–52.

———. "Social Sin: Social Reconciliation?" In *Reconciliation, Churches and Nations in Latin America*, edited by Iain MacLean, 171–89. London: Ashgate, 2006.

Pieper, Josef. *The Silence of St. Thomas*. Translated by John Murray and Daniel O'Connor. South Bend, IN: St. Augustine Press, 1999.

Pius XI. *Ubi arcano Dei consilio*. Encyclical Letter, 1922. www.vatican.va.

Pius XII. *Humani generis*. Encyclical Letter, 1950. www.vatican.va.

———. *Summi pontificatus*. Encyclical Letter, 1939. www.vatican.va.

Pontifical Council for Justice and Peace. *Compendium of the Social Doctrine of the Church*. London: Continuum, 2012.

Porter, Jean. *Natural and Divine Law: Reclaiming the Tradition for Christian Ethics*. Grand Rapids, MI: Eerdmans, 1999.

Puhl, Louis. *The Spiritual Exercises of St. Ignatius: Based on Studies in the Language of the Autograph*. Chicago: Loyola Press, 1951.

Quigley, Thomas, ed. *Guatemala Never Again! REMHI Historical Memory Project: The Official Report of the Human Rights Office, Archdiocese of Guatemala*. Maryknoll, NY: Orbis Books, 1999.

Rahner, Karl. "Christian Pessimism." In *Theological Investigations*, vol. 22: *Human Society and the Church of Tomorrow*, 155–62. Translated by Joseph Donceel. London: Darton, Longman and Todd, 1991.

———. "Concerning the Relationship between Nature and Grace." In *Theological Investigations*, vol. 1: *God, Christ, Mary and Grace*, 297–317. Translated by Cornelius Ernst O.P. London: Darton, Longman and Todd, 1969.

———. "Ignatian Spirituality and Devotion to the Sacred Heart of Jesus." In *Mission and Grace: Essays in Pastoral Theology*, vol. 3, 176–210. London: Sheed and Ward, 1966.

———. "The Theological Concept of Concupiscentia." In *Theological Investigations*, vol. 1: *God, Christ, Mary and Grace*, 347–82. Translated by Cornelius Ernst O.P. London: Darton, Longman and Todd, 1969.

Radcliffe, Timothy. *Sing a New Song: The Christian Vocation*. Dublin: Dominican Publications, 1999.

Ratzinger, Joseph. "Commentary on Part I, Chapter I." In *Commentary on the Documents of Vatican II*, vol. 5: *Pastoral Constitution on the Church in the Modern World*, edited by Herbert Vorgrimler, 115–64. London: Burns & Oates, 1969.

———. *Die Letzte Sitzungsperiode des Konzils*. Köln: Bachem, 1966.

Reagan, Ronald. "Address to the British Parliament, House of Commons, London." In *The Last Best Hope: The Greatest Speeches of Ronald Reagan*, edited by Michael Reagan, 99–105. West Palm Beach, FL: Humanix Books, 2016.

Reichberg, Gregory M. *Thomas Aquinas on War and Peace*. Cambridge: Cambridge University Press, 2016.

Rios-Oyola, Sandra M., and Thania Acarón. "Peacebuilding and Dance in Afro-Colombian Funeral Ritual." In *Peacebuilding and the Arts*, edited by Jolyon Mitchell, Giselle Vincett, Hal Culbertson, and Theodora Hawksley, 395–413. London: Palgrave Macmillan, 2019.

Rosenthal, Alexander S. "The Problem of the *Desiderium Naturale* in the Thomistic Tradition." *Verbum* 6, no. 2 (2004): 335–44.

Rowland, Tracey. *Culture and the Thomist Tradition: After Vatican II*. Abingdon: Routledge, 2003.

Rowlands, Anna. *Catholic Social Teaching: A Guide for the Perplexed*. London: T.&T. Clark, 2018.

Rutikanga, Bernard Noel. "Rwanda: Struggle for Healing at the Grassroots." In *Artisans of Peace: Grassroots Peacemaking among Christian Communities*, edited by Mary Ann Cejka and Thomas Bamat, 132–65. Maryknoll, NY: Orbis Books, 2003.

Schirch, Lisa. *The Little Book of Strategic Peacebuilding*. Intercourse, PA: Good Books, 2005.

Schneiders, Sandra. "New Testament Reflections on Peace and Nuclear Arms." In *Catholics and Nuclear War: The US Catholic Bishops' Pastoral Letter on War and Peace*, edited by Philip J. Murnion, 91–105. London: Geoffrey Chapman, 1983.

Schreiter, Robert J. "The Catholic Social Imaginary and Peacebuilding." In *Peacebuilding: Catholic Theology, Ethics and Praxis*, edited by Robert Schreiter, R. Scott Appleby, and Gerard F. Powers, 221–39. Maryknoll, NY: Orbis Books, 2010.

———. *The Ministry of Reconciliation: Spirituality and Strategies*. Maryknoll, NY: Orbis Books, 1998.

———. "A Practical Theology of Healing, Forgiveness and Reconciliation." In *Peacebuilding: Catholic Theology, Ethics and Praxis*, edited by Robert Schreiter, R. Scott Appleby, and Gerard F. Powers, 366–95. Maryknoll, NY: Orbis Books, 2010.

———. *Reconciliation: Mission and Ministry in a Changing Social Order*. Maryknoll, NY: Orbis Books, 1992.

Schwöbel, Christoph. "Reconciliation: From Biblical Observations to Dogmatic Reconstruction." In *The Theology of Reconciliation*, edited by Colin Gunton, 13–38. London: T.&T. Clark, 2003.

Shadle, Matthew A. *The Origins of War: A Catholic Perspective*. Washington, DC: Georgetown University Press, 2011.

Sobrino, John. *Witnesses to the Kingdom: The Martyrs of El Salvador and the Crucified Peoples*. Maryknoll, NY: Orbis Books, 2003.

Stauffer, Jill. "An Interview with Judith Butler." *Believer Magazine* 2 (2003). https://believermag.com/an-interview-with-judith-butler/.

Stoebe, H. J. "Nḥm (Pi) to Comfort." In *Theological Lexicon of the Old Testament*, edited by Ernst Jenni and Claus Westermann, 734–39. Translated by Mark E. Biddle. Peabody, MA: Hendrickson, 1997.

Stuhlmacher, Peter. "Isaiah 53 in the Gospels and Acts." In *The Suffering Servant: Isaiah 53 in Jewish and Christian Sources*, edited by Bernd Janowski and Peter Stuhlmacher, 147–62. Grand Rapids, MI: Eerdmans, 2004.

Suárez, Francisco. *Selections from Three Works*. Edited by Thomas Pink. Indianapolis, IN: Liberty Fund, 2014. Online edition at https://muse.jhu.edu /book/39724.

Sullivan, A., D. Voas, and M. Brown. *The Art of Asking Questions about Religion*. London: Centre for Longitudinal Studies, 2012.

Synod of African Bishops. "The Church in Africa in Service to Reconciliation, Justice and Peace." Instrumentum Laboris, 1999. www.vatican.va.

Tanner, Kathryn. *Theories of Culture: A New Agenda for Theology*. Minneapolis, MN: Fortress Press, 1997.

————. "Trinity." In *The Blackwell Companion to Political Theology*, edited by Peter Scott and William T. Cavanaugh, 319–32. Oxford: Blackwell, 1996.

Tertullian. *Apologia, De Spectaculis*. Edited by T. R. Glover, Gerald Henry Rendall, and Walter Charles Alan Kerr. London: Heinemann, 1931.

Te Selle, Eugene. *Living in Two Cities: Augustinian Trajectories in Political Thought*. Scranton, PA: University of Scranton Press, 1998.

Theos. *The Spirit of Things Unseen: Belief in Post-Religious Britain*. London: Theos, 2013.

Tillich, Paul. *Theology of Peace*. Edited by Ronald H. Stone. Louisville, KY: Westminster John Knox Press, 1990.

Turner, Denys. *Thomas Aquinas: A Portrait*. New Haven, CT: Yale University Press, 2013.

United Nations Truth Commission. "From Madness to Hope: The 12 Year War in El Salvador." Equipo Nizkor, 1993. www.derechos.org/nizkor/salvador/informes/truth.html.

United States Conference of Catholic Bishops (USCCB). *The Challenge of Peace*. Episcopal Letter, 1983. www.usccb.org/issues-and-action/human-life-and-dignity/war-and-peace/nuclear-weapons/upload/statement-the-challenge-of-peace-1983-05-03.pdf.

————. *The Harvest of Justice Is Sown in Peace*. Episcopal Letter, 1993. www.usccb.org/beliefs-and-teachings/what-we-believe/catholic-social-teaching/the-harvest-of-justice-is-sown-in-peace.cfm.

Vanier, Jean. *Our Life Together: A Memoir in Letters*. London: Darton, Longman and Todd, 2008.

Vatican II. *Gaudium et spes*. Pastoral Constitution, 1965. www.vatican.va.

————. *Optatam totius*. Decree, 1965. www.vatican.va.

————. *Sacrosanctum concilium*. Constitution, 1963. www.vatican.va.

————. *Unitatis redintegratio*. Decree, 1964. www.vatican.va.

Vitoria, Francisco de. *De Indis*. In *De Indis et De Jure Belli*. Edited by Ernest Nys. New York: Oceana, 1964. Online edition at https://en.wikisource.org/wiki/De_Indis_De_Jure_Belli.

Vladisavljevic, Anja. "Austria Church Bans Mass at Bleiburg Commemoration." Balkan Insight, 8 March 2019. https://balkaninsight.com/2019/03/08/austrian-church-bans-mass-at-bleiburg-commemoration/.

Volf, Miroslav. *The End of Memory: Remembering Rightly in a Violent World*. Grand Rapids, MI: Eerdmans, 2006.

Wagner, J. Ross. *Heralds of the Good News: Isaiah and Paul "In Concert" in the Letter to the Romans*. Boston: Brill, 2002.

Watts, John D. W. *Word Biblical Commentary: Isaiah 34–66*. Waco, TX: Word Books, 1987.

Weaver, Darlene Fozard. "Vatican II and Moral Theology." In *After Vatican II: Trajectories and Hermeneutics*, edited by James L. Heft and John O'Malley, 23–42. Grand Rapids, MI: Eerdmans, 2012.

Webster, John. "The Ethics of Reconciliation." In *The Theology of Reconciliation*, edited by Colin E. Gunton, 109–24. London: T.&T. Clark, 2003.

Weigel, George. *Tranquillitas Ordinis: The Present Failure and Future Promise of American Catholic Thought on War and Peace*. Oxford: Oxford University Press, 1987.

Westermann, Claus. *Isaiah 40–66*. London: SCM, 1969.

Whitfield, Teresa. *Paying the Price: Ignacio Ellacuría and the Murdered Jesuits of El Salvador*. Philadelphia: Temple University Press, 1995.

Whitmore, Todd. "Peacebuilding and Its Challenging Partners." In *Peacebuilding: Catholic Theology, Ethics and Praxis*, edited by Robert J. Schreiter, R. Scott Appleby, and Gerard F. Powers, 155–89. Maryknoll, NY: Orbis Books, 2010.

Williams, Rowan. "'Good for Nothing?' Augustine on Creation." *Augustinian Studies* 25 (1994): 9–24.

———. "Politics and the Soul: A Reading of the *City of God*." *Milltown Studies* 19–20 (1987): 55–72.

———. *Resurrection: Interpreting the Easter Gospel*. London: Darton, Longman and Todd, 2002.

———. "Saving Time: Thoughts on Patience, Practice and Vision." *New Blackfriars* 73, no. 861 (1992): 319–26.

———. "The Suspicion of Suspicion: Wittgenstein and Bonhoeffer." In *The Grammar of the Heart*, edited by Richard H. Bell, 36–53. San Francisco: Harper and Row, 1988.

———. *The Truce of God: Peacemaking in Troubled Times*. Norwich: Canterbury Press, 2005.

Wittgenstein, Ludwig. *Philosophical Investigations*. Translated by G. E. M. Anscombe. Oxford: Blackwell, 2001.

Wojtyła, Karol, and Anna-Teresa Tymieniecka. *The Acting Person*. Translated by Andrzej Potocki. Dordrecht: D. Reidel, 1979.

Yzermans, Vincent A. *American Participation in the Second Vatican Council*. New York: Sheed and Ward, 1967.

Zechmeister, Martha. "The Authority of Those Who Suffer." Congregatio Jesu, May 2013. www.congregatiojesu.org/en/docs_talks_public.asp.

INDEX

Acting Person, The (Wojtyła), 115–17, 259n36, 259n38

Ad beatissimi apostolorum (Benedict XV), 46–48, 58, 245n81, 248n112

Africae munus (Benedict XVI)
on bonds through the Eucharist, 194, 260n53, 279n87
on demands of justice and charity, 278n69
on midlevel and grassroots actors, 250n7
peace and peacebuilding in, 65
reconciliation in, 170–74, 191, 194, 260n53
tension between the spiritual and political in, 172–73, 194, 196, 277n48

"Agenda for Peace, An" (Boutros-Ghali), 256n5

Algerian civil war, 198–200

Alison, James, 101, 223, 253n50, 285n56
Knowing Jesus, 254n52
On Being Liked, 285n60

Allorché fummo chiamati (Benedict XV), 241n31, 247n106

Ambrose, Saint, 25

Anabaptist churches, 24

Apologia (Tertullian), 235n2, 235n9

Appleby, Scott, 5–6, 7–8, 256n8

Aquinas, Thomas
on the common good, 35–38, 109, 239n65
compared to Augustine, 36–38
De Regno, 35, 41
on free will, 266n31
on happiness, 35–36, 43–45, 239n62, 266n31
influence on Church teaching, 39, 41, 44–45, 48, 49
influence on *Pacem in terris*, 51–52, 53, 54, 55, 109
influence on Vatican II, 56–57, 59
on just war, 37, 39–40, 42, 63
on natural and eternal law, 35–38, 42–43, 238n57, 281n12
on nature and grace, 43–45, 239n58
on peace, 34–38, 192, 208, 239n68
on sin, 281n12
Summa Theologica, 35–37, 44, 239n65, 281n12
theory of human knowledge, 238n48
use of scripture, 42
on virtue, 35, 239n58

L'Arche community (Israel), 103

Ariccia text (*Gaudium et spes*), 59–60, 246n89

Atlacatl battalion (Salvadoran army), 122–23

THEODORA HAWKSLEY

is head of social and environmental justice programming at the London Jesuit Centre. She is co-editor of *Peacebuilding and the Arts*.

9 780268 108465